UNSHAVED

UNSHAVED

RESISTANCE AND REVOLUTION IN WOMEN'S BODY HAIR POLITICS

BREANNE FAHS

UNIVERSITY OF WASHINGTON PRESS | *Seattle*

Composed in Iowan Old Style, typeface designed by John Downer

26 25 24 23 22   5 4 3 2 1

Printed and bound in the United States of America

UNIVERSITY OF WASHINGTON PRESS
uwapress.uw.edu

LIBRARY OF CONGRESS CATALOGING-IN-PUBLICATION DATA
Names: Fahs, Breanne, author.
Title: Unshaved : resistance and revolution in women's body hair politics / Breanne Fahs.
Description: Seattle : University of Washington Press, [2022] | Includes bibliographical references and index.
Identifiers: LCCN 2021043715 (print) | LCCN 2021043716 (ebook) | ISBN 9780295750279 (hardcover) | ISBN 9780295750286 (paperback) | ISBN 9780295750293 (ebook)
Subjects: LCSH: Body hair—Social aspects. | Hair—Removal—Social aspects. | Beauty, Personal—Social aspects.
Classification: LCC HQ1219 .F35 2022 (print) | LCC HQ1219 (ebook) | DDC 646.7/042—dc23
LC record available at https://lccn.loc.gov/2021043715
LC ebook record available at https://lccn.loc.gov/2021043716

∞ This paper meets the requirements of ANSI/NISO Z39.48-1992 (Permanence of Paper).

For Chris Bobel

The worst thing is not that the world is unfree, but that people have unlearned their liberty.

—MILAN KUNDERA, *LIFE IS ELSEWHERE*

but once, i dreamed i had no teeth
just a mouth to hold
other people's things . . .
tell them i grew a new tongue

—DENICE FROHMAN, "A WOMAN'S PLACE"

CONTENTS |

UNSHAVED

Introduction |

Revolting Bodies or Bodies in Revolt?

It was in the air . . . this hatred of women and their bodies—it
seeped in with every draught in the house; people brought it home
on their shoes, they breathed it in off their newspapers. There was
no way to control it.

—ZADIE SMITH, *On Beauty*

I HAVE NO MEMORY OF THE FIRST TIME I SHAVED MY LEGS OR
underarms. Though I have asked many women about their stories of hair
removal, I cannot summon to my memory anything about my first shaving experiences. I see only a vague compilation of half memories: my
mother explaining how to use a razor without cutting myself, skin irritation and prickliness, the weird gel that came out of the top of my pink
(women's!?) razor, and the sense of having smooth legs. I don't remember it as a conscious choice, a mandate from friends at school, an event at
the urging of my mother, or even an internal tension. Removing body
hair felt like something girls always *had to do*, something so ingrained in
adolescent girl culture that it left almost no imprint on my mind. It was,
for that period of my life, the most mundane of chores. Like so many
other girls, I complied with shaving without registering it as an actual
decision.

I only saw hair removal as strange and peculiar a few years later, when,
as a competitive teenage swimmer, our entire mixed-gender team grew
out our body hair for the season and then had a celebratory shaving party
right before the big races. Body hair moved from unconsciously managed

1

to a training technique, a way to induce the sensation of "drag" on the body—in this case, extra weight that must be dragged through the water (though it was also "drag" in the sense of a very particular kind of athletic gendered performance). Swimmers imagine that when they suddenly shave their bodies before the big races, they will swim faster because they glide through the water like sleek, futuristic human fish. Though it was a training ploy, and though I complied with all of this growing and then shaving, year after year, I also developed a newfound appreciation for my body hair. It never felt gross or dirty or unusual to me; I rather liked the way that I looked and felt with body hair. I marveled at the way I grew armpit hair in a pattern exactly like my father's, and later, when we traveled to Germany to train there for part of a summer, I felt kinship with the German girls who had abundant body hair. In a strange twist of good adolescent luck, swimming allowed me to keep my body hair without the social penalties other adolescent girls might have faced; I had body hair because I was a varsity athlete maximizing my training regimen. *I had an excuse.*

So began my lifelong interest in the social construction of women's body hair and the curious ways that women comply with a norm that is purely aesthetic instead of functional or health related. What did it mean that so many cultural messages targeted girls' and women's body image, barraging them with the idea that their natural bodies were disgusting, smelly, dirty, in need of management, and wholly unsatisfying without hair removal, abundant beauty products, and labor-intensive grooming and maintenance?[1] Why had women in other countries been easily able to resist the norms of women's hairlessness while American women shaved and waxed in a compulsory manner? Why had something so straightforward and mundane become so *emotional*, even to the feminist women I knew? What would happen if women chose to resist this norm?

EXTRAORDINARY COMPLIANCE

The social norm of women removing their body hair has a compliance rate of between 92 and 99 percent in many countries, including the United States, the United Kingdom, Australia, New Zealand, and much of Western Europe.[2] Over 91.5 percent of women in the United States regularly remove their leg hair and 93 percent regularly remove underarm hair.[3] A recent Australian study found that approximately 96 percent of women regularly removed their leg and underarm hair, 60 percent removed at least some pubic hair, and 48 percent removed all pubic hair.[4] One UK study found that over 99 percent of women reported removing body hair at some point in their lives, and a study of Australian women found that 98 percent of them were removing both leg and underarm hair.[5] Pubic hair removal, too, has sharply increased in frequency in the past decade, with anywhere from 50 percent to 98 percent of American and Canadian women reporting that they remove some or all pubic hair, with one recent study finding that 50 percent of women said their "typical status" is hair-free.[6] A study in *JAMA Dermatology* found that only 16 percent of women have left their pubic hair alone and have gone completely natural and that sizable numbers of women remove their pubic hair in order to meet their partners' preferences.[7] Further, women remove their hair at great cost: American women who shave spend in their lifetimes more than $10,000 and two months of their lives managing unwanted hair; that number increases to a full $23,000 for women who wax once or twice per month.[8] In all, these estimates across numerous cultures in the global north show extremely high rates of body hair removal for women.

Looking more globally, women in countries around the world have also seen increases in the mandate for their body hair removal. In China, women rarely routinely shaved their body hair until the late 1990s; compliance with this norm has risen sharply in the previous ten years, with hair removal products being advertised widely and Chinese women becoming targets of advertising campaigns that teach them to feel shame about their bodies.[9] Japanese women routinely remove leg and underarm hair and have become huge proponents of IPL (intense pulsed light) laser hair removal. Hair removal in India has become ubiquitous, with increased use of depilatories and laser hair removal for the chin, upper lip, underarms, cheeks, and bikini area.[10] Though German women were once averse to body hair removal, 69 percent of them now remove their body hair.[11] Given what is known about the influence of American television on body shaming and eating disorders in women throughout the world, one can also surmise that norms of hairlessness are also being exported with equal intensity.[12]

Though I have studied the social norm of body hair removal for nearly fifteen years, I continue to find it remarkable that women have been so wholly convinced to comply with a norm that is purely social and aesthetic, with no notable health or hygiene benefits. In fact, doctors have recently begun to urge women to reconsider removing body hair, especially pubic hair, due to the link between hair removal and adverse medical risks, including shaving injuries, lacerations, rashes, abscesses, and abrasions. They also caution about the risk of unnecessary and risky hospitalizations for uncontrollable staph infections due to body hair removal.[13] Another study found that a full *60 percent* of women reported having at least one health complication as a result of pubic hair removal, suggesting that pubic hair removal poses some danger to women on a regular basis.[14] Links between pubic hair removal and cancer have also been documented, with scientists urging people to understand that partial or complete removal or pubic hair with a razor could create "genital inflammation, vulvar dysplasia, and malignancies."[15] Further, two systematic reviews of studies about presurgical shaving—a routine practice where pubic hair is removed before Cesarean sections, for example—suggest that such hair removal increased women's risk of infection because organisms thrive in the small cuts created by shaving. Doctors have seriously discouraged this practice.[16] Less seriously, 80 percent of women reported experiencing genital itching related to pubic hair removal.[17]

These risks are not unique to pubic hair removal. One key study from 2003 found that the combination of shaving underarms and applying antiperspirant deodorant increased risk of breast cancer and led to younger age of first diagnosis for breast cancer, again reinforcing the notion that shaving body hair has direct health consequences.[18] And yet, women who removed their body hair reported feeling cleaner, more hygienic, sexier, more attractive, smoother, and more "normal."[19] Most women remove their body hair not because someone else tells them to, but because they *want* to. Many women argue that removing their body hair is their personal choice, that they enjoy it, and that they would feel "dirty" or "gross" without removing it.[20]

This internalized sense of want and need for a norm that lacks health and hygiene benefits is also remarkable when compared to compliance rates with other norms. For example, Americans are generally notably resistant toward complying with social norms that have direct health benefits: only 55–65 percent of US adults complied with mask wearing during the peak of the COVID-19 outbreak, 66 percent of Americans showered daily, 18 percent of US adults ate five servings of fruits and vegetables daily, 23 percent exercised for at least seventy-five minutes per week, 85.9 percent wore seatbelts, and 86.3 percent did not smoke.[21] For norms that lack health and hygiene implications and that are strictly related to gender and power, compliance was remarkably high in comparison to health behaviors. For example, 73 percent of women have worn high heels, between 39 and 49 percent wore them daily, and a whopping 71 percent complained that these shoes hurt their feet.[22] Further, while 41 percent of American women wore makeup on a daily basis and another 25 percent wore makeup several times per week, a full 44 percent of women felt more unattractive and uncomfortable when not wearing makeup than when they did, and 14 percent reported feeling "naked" without makeup.[23] (Additionally, women rated other women wearing makeup as more attractive, healthy, competent, and confident, suggesting that gender norms impacted not only how individuals felt about themselves but also how they judged others.)[24]

But, of course, that isn't really the story. People do not typically make informed and rational choices about grooming, beauty, and aesthetics based on logical outcomes or careful personal analysis, and choices are not all equally *choosable*. Much in the same way that certain sexual practices feel like choices but then become compulsory—particularly heterosexuality, in Adrienne Rich's classic analysis, or perhaps even bisexuality, as women feel pressured to hook up with women in order to please men, or being sexual itself, according to feminist scholar Ela Przybylo—body hair removal for women has shifted to a compulsory status.[25] Those nonconformists who choose to go against the grain—to engage in same-sex attraction, love, and sex, to resist having sex entirely, to grow out their body hair, and many, many other examples—often face great social penalties. They find themselves in a condition of, at minimum, swimming upstream, exerting effort just to be themselves. At times, they face even more severe forms of social punishment, including derogatory comments, discrimination, social isolation, harassment, threats, and assault. These are the conditions to which we subject women who defy social norms and expectations, who delineate the boundaries of their own bodies on their own terms rather than someone else's. These are also the conditions within which people make routine, everyday choices about their bodies, as expectations of possible rejection, disapproval, and social punishment *create* the mundane experiences of the body and the daily choices people make.

The story of women's body hair removal connects at its core to the story of women's oppression itself, to the insidious ways that women's bodies are controlled, managed, shaped, restricted, constrained, and dictated by forces they did not choose or decide. Hair is tangled up with a wide variety of powerful institutions that shape and mold the choices women make about their bodies—cultural practices, institutions, formal organizations, families, workplaces, relationships, the beauty and fashion industries, governments, and capitalism, to name a few. Cultural stories about hair—particularly women's body hair—have their roots in the fundamental belief in the gendering of subject/object relations, where women are told (and then internalize) the story that their bodies are fundamentally *wrong* in their natural state and, in tandem with this, that they must alter their bodies in order to be seen as beautiful, acceptable, attractive, worthy of love, and inoffensive.

Through this process, women and their bodies become both subjects and objects, imposed upon by culture and also working to undo and remake culture itself; in short, byproducts and creators of culture. As feminist scholar Elizabeth Grosz writes, "The body must be regarded as a site of social, political, cultural, and geographical inscriptions, production, or constitution. The body is not opposed to culture, a resistant throwback to a natural past; it is itself a cultural, *the* cultural, product." She goes on to add, "What is needed are metaphors and models that implicate the subject in the object, that render mastery and exteriority undesirable."[26] To understand women's relationships to their bodies, a closer look at how the subject operates within a mode of being objectified (becoming an object) is necessary.

In this book, I look at women's body hair as precisely that—*the subject in the object*—in order to better understand the conditions in which women imagine hair removal—itself a kind of ordinary body modification—as necessary, important, and desirable. More importantly, I examine the ways in which women resist this norm individually or collectively, even temporarily, as a literal and metaphorical representation of how bodies can serve as tools of resistance to the broader forces of oppression—patriarchy, misogyny, racism, white supremacy, classism, homophobia, fat phobia, ableism, ageism, and transphobia. I want to think big while looking at something small; I want to work ambitiously with something seemingly trivial and certainly mundane. It is my hope that a book about women's body hair can pull back the curtain on some of the more complicated, difficult, contentious, and largely invisible dimensions of body politics. In essence, this book serves as a meditation on how people make choices about their bodies in a culture that has disdain for their bodies and how people can and should continue to direct their energies toward full-fledged revolts against body shaming, body hatred, and the narrowing of beauty norms. It is within this tension—between compliance and resistance—where the "subject in the object" is most vividly seen and felt.

THE FRENZY AROUND BODY HAIR

As I illuminate in chapters 1 and 2, I have spent a sizable amount of time fielding media inquiries about women's body hair, particularly after a story about an assignment I do with students went viral throughout right-wing media in 2014. Consequently, I have agreed to do numerous interviews about women's body hair and have responded to questions from reporters and scholars patterned in similar ways over time. Specifically, I have been asked repeatedly the following groups of questions: First, how (and why) did body hair removal for women start, and why was this norm introduced to women? Second, why do women comply with removing their body hair? What does it mean in a symbolic sense? Is hairlessness connected to femininity, and is hair connected to masculinity? Third, isn't hair removal a personal choice? What if women enjoy removing their body hair? What if it brings women pleasure? And fourth, isn't this a trivial/silly/dumb topic? Shouldn't you spend time working on something more substantial, meaningful, serious? In this introduction, I reflect on each of those areas to better explore the common ways that people think about, imagine, and enter the conversation about women's body hair.

A BRIEF HISTORY OF WOMEN'S BODY HAIR REMOVAL

> History produces not only the forces of domination but also the forces of resistance that press up against and are often the objects of such domination. Which is another way of saying that history, the past, is larger than the present, and is the ever-growing and ongoing possibility of resistance to the present's imposed values, the possibility of futures unlike the present, futures that resist and transform what dominates the present.
>
> —ELIZABETH GROSZ, *THE NICK OF TIME*

The question of how and why body hair removal for women began, along with why this norm was first introduced to women, is a seemingly straightforward question with deceptively complex answers. The question seems to imply that the history of women's body hair removal essentially means the history of *voluntary* body hair removal. While forced body hair removal had long been used as a tactic of war and colonialism for centuries prior, women's *voluntary* body hair removal gained in popularity in the 1920s and permeated American culture so thoroughly that, by the late 1950s, women's body hair removal transformed into a compulsory cultural practice. Scholar Christine Hope reiterates that women's voluntary hair removal is a new practice: "Most women in the United States did not remove hair from underarms or legs prior to World War I."[27] As scholar Rebecca Herzig writes in her exceptional study of the history of hair removal, "Where eighteenth-century naturalists and explorers considered hair-free skin to be the strange obsession of indigenous people, Cold War–era commentators blithely described visible body hair on women as evidence of a filthy, 'foreign' lack of hygiene. The normalization of smooth skin in dominant US culture is not even a century old."[28]

Women's hair removal became a lucrative moneymaker for companies seeking to profit off women's newfound insecurities about their body hair. At the turn of the twentieth century, advertisements and popular culture equated razors with masculinity, as the shaving of facial hair was equated with professionalism and career success for men. Seeing an opportunity to grow their potential market base, the popular razor company Gillette set out to transform the market and introduce shaving to women, though it took twenty years before women adopted shaving as a regular beauty practice. The introduction of razors to women had a bumpy start.

The appeal of shaving for women increased when municipal water supplies were established and when private, indoor bathrooms became more normative and widely available in middle- and upper-class homes. Women and children no longer had to expend the enormous energy required to fetch containers of water to have on hand for shaving and rinsing their razors. Instead, as water was piped into their homes, the regularity of bathing eventually increased along with its symbolic impact. By the turn of the century, bathing was no longer an activity of the wealthy but a regular practice for everyday people. (This shift was driven, in large part, by contagious outbreaks that drove people away from infrequent bathing in communal municipal bathhouses.) Herzig writes of this shift, "Maintaining a separate, private area of the home for body washing—a 'bathroom'— became a way to mark class status, and middle-class Americans strove to attain that luxury."[29] Home bathroom sets appeared in the Sears catalogue in 1908, and many included mirrors, which allowed people to inspect and manage their hair growth. Added to this, new home construction emphasized private bathrooms rather than municipal bathhouses, particularly as bathrooms became thought of as necessary and normative.[30]

These societal shifts meant that shaving moved from barber shop to bathroom, from infrequent to often, and most importantly, it could now be done in solitude. Shaving went from a relatively infrequent activity to a daily norm, particularly for men, with expectations that individuals would learn to shave their own faces (or, in women's cases, bodies). Men learned how to shave on their own, a skill necessary during World War I, when beards were considered to be both unsanitary because of lice and a safety hazard because they prevented a tight seal on gas masks. Every US soldier was required to carry a shaving device of some kind, which pushed Gillette to sell its compact pocket razor and blade sets en masse.[31] Gillette strategically targeted men with its products and, by 1921, convinced a whole generation of men to shave their faces daily, transforming it into a new cultural norm.[32]

This period, marked by intense changes in women's fashion and dress in the 1910s and 1920s, also brought about a new self-consciousness about women's underarm hair. Fashion photography had recently been invented, meaning that women more routinely interacted directly with images of celebrities and celebrity fashion. A dramatic shift had begun in women's dress, and sleeveless fashion became appealing and highly sought after, as did sheer-sleeved clothing that exposed the underarms. This meant that a whole new market opened up for women to maintain their newfound hairlessness. The magazine *Harper's Bazaar* began running instructional advertisements in May 1915 about the fashionable qualities of removing underarm hair, complete with phrases like "Summer Dress and Modern Dancing combine to make necessary the removal of objectionable hair."[33] *McCall's* began running similar instructional underarm hair removal advertisements in January 1917, broadening the target audience to a wider range of social classes.[34] The idea of *needing* to remove body hair was a new concept, and the advertisements for hair removal products reflected this. Around this same time, Gillette began its aggressive campaign for women's hairlessness by introducing the first women's razor, the Milady Décolletée, pitched as a toilet accessory rather than a (highly masculine) razor with sharp blades. When men came back from the war, women began to borrow men's razors rather than rely on the sometimes dangerous and often foul-smelling depilatory creams they had used before. The purchase of "women's razors," then, became pitched as a way to avoid women's "razor-napping" of men's products.[35]

To a certain degree, the norm of women's hairlessness had successfully been introduced to American culture by the late 1920s. Sears began offering dresses with sheer sleeves in 1922, and sleeveless dresses appeared in 1925; the first beauty books mentioning underarm hair removal appeared in 1922.[36] Many women removed their underarm hair, and most women had internalized self-consciousness about their leg hair. (Still, as Hope mentions, "At no time is there a campaign against leg hair comparable to the earlier campaign against underarm hair.")[37] By 1930, an article appeared in *Hygeia* labeling the removal of leg, arm, and underarm hair a "social convention" and claiming that such hair removal was "as much a part of the routine of every woman as washing her hair or manicuring her nails."[38] Also of crucial importance during this time was the general assault on women's bodies via teaching women to feel self-conscious about all aspects of their so-called hygiene. As Hope notes, "Women during this period were not only being told that their body hair was unfashionable, but also that their breath was bad, that they were probably turning away suitors because of body odor, that 'feminine daintiness' demanded a certain type of sanitary napkin, and that being a good mother meant using soft toilet tissue. In short, one's goodness and value as a human being came to be identified with one's attention to rather stringent personal hygiene routines."[39] The stakes had grown ever more severe for women to comply with new norms of body "management" and hygiene.

While many women removed their leg hair in the 1930s, an even greater number relied on thick nylon stockings to conceal their leg hair. But, as World War II made nylon shortages more common, nylon production moved from an optional fashion garment to an essential of military operations instead in the United States (unlike England, which prioritized women's nylon stockings as an "essential" element of life). Herzig writes of this dramatic shift in nylon production, "Within a single year beginning in September 1941, production of all-silk hosiery declined 99.1 percent and all-nylon hosiery by 97.1 percent."[40] Women reacted negatively to this sudden shift: they painted on "liquid" stockings and applied lotions and creams to their legs, penciling on stocking seams to their legs and affixing fake decals of stocking seams to give the illusion of wearing stockings. This tactic, however, only worked if legs had been recently shaved, and because women had been sold on hairlessness (and stockings) as a requirement for professionalism, they began to use "leg cosmetics" as a quick substitute for real nylons. These, too, quickly fell out of fashion when lotions and cosmetics were deemed nonessential during WWII, leaving women with the general sense that shaving (and, for white women, tanning) was easier than bothering with leg cosmetics.[41]

The remarkable speed of increase in women's body hair removal practices presents a staggering picture of how quickly the norm of hairlessness was adopted, internalized, and deployed onto the body. By 1964, a full 98 percent of all American women ages fifteen to forty-four routinely shaved their legs, a trend that continued until the start of the women's movement in the late 1960s when, due to the momentum of the black power movement and the embrace of natural (decolonized) black hair, women's body hair began to be seen as a symbol of internalized beauty norms and unnecessary meddling with the natural body.[42] Further, because the second wave—particularly the radical feminist versions of the second wave—prioritized the personal as political and wanted to revolutionize the notion of the public/private divide, body hair served as a symbol of patriarchal intrusions onto the body.[43] Feminists wanted to explain the way that the domestic sphere shaped and defined women's options, particularly about reproductive labor, sexual politics, and marriage/family relationships. Control and autonomy over the body, particularly as recognized through the struggles over abortion, sexual liberation, natural childbirth, and freedom from violence, could be seen through the politics of women's body hair, as women revolted against compulsory hair removal, groomed their head hair differently (longer hair, less alteration, less dyeing), and used visible armpit hair as a statement of feminist politics.[44] As Herzig writes, "Body hair provided a convenient stand-in for larger disputes over which elements of the self were (or should be) subject to the woman's individual control."[45]

After the peak of the women's movement, body hair removal moved aggressively into the corporate framework, with women's magazines, advertisements, and products targeting women's insecurities about their bodies and reminding them that hair removal was both necessary for "proper" femininity and required in order to present as beautiful and professional. This "liberation through consumption" model dangerously equated hairlessness and consumerism.[46] Fortunately, feminists have consistently resisted the hairlessness mandate since the beginning of the women's movement in the late 1960s. This makes sense, as feminist psychologist Susan Basow found that feminist women and lesbians were the least likely to comply with social norms of women's hair removal and were the most likely to grow their body hair.[47]

Feminists have resisted not only by refusing to shave but also by engaging in more collective forms of resistance focused on anticorporate, anticonsumerist models of advocacy (mirroring menstrual activism's takedown of the pharmaceutical industry and the corporate landscape of menstrual products and menstrual product advertisements).[48] For example, since the 1970s, an increasing number of older women, particularly feminist-identified older women, have chosen to keep (and show) their gray head hair, claiming it as authentic and pushing back against the "old = incompetent" model of aging; many women with visibly gray hair feel that people take them more seriously with gray hair and that they have revised the rules of gender by rebelling against the beauty industry.[49] Older women also grappled with a loss of body hair in general, particularly pubic hair and leg hair, relative to younger women.[50] More recently, nonbinary and trans people have upended the gender binary and have actively changed the cultural conversation around gender and body norms, including norms around hair, hairiness, and hairlessness, the costs and benefits of nonconformity, and the euphoria/dysphoria of resistance.[51] That said, aggression and hostility toward hairy people (especially hairy feminists) also intensified, as women's hairy legs became linked to violent radicalism and "extreme" animal rights activism, and hostility toward "bearded terrorists" appeared rampantly following the 9/11 attacks on New York's World Trade Center.[52]

Still, this historical treatment of women's voluntary hair removal practices largely neglects the broader story of *forced* hair removal that has permeated much of the colonial and military histories of the United States. While not unique to women per se, forcible hair removal has been used throughout US history on prisoners, students, and soldiers and in colonial forms of violence for centuries. As scholar Rebecca Herzig notes, the United States government frequently utilized forced shaving as one of its normative tactics for torturing detainees at Guantánamo, alongside sleep deprivation, exposure to cold temperature, confinement in a box, beatings, prolonged stress standing, and suffocation by water.[53] Writing about forced shaving as a military tactic of torture, Herzig asks, "When exactly does a practice cease to be merely 'unpleasant' and become 'cruel,' 'inhuman' torture? What distinguishes trivial nuisances from serious problems? Who gets to determine the parameters of true suffering, and of real violence?"[54] She goes on to add that the history of hair removal has been not on the periphery of our political world, but at the *center* of it: "Hair removal has preoccupied public and political figures in the United States from Thomas Jefferson to Donald Rumsfeld, has shaped practices of science, medicine, commerce, and war, and has elicited breathtaking levels of financial, emotional, and ecological investment."[55]

Thus, the history of women's body hair removal is a complicated one, mired by the broader histories of hair and hair removal as social and political weapons. Body hair has been used, historically and currently, as a way to delineate rights and privileges based on distinctions between sexes, races, and species, and it has defined all sorts of social statuses: "mental instability, disease pathology, criminality, sexual deviance, and political extremism."[56] The biomedical categorization of individuals based on their body hair growth, for example, has furthered racist and classist practices of categorizing people according to their perceived level of humanness or animality. The measuring of the skull alongside notations about head hair and body hair, for example, was commonly practiced among scientists and anthropologists engaged in racist and imperialist work to discover the "superior" race.[57] The eroticization of the body hair of women of color, often mixed with violence and dominance, also informed the gender practices of colonialism and imperialism.[58]

Still more, relationships of domination have been solidified through practices of hair removal and inspection of body hair. For example, during times of slavery, slave traders would shave the beards and faces of enslaved men who were being prepared for sale because "younger" appearing men drew higher prices.[59] (Herzig found an appalling eighteenth-century engraving of an Englishman licking the face of an enslaved man being auctioned in order to test whether he had stubble on his face and thus was secretly older than slave traders had suggested.) As a more recent example, in the mid-1990s French officials began to require that all immigrants, including students and refugees, from Africa undertake a medical exam, which included full inspection of their bodies in order to identify "abnormalities." One Senegalese woman described how inspectors smelled the odor of her armpits, counted the holes in the lace of her underwear, and measured the length of her body hair.[60] As Herzig eloquently argues, "By examining that labor [of body hair management] more closely, we might better perceive the implicit values suffusing social life."[61]

THE SYMBOLIC MEANING OF WOMEN'S HAIRLESSNESS

To better understand these implicit values that inform and shape social life, a consideration of the symbolism of hair—and the symbolic meaning of women's hairlessness—is warranted. I am often asked, "Why do women comply with removing body hair? What does it mean in a symbolic sense?

Is hairlessness connected to femininity, and is hair connected to masculinity?" Understanding the frameworks surrounding head hair helps to better contextualize the symbolic roots of women's body hair.

Deep historical and symbolic links between hair and power have permeated religious and cultural stories for centuries. Many early depictions of Christ, for example, portray him with long, flowing hair, and this iconography has persisted throughout the contemporary period.[62] In many religious traditions, the voluntary removal of hair ("tonsure") has been linked to deference to God and religious submission. (The Catholic Church has also made a small fortune on selling the removed hair from nuns, and the custom of tonsure has been exploited for profiting off hair produced from traditions of women's religious deference.)[63] Monks and, in some cases, nuns still routinely shave their heads in many religious traditions such as Buddhism, Hinduism, Catholicism, and Eastern Orthodoxy.[64] Orthodox Jewish women who leave parts of their hair showing under hats and scarves are seen as less pious or modest than those who cover their hair completely with tight turbans or wigs.[65] As another example of religious hairlessness as an act of deference, Hasidic Jewish women shave their heads completely after getting married, subsequently covering their shaved heads with wigs or long scarves.[66]

In part, this covering or removing of hair stems from the belief that longer, uncovered hair tempts men and exposes women as vulnerable and eroticized. Long hair on women has become associated with sexuality, seduction, and desire rather than actual political and social power.[67] This has its roots in the historical depictions of Eve as a long-haired temptress to Adam and folkloric tales of mermaids and sirens with long tresses that would seduce and entrap sailors, often leading them to their untimely deaths.[68] Veiling of women's hair—in the form of nuns wearing veils (a tradition that continued until the 1960s) and brides wearing veils during and after their wedding ceremonies—has roots in ancient Greek, Roman, and Jewish cultures.[69] (Remember that the word *nuptial* means "to veil".)[70] Christian and Jewish cultures continued for centuries to require the covering of hair, just as most Muslim cultures implore women to wear veils and hair coverings when outside of the home.[71] Typically, powerful women world leaders—particularly older women leaders—crop their hair short (and consistently dye it to hide their gray hair) in order to be perceived as serious leaders, as seen with key figures like Hillary Clinton (United States), Angela Merkel (Germany), and Tsai Ing-wen (Taiwan). (Notable exceptions, like Alexandria Ocasio-Cortez, have also become simultaneously deeply sexualized, objectified, and mistreated in vile ways by Republican men, though Ocasio-Cortez's reactions and responses have been epically brave and courageous.)[72]

Hairlessness, then, has also become associated with powerlessness, particularly when people have had their hair removed against their will. Historically, forced hair removal for women often intensified based on the racial and ethnic backgrounds of the women involved. In addition to the examples above from the times of slavery, or the colonial conquests of Indigenous cultures in the Americas, many other examples of forcible hair removal have revealed the links between hairlessness and powerlessness. British inmates in prisons, workhouses, and hospitals had their hair forcibly removed until the 1850s.[73] Hindu tradition dictated that widows shave their heads upon the death of their husbands and remain that way for life.[74] Native American children, forcibly removed by agents of the US government, had their hair cut and their clothing and customs stripped and were detained in boarding schools ("Indian schools") from 1879 until the mid-twentieth century.[75] Aggressive hair "dealers" gave poor immigrants sailing from Europe to New York business cards detailing where they should go to sell their hair upon arrival, resulting in over fifteen thousand pieces of hair being cut directly from new immigrants' heads after they came to America; desperation often led to women selling their hair for a fraction of what it was worth.[76] (The practices of preying on poor, vulnerable, and immigrant women continues today in South Korea, China, Indonesia, Cambodia, Vietnam, Laos, Mongolia, and Burma, with racist narratives of "contaminated" hair making the situation all the more reprehensible.)[77] During World War II, the French military frequently shaved the heads of women who had engaged in sex with German soldiers in order to shame and humiliate them.[78] Historically, Polynesian cultures dictated that men had long hair and women had short hair, a trend that only shifted when they faced European colonization and the forced removal of men's hair.[79]

That said, notable differences exist between head hair and body hair, as head hair has become a symbol of femininity while women's body hair has been framed since the 1920s as unfeminine, excessive, dirty, unwanted, and unhygienic.[80] Symbolically, women's hairlessness positions them as feminine, within bounds, clean, desirable, and worthy, or, put more succinctly, *properly* gendered. The act of body hair removal, and the resulting smoothness and hairlessness, is seen as not just a personal grooming choice but an act of conformity to gendered expectations that permeate adolescent and adult life. Refusing to remove body hair also has different meanings from refusing to cut head hair, symbolically, politically, and culturally. This is not to suggest that growing body hair somehow reconfigures women from the framework of cultural and social norms. As scholar Daniella Caselli argues, "A female body with hair does not overcome cultural normativity; rather, it situates itself in a different position in relation to it."[81]

Related to this, a sizable body of work has examined the fetishization of girls' hairlessness that translates into pressures for adult women to be "baby soft" and "clean," particularly as girls and women are objectified within the media and by boys and men themselves.[82] Objectification theory, which argues that girls and women become accustomed to internalize an observer's perspective as their primary view of their physical selves, suggests that as women and girls become *objects* for the male gaze rather than *subjects* in their own right, their bodies (and presumably their body hair) are placed under increasingly intense self-scrutiny. This results in women's self-loathing, depression, internalized shame, poor body image, beliefs in their natural bodies as disgusting or inadequate, and compliance with socially constructed body norms.[83] Internalizing cultural messages about women's and girls' bodies can be hazardous for their well-being.

In a related way, pressures for women to have prepubescent genital appearance have also increased, with cultural messages repeatedly reinforcing the idea that a hairless vulva is essential to sexual appeal and self-care.[84] Within pornography, the hairlessness norm is particularly insidious, as hairy vulvas often constitute a "fetish" market while hairless women's genitals have become ubiquitous.[85] These trends have resulted in a vast increase in women internalizing the message that they must remove their pubic hair and conform to hairlessness norms, even if they find pubic hair removal to be uncomfortable, expensive, or problematic.[86] Further, women who removed their pubic hair reported less condom use with partners, more self-objectification, and more thin-ideal internaliza-tion.[87] In short, the ability to distinguish between personal beliefs or desires and cultural mandates has become increasingly difficult as sexual objectification and self-objectification have intensified.[88]

THEORIZING BODY HAIR AS ABJECT

In this way, Mary Douglas's theory of pollution and dirt, coupled with Julia Kristeva's notion of abjection and abject bodies and Emily Martin's anthro-pological work on reproduction, can help to more fully explain the power-ful hostility people have toward women's body hair, and it can shed light on the true stakes of refusing to comply with social norms of women's hairlessness. In Mary Douglas's work—and it is nearly impossible to over-state how influential she has been in shaping understandings of bodies and culture—she argues that strong negative feelings emerge when dichot-omies and categories are breached, muddied, or polluted and that cul-tural beliefs about women often position themselves in reference to the notion of pollution. Douglas writes, "Ideas about separating, purifying, demarcating and punishing transgressions have as their main function to impose system on an inherently untidy experience. It is only by exagger-ating the differences between within and without, above and below, male and female, with and against, that a semblance of order is created."[89] In short, when there is dirt or pollution or some kind of "matter out of place," thus dis-ordering culturally accepted hierarchies, it exposes the bound-aries between order and chaos, self and other, as fragile, permeable, and easy to breach. Dirt, in this case, originates from the body; thus, people often adopt the euphemisms of *clean shaven* or *fresh and clean* to describe their shaved bodies and faces.[90] Women's body hair, too, can serve in this role of Douglas's pollutant and disrupter. As scholar Alice Macdonald writes, "These women are treated with social disapproval, since the fail-ure to remove the offending hair—the 'matter out of place'—will be seen as a sign that she wishes to destabilise society itself."[91]

Adopting some of these same themes, Julia Kristeva has argued in her groundbreaking work on abjection that simple aspects of the body like bodily fluids, along with aspects of the material world like the cream on top of a glass of whole milk or, in more extreme cases, corpses themselves, can all represent that which "disturbs identity, system, order. What does not respect borders, positions, rules."[92] These borders are established when children try to pull away from their mothers and establish their own identities. People go to great lengths to preserve their sense of autonomy and selfhood, she argues. Consequently, the abject serves to "erupt the Real" into our sanitized, orderly, and body-denying lives, forcing people to confront not the cerebral or philosophical/religious knowledge of, or meaning of, death, but rather, the "sort of materiality that traumatically *shows you* your own death."[93] Body hair, then, when it moves into an abject status, can push people into having to *experience* the collapse of order and of self-other distinctions, resulting in a heightened emotional reaction to something seemingly small, trivial, and mundane. Hair moves from the inside to the outside of the body and might be regarded, as Macdonald writes, as "bodily excreta, which provides one account of the fears it may evoke. For, viewed in this way, the appearance of hair on a body surface can both constitute the animal within, which constantly threatens to overwhelm the human, and, in gender terms, may trigger anxiety about sexual identity."[94] Remember, too, that what makes something abject is often connected to the (monstrous) feminine, as women's bodies and their fluids, hair, and menstrual blood are, in the patriarchal imagination, disorderly by nature.

Though less theoretical and more situated in grounded, qualitative anthropological work, scholar Emily Martin's work also sheds light on the ways that women begin to imagine their bodies as outside of themselves, in part because of the cultural stories made about women's reproduction. Women do not themselves *deliver* their babies, but rather, their babies *are delivered* by the (authoritative) doctors; women and their uteruses are not seen as inseparable and fused together, but rather, uterine contractions *happen to* them and they *go through* labor rather than experience it as something they *do*.[95] As Martin says, "Often these assumptions are deeply buried, not hidden exactly, but so much a part of our usual experience of the world that they are nearly impossible for a member of the same cultural universe to ferret out."[96] These distinctions may very well extend into the way that women are taught to see their body hair—as an extension of themselves rather than as a part of themselves, as something external to be managed rather than as something folded into their entire embodied self.

AGAINST NEOLIBERALISM: BODY HAIR AS "PERSONAL CHOICE"?

Women's body hair is theoretically imagined as disruptive, chaos produc-
ing, outside of the self, and as something women must therefore manage
and control. The cultural story about body hair removal as a "personal
choice" then emerges and pivots attention away from the cultural and societal expressions of control over women's bodies. If people imagine their
body hair as merely something they can alter, modify, and remove if they
choose to, this suggests, as stated earlier, that all choices are choosable
and that women merely select from a buffet of possible options during
their routine grooming practices. Journalists have repeatedly asked me,
"Isn't hair removal a personal choice? What if women enjoy removing their
body hair? What if it brings them pleasure?" The answers to these questions are surprisingly tricky, particularly because we so poorly theorize
the concept of pleasure as a site worthy of critical attention.

The complex ways that cultural stories transform into rhetoric of "personal choice" owe much to the traditions of neoliberalism and the ease with
which neoliberal philosophies translate onto people's embodied experiences.[97] Neoliberalism essentially argues that free-market capitalism should
guide the choices individuals make, and that individual choices should be
unfettered and driven by self-interest while being situated in reference to
the logics and sensibilities of capitalism. (One infuriating extension of this
logic has been the notion that women have sexual or erotic capital and
should intentionally maximize the utility of this in all interactions, personal
and professional.)[98] In this way, even though women's body hair removal
has staggeringly high levels of compliance, and even though women who
grow their body hair might experience punishment, denigration, and rejection, and even though corporate and pharmaceutical industries stack up in
favor of pushing for more products and more drugs in order to maintain a
"normal" body and a "normal" appearance, all of this gets funneled toward
the simple suggestion that people have individually chosen this. And, more
insidiously, coupled with the emphasis on individual personal choice is the
even thicker layer that people enjoy and find pleasure in these various forms
of body modification. *It brings me pleasure! I like the way my legs feel after I shave!
Being smooth makes me feel feminine! It feels good!*

The entire enterprise of neoliberalism requires individuals to self-manage and self-regulate, particularly as states cede their power to the markets, a process that then renders bodies as subject to market demands and whims. The shaping of our individual bodies to meet these market demands—to engage in labor to "improve" ourselves, to get an education in order to maximize desirability as a future job candidate, to shape and groom the body in order to maximize success on the dating market—has informed nearly all aspects of contemporary American life, including the mundane choices people make about their body hair. Rebecca Herzig writes convincingly of the influence of neoliberalism on women's body hair choices, "Nourished by pervasive commercial media, the opacity of global commodity chains, and consistently lax regulation of so-called elective care, ever more emphasis is placed on individual 'freedom.'"[99] She goes on to add, "Shave or wax, laser or pluck: we are empowered to decide, and responsible for our own outcomes."[100] Or, as Louise Tondeur writes, "Everyday, normalising, mundane, trivial consumption forms part of a system which supports the global market-place."[101]

What neoliberal ideologies of "personal choice" leave out, of course, is the incredibly disruptive and rebellious power of opting out, of choosing not to purchase shaving products, or to not imagine one's body as deficient and disgusting for having hair on it. Something isn't really a choice if people can't choose to abstain from it, and in large part, much of this book takes up the question of what happens when women nevertheless abstain from shaving and waxing. What does it look like, both for the women who do this and for those who confront hairy women, when women refuse to submit to the false choices of neoliberal and market-driven body hair removal options?

When women internalize the need to remove their body hair and become tools for ensuring that other women also comply, they most often do this by using the rhetoric of "personal choice." Power is exercised most effectively in this way—not by heavy-handed, top-down, out-loud, explicit enforcement of shaving mandates but instead through the slow and subtle infiltration of power into our everyday practices. Hair removal choices feel pleasurable because women are actively complying with the hairless ideal. This is similar to how people do not necessarily intentionally *mean* to cede control over their lives to megacorporations and big technology companies and pharmaceutical companies but often do so nevertheless through the gradual process of those things starting to feel easier and easier (e.g., "It's so much easier to just order food online from Amazon instead of going to a grocery store!" or "I feel so much happier when I use this kind of shampoo"). For anyone who has ever tried to resist social conventions and traditional gender roles—whether through coming out as queer or trans, making unconventional choices about the body, or inventing different ceremonies or holidays or customs—the difference between swimming upstream and swimming downstream can be intense.

That said, women often do take immense pleasure in the act of refusing and resisting social norms. The unruliness of women's body hair, and women's expressions of wanting to make space for themselves in a world that insists on restricting their bodily choices, is delightful to look at up close. Growing body hair means different things to different people; it can feel easy or fun, trivial or profound, and it can make a powerful political or personal statement. For women, having body hair can be freeing in all of the best ways—more time, more energy, more body love, more solidarity with others who resist by using their bodies, more space for gender diversity, more claiming of space for rambunctious and playful forms of rebellion. I want to at least posit here that, while pleasure is often a poor metric for making choices about the body, pleasure can nevertheless be found *both* in conformity (swimming downstream) and in rebellion (swimming upstream). The better people get at understanding the social contexts in which they make personal choices, the more they can demystify those choices and understand them as complicated and tangled up with structures of power and pleasure.

REIMAGINING THE MUNDANE

> As Cixous reminds us, if something is being called silly, there is likely to be a political motivation, an attempt at subjection and the removal of power involved in the process. Pubic hair is silly, masturbation is silly, women's writing is silly, because to call them anything else would be to allow them to unleash their power.
>
> —LOUISE TONDEUR, "A HISTORY OF PUBIC HAIR"

Though I would like to believe that the answers to the question "Why do the mundane experiences of the body matter?" would be self-evident—particularly given that so much of feminist history, and radical feminist history in particular, has targeted the intimate, personal, and domestic experiences of women as valid and important—I very often get asked questions about the lack of importance and significance of studying women's body hair. Questions like "Isn't women's body hair a trivial, stilly, dumb topic? Shouldn't you spend time working on something more substantial, meaningful, and serious?" have appeared frequently in professional contexts (e.g., the editor of a well-known and respected journal prefaced her acceptance of my article with a claim that she initially thought it was unworthy and trivial) and with journalists who often want to disparage the status of American intellectuals and their "frivolous" subjects of research.

To answer these questions, I have been particularly aware that, while the field of body hair research is small, nearly all of the other feminist writers on women's body hair have faced similar questions (attacks?) and accusations as well. Louise Tondeur wrote an entire chapter on the subject, responding critically to Terry Eagleton's claim that theorists should move away from the trivial and everyday realities and instead focus on subjects with more existential and transcendental heft.[102] (Her response, a brilliant evisceration of Eagleton, is in fact a wonderful exposé on the importance of feminist work on the so-called mundane.) Rebecca Herzig encountered, in numerous professional contexts, people eager to shame and embarrass her for writing on the history of hair removal. She also brilliantly responds to them by noting, "The boundaries of 'serious' bioethical concerns, and of medical 'necessity,' are continuously remade, symbolically and materially, in relation to the trivial and the superfluous. Much as masculinity co-constitutes femininity or the human co-constitutes the animal, the serious and the trivial are predicated on one another, even while continuously excluded from one another."[103] Scholar Rose Weitz faced constant assumptions that studying hair was trivial and silly, to which she replies, "Far from being trivial, these concerns reflect deeper truths about women's lives, truths so embedded in our culture that they can be as difficult for us to see as for fish to see water."[104]

I could not agree more with these refutations of the argument that the study of women's body hair is too trivial to be worthy of serious attention. To put this forth as a topic of scholarly inquiry pushes back against systems of power that separate out the serious and the trivial, the worthy and unworthy. As hair scholar Karin Lesnik-Oberstein writes in her insightful analysis of women's body hair as compared to the treatment of women's fatness, "Any consideration of women's body hair, in short, is clearly regarded as a legitimate subject of only medical and cosmetic interest, with the two aspects being extensions of each other, as both have the aim of removing the hair. Otherwise, women's body hair is seen as, apparently, either too ridiculous and trivial—or too monstrous—to be discussed at all."[105]

I would add that it is precisely this backlash, this emotional reactivity to the study of women's body hair, that animates this book and that has animated me in teaching and writing about body hair for over fifteen years. I have written about numerous subjects during my career, many of which could be seen on the one hand as trivial, stupid, and silly and on the other as outrageous, obscene, dirty, outlandish, and controversial. None of those topics has incited more emotional aggression from right-wing reactionaries than my work on women's body hair. That suggests that my speaking and writing about women's experiences with growing body hair has hit some kind of nerve and that the subject is not only worthy of scholarly attention but also worthy of serious analysis in the broader landscape of feminist politics. What (*the fuck*) is going on when writing about body hair provokes responses like death threats and calls for my firing? While right-wing aggression and trolling has become itself more common in the lives of left-wing women,[106] I would still argue that its appearance over a scholarly subject like body hair suggests an underlying hatred, fear, and disdain for women and their bodies, especially if those bodies operate outside of patriarchal mandates for grooming, hygiene, and hairlessness.

WHY WRITE A BOOK ABOUT BODY HAIR REBELLIONS?

This book addresses the central quandary that women's bodies sit in a permanent state of tension between, on the one hand, the seemingly insignificant and, on the other hand, deeply entrenched views about gender, identity, beauty, and social norms. This very tension—the triviality and inconsequentiality of hair combined with the ways that it is persistently regulated while eliciting emotional responses from people—animates and underlies each chapter of this book. I look closely at the politics of women's body hair; that is, how body hair moves from a personal grooming choice to something with much wider resonance in the broader cultural stories about women's reproductive rights, feminist battlegrounds about autonomy, neoliberal intrusions onto beauty regimens, and even global tensions around women's "place" in society. In this sense, I work in this book to move away from thinking *about* the existing practices of body hair and instead look specifically at the reverberations of women's body hair *rebellions*. What happens when women use body hair as a form of hidden or public revolt? How can body hair map onto bigger stories about patriarchy, power, and the necessity of embodied resistance?

Body hair is an emotional subject. In every interview I have done on body hair and in every piece I have ever written on this subject, my overwhelming impression is that body hair incites fervor. People feel strongly about their own hair choices and often react badly when women use body hair as a form of rebellion against the status quo. Body hair is also a *tool*, something that peels away the layers of the culture people live in, revealing its deeply held beliefs about rigid gender roles and normative body choices. Consequently, I illuminate here the ways that body hair rebellions carry deep emotional and cultural weight.

Tying this book together are chapters that examine conformity and resistances to body hair norms and the deeply entrenched feelings people have about creating, existing within, and being subjected to norms about "appropriate" and "proper" bodies. I incorporate historical material, new qualitative interviews with body hair rebels, body hair art, zines about body hair, global political battles over body hair, and conversations with women who temporarily or permanently resist the hairlessness norm for women. This book is intentionally interdisciplinary, leaping across subjects and styles, methods and manners of looking and seeing. I draw from critical feminist psychology, sociology, cultural studies, women and gender studies, queer studies, history, sexuality studies, art history, and health studies, intentionally and joyfully. I work here to integrate material on abject bodies, embodied resistance, and bodies marked as "outsider" or "Other." I work across geographical spaces and take seriously the stakes of rebellion. Ultimately, I showcase the possibilities of bringing together the mundane and the extraordinary, the everyday and the revolutionary.

Body hair is also a site of possibility. It is the perfect site for exposing readers to the allure of social norms, the invisible workings of power, and the possibilities of resistance. To date, very little work has addressed the kinds of issues interrogated within this book, particularly the nexus between individual choices about body hair and cultural/political implications of breaking body hair norms. And, because everyone can relate to a book about hair—as we all negotiate the tiny daily choices around managing and grooming our body hair—this work serves as a springboard for more serious conversations about oppression, social identity, patriarchy, biopolitics, and power. This book provides an examination of the complexity of body hair and bodies in revolt as written into this contemporary cultural moment, particularly as its subjects provide a window into *what is possible* for bodies when they revolt. I want readers to invest in the notion that small aspects of our bodies have wide reverberations in the political and social landscape; more importantly, I want that fact—that decisions about bodies matter not just to us as individuals but also to the wider political landscape—to feel exciting and pregnant with possibilities rather than limiting and daunting.

BOOK ORGANIZATION

This book approaches its subjects through critical frameworks that move the boundaries of how people typically see women and their body hair choices. I focus the book's eight main chapters on three clusters, first considering, in part 1, Revolting Bodies, the implications and significance of *temporary* body hair rebellions, followed in part 2, Art and Activism, by the role of art *as* activism in moving the discourse around gender and body hair. I conclude the book with three chapters that look at people who engage in more sustained, sometimes lifelong body hair rebellions, including a series of twenty-two interviews with women and nonbinary people who already resist body hair norms. A short epilogue ties together the book and offers some thoughts about the necessity of activism and the future of body hair rebellions. This organization for the book captures body hair resistance when it first happens (that is, the first time women might consider not removing their body hair and the consequences for not removing hair), followed by a closer look at how body hair has been taken up as a cultural form of resistance in zines, photographs, drawings, and political activism, and concluding with a close reading of recently collected qualitative narratives from longtime body hair rebels.

More specifically, part 1, Revolting Bodies, includes two chapters that look at the reverberations and consequences for undergraduate students who *temporarily* engaged in body hair rebellions during the course of a single semester. I drew from hundreds of narratives from college students who experimented with growing out their body hair and writing about it. Since 2007, I have given students in some of my courses an optional extra credit assignment where they grow their body hair (women), remove their body hair (men), or creatively rebel with body hair (trans/nonbinary folks) and write about the experience throughout the semester by keeping a log of their experiences and writing a short paper at the end of the semester. These rich narratives serve as the basis for this section of the book, as I explore a plethora of subjects that arose during this assignment: differences between imagining a body hair rebellion and engaging in one, women's experiences with homophobia and heterosexism, race and class differences in students' reactions to body hair, and the media reactions and experiences resulting from these body hair rebellions.

Chapter 1, "Hairy Subjects," closely examines the social identity implications for women's body hair rebellions, particularly for race, class, sexuality, and gender. I consider body hair as a "hairy subject"—one in which we get entangled in the workings and trappings of power as it plays out both in social life and in our own minds. Most centrally, I contrast a diverse community sample of women asked to *imagine* their own, and others', reactions to their hypothetical body hair growth, as compared with the response papers from sixty-two undergraduate women who grew their body hair for an assignment. Both groups showed overwhelming negativity toward women growing body hair in both studies, but they differed in perceptions of social control and individual agency. Women who imagined body hair growth described it more nonchalantly and individualistically, citing personal choice and rarely acknowledging social pressures placed upon women even when they were disgusted by other women's body hair. Women who tried growing their body hair regularly discussed unanticipated social pressures and norms, rarely discussed personal choice, and reported a constellation of difficulties, including homophobia, family and partner anger, and internalized disgust and "dirtiness." Ultimately, the differences between the results of these studies point to gaps between how we might *imagine* being marked as "Other" and how it feels to *live* as "Other." Further, this chapter highlights the invisibility of omnipresent sexism directed toward those who violate practices to "maintain" the female body.

Chapter 2, "Body Hair Battlegrounds," extends my earlier work on the body hair assignment by revisiting the question "What do women's overt body hair rebellions provoke in others?" Instead of looking only at the specific individual experiences of students in my courses who have chosen to grow out their body hair (see chapter 1), in this chapter I also examine the 2014 public media attention that this assignment received in the (mostly conservative) news media. I examine the most significant findings from the body hair assignment from 2007 to 2020, including the interplay between internalized versus externalized oppression, the politics of respectability, patriarchal control of women's bodies, the links between homophobia and heterosexism, the anxieties about "masculinizing" body hair removal for men, and most significantly, the ways that the emotional and affective implications of body hair continue to govern our thinking about, and practices surrounding, body hair removal for women. This chapter is meant to introduce readers to the politics of body hair assignment and its various implications from its inception in 2007 through today. I conclude the chapter by looking at four recent semesters of women and gender studies students who participated in this assignment and lay out some of the more interesting patterns of their reports on the experience. I also imagine the *future* of body hair rebellions, both on and off campus.

Part 2, Art and Activism, includes three chapters that situate the artistic dimensions of body hair resistance as a form of activism. I examine, from a cultural studies perspective, the wider breadth of how body hair serves as a form of resistance in artistic and activist work. The section begins by looking at body hair zines and drawings as an effort to normalize abject bodies and move them more to the center of feminist thought and activism. I then consider the role of body hair art photography and the complex ways that notions of the "natural" are nuanced and reimagined through such photographs. I conclude by discussing China's "armpit hair contest" from 2015 and the political implications of engaging in body hair protest en masse by weaponizing abject bodies on social media as a force of social justice. Ultimately, this section asks how art and activism work in tandem, and how body hair can provoke political and social change.

Chapter 3, "Hairy, Not So Scary," examines fifteen recently published (2015–20) body hair zines (e.g., *Body Hair: A Love/Hate Story, Frida at My Table, Hairy & Happy*) and a series of drawings about body hair by Pakistani American artist Ayqa Khan in order to situate these creative works as activist efforts. By seeing them as a mechanism to normalize women's body hair and bring body hair into the public conversation about feminism, choices about the body, and resistance to patriarchy, I recast these zines and drawings as politicized and distinctly feminist. I theorize these zines and drawings of hairy bodies as an integral part of contemporary feminist politics and activism. I also extend the existing parameters of how artists imagine body politics by including art that is often marginalized or ignored as "trivial" or "silly." Ultimately, this chapter works to reimagine body hair zines and drawings as a contemporary reflection on abjection and, more importantly, *resistance* to the sidelining of abject bodies.

Chapter 4, "Expanding the Body Hair Imaginary," positions art photography that features women with visible body hair as an emerging mode of artistic expression. Given that widespread body hair removal, for women, largely began in response to the development and circulation of fashion photography between 1915 and 1919,[107] the relationship between women, body hair, and photography is fraught and significant. As photographers grapple with abjection, discourses of the natural body, and the visually arresting possibilities of women's body hair, they also visually document—both by rebelling against them and by in some ways reinforcing them—the powerful social norms of women's hairlessness. I specifically argue that body hair photography is itself a *social intervention*, working against the operations of making body hair invisible, silent, and secret. I examine in this chapter several photographers whose work captures the complexities and contradictions of visually documenting women's body hair, including British photographer Ben Hopper's series called *Natural Beauty*, in which he contrasts the highly stylized traditions of fashion models and fashion modeling with the natural, makeup-free, diverse bodies of women with body hair; Oaxacan American artist Zuly Garcia's photographs called *The Valentine's Day Series*, in which she features Mexican and Sikh women revealing body hair against a backdrop of traditional campy femininity; and Marilyn Minter's images of pubic hair in *Plush*, where she features an array of slick, textured, explicitly erotic photos of women's pubic hair. I conclude by looking at historical and contemporary feminist performance art—in particular, Eleanor Antin's 2017 reimagining of her classic 1972 piece, *Carving*—to deeply consider how the notion of the *natural* is an inadequate framing to capture the subversive qualities of body hair photography. Ultimately, I argue in this chapter that photography of the body can serve as a social intervention, one that embraces rather than erases contradictions while better understanding the time and context of its subjects.

In chapter 5, "China's Armpit Hair Contest," the final chapter in part 2, I look at the cultural context of China's gender politics, particularly surrounding the conflicted messages around the Communist Party gender equity claims as contrasted with newer pressures for Chinese women to embrace traditional gender roles, marriage, and child-rearing, largely a consequence of China's one-child policy and the imbalances of men and women that resulted from this. I then look closely at the political protests and performative activism that occurred in response to these changing gender role norms from 2012 to 2015, focusing heavily on the work of feminist activist and women's rights advocate Xiao Meili and her colleagues. I examine the rationale for, and consequences of, the 2015 "armpit hair contest" in China started by Xiao Meili on the social media website Sina Weibo. Subsequently, I consider the slippage between the polarities in which this contest operated, as it moved between the silly/campy and the serious/impactful. In tandem with this, I focus on the March 2015 arrest of five Chinese women activists called the Feminist Five, three of whom participated in the contest, and the international impact of these arrests on Chinese feminist activism in the subsequent months and years. By looking at the frenzied media coverage of both the armpit hair contest and the arrest and detention of the Feminist Five, I explore the ways that feminist resistance, especially around body hair, can move across geographical and cultural spaces with remarkable speed and impact. I also consider the value of performative activism around body hair, particularly as these protests posed a threat to the status quo both in China and throughout the world.

In part 3, Body Hair Rebels, I look at the narratives of those who have engaged in long-term body hair rebellions, drawing from a series of twenty-two interviews with women and nonbinary people from diverse backgrounds—race, class, sexual orientation, age, parental and relationship statuses, and geographical locations across the United States—who have intentionally grown out their body hair for long periods of time. Unlike the narratives of college students in part 1 of the book, these stories highlight the lives of those who intentionally became long-term body hair rebels. I use these qualitative interviews to expand the conversation on body hair to a variety of subjects, including gender, power, emotions, embodiment, social identities, and the impact of bodies in revolt. This section is meant to showcase the extended narratives of those grappling with how to use their bodies as a form of resistance, and the costs and benefits of doing so. In this way, these chapters serve as a meditation on the freedoms people have with their bodies and the trappings that create barriers for all people struggling for self-definition, autonomy, and liberty.

Chapter 6, "Growing a Thicker Skin," highlights the *emotional qualities* of women's body hair and the deeply entwined relationship between body hair and affect. First, I look at the key reasons women chose to grow their body hair, highlighting the diverse range of reasons that women chose to reject the social norm of women's hairlessness. I then consider the emotional experiences of hair, particularly the joy and ambivalence women feel about their hair, alongside the different meanings women assign to different regions of their body hair, including armpit hair, leg hair, pubic hair, facial hair, and "rogue" body hairs. I conclude by examining why women feel emotional about their hair, and what this says about gender and power. The political implications of emotions, and how emotions govern our aesthetic and beauty choices, are explored in this chapter.

In chapter 7, "The Only Opinion That Matters Is My Own," I examine the ways that women struggle with, and have reflected on, the painful dynamics of how they negotiated their body hair in different social and relational spaces. From decisions about whether to wear long pants or skirts at work to conversations where they worried about dating new partners and wondering about their body hair preferences, women constantly navigated complicated and tricky terrain around the social regulation of women's body hair. This tension—between the social and the personal, the contextual and the individual—forms the basis of this chapter. Ultimately, this chapter highlights the contradictions and complexities of working to undermine patriarchal control of women's bodies, all while struggling within the weighty and difficult parameters of the social contexts in which women live.

In the final full chapter of the book, chapter 8, "In the Revolution, We Will All Be Hairy," I work to explore the fraught relationship between the body as natural versus cultural, inherent versus produced, real versus symbolic, which plays out vividly in the politics of women's body hair. Here, the portrait of bodies being *produced* by their cultural and social world, shaped and molded—or in this case, shaved and waxed—conjures the story of bodies as *products*, bodies as embedded within the scaffolding of culture, within patriarchal, racist, misogynist, classist, and homophobic lenses, within the battle between individual autonomy and social sculpting. I look in this chapter at the question of how body hair connects to gender, power, and politics, particularly as body hair moves into an explicitly rebellious and revolutionary framework. Unlike the previous two chapters on the emotions surrounding body hair and the social and relational frameworks of body hair, the material in this chapter was explicitly political and ideological, as women constructed their body hair choices within this conservative political landscape, at the peak (or valley?) of the Trump presidency, in the middle of COVID-19 and the Black Lives Matter protests and activism of 2020. These meditations on how body hair rebels imagined the hope and possibilities of body hair as a political tool also undermine neoliberal "individual choice" rhetoric and instead situate body hair as part of a broader social context that strips women of their power and engenders a host of new forms of resistance written onto the body.

Ultimately, I hope this book will resonate with readers across a range of identities, body choices, hair statuses, and geographies. Body hair has the rare status of being something that people almost universally negotiate, contemplate, and make choices about on a daily basis.

In this way, hair unites people and reveals a common language of expression of self, culture, and society. In another way, body hair—especially on women—provokes, unsettles, disrupts, and at times, offends. It evokes divisions between people, demarcates categories and classes, and showcases deeply held historical beliefs about power and the exercise of power onto bodies. But it is precisely this uneasiness and potential reactivity to women's body hair that invests it with its power.

Dorothy Allison once wrote, "Two or three things I know for sure, and one is that I would rather go naked than wear the coat the world has made for me."[108] In this most delicate of borders, between self and other, person and culture, body and world, there is a window into the operations of power, into how to wiggle free from the coat that the world has made for each of us. The workings of how gender operates, how the deep imprint of culture is felt in the individual's experience of the body, and how cultural stories are made and remade become visible when looking closely at the story of women's body hair. And maybe, though this work is never complete, by seeing these stories more clearly, we can render them fragile and vulnerable, and we can see how easily they break apart and are remade anew.

PART I |

REVOLTING BODIES

Hairy Subjects: Imagining versus Experiencing Body Hair Rebellions

The space between the idea of something and its reality is always wide and deep and dark. The longer they are kept apart—idea of thing, reality of thing—the wider the width, the deeper the depth, the thicker and darker the darkness. This space starts out empty, there is nothing in it, but it rapidly becomes filled up with obsession or desire or hatred or love—sometimes all of these things, sometimes some of these things, sometimes only one of these things.

—JAMAICA KINCAID, "On Seeing England for the First Time"

IN *THE HISTORY OF SEXUALITY*, VOLUME 1, MICHEL FOUCAULT writes that "power is tolerable only on condition that it mask a substantial part of itself. Its success is proportional to its ability to hide its own mechanisms."[1] By this, he means that power can only thrive in contexts that conceal the workings of how power operates, and that it is immediately destabilized and thrown off balance by an interrogation of how power works. The nature of power, according to Foucault, lies in its incessant reproduction within social systems, its replication, expansion, and dissemination through discourse. In other words, we cannot always *see* power and its workings, but we are nevertheless trapped within those workings. To challenge power—to directly interrogate it, reveal it, and undermine it—makes power less tolerable, more exposed, more vulnerable.

Body hair is deeply connected to the story of how power operates. Writing and thinking about the contemporary politics of body hair reveals the heavy-handed exertions of power and the always-multiplying forms of resistance to that power. In many ways, body hair serves as a microcosm of how to understand power on a much larger and broader scale; it is the tiniest of subjects with enormous implications. For this reason, I work in this chapter to consider body hair as a "hairy subject"—one in which we get entangled in the workings and trappings of power, both as it plays out in social life and in our own minds.

I first consider body hair as connected to the study of power itself, particularly the work of Michel Foucault, followed by an analysis of the body as a key site of resistance for marginalized people. I then examine the most significant findings from an assignment I have given to students since 2007 that asks them to experiment with their body hair and then reflect on gender norms. In particular, I look at the interplay of internalized versus externalized oppression, the politics of respectability, patriarchal control of women's bodies, the links between homophobia and heterosexism, the anxieties about "masculinizing" body hair removal for men, and most significantly, the ways that the emotional and affective implications of body hair continue to govern our thinking about, and practices surrounding, body hair removal for women. I ask in this chapter, Is body hair a symbol of freedom or a marker of oppression? Does it reveal power as weak and vulnerable (and thus easily changed and rebelled against) or as strong and fixed (and thus a behemoth force against which people struggle)? Such paradoxes inform the volatile politics of body hair and show body hair as both a material experience of the physical body and a symbol of how power operates.

Foucault has implied that we are much freer than we feel and, perhaps paradoxically, that we are constrained by forces we cannot see or sense or fully understand. Here Foucault suggests there are twin forces at work when we unpack the mechanisms of power—we are freer than we feel; that is, able to radically change and alter the terms in which we experience or understand our bodies, and paradoxically, we are also simultaneously constrained by invisible forces, trapped in a sticky spider web of invisible lines that form all around us. Power is deployed without our permission, invisible, insidious, and it is also possible for us to at least partially implode these working with relative ease. We can slyly attack the workings of power within discourse, dislodge the "truth" of those workings, and make something new. (One could easily see this as COVID-19 first took hold, when so many aspects of life that seemed fixed and immutable suddenly failed or became exposed as weak and vulnerable—capitalism, food supply networks, health care, decision-making around federal spending, or even safety itself.) These paradoxes form the crux of the chaotic biopolitics of body hair, in part because these are some of the great complexities and contradictions that underlie the social text of the body and its relationship to power.

HAIR AS EMOTIONAL

While hair in general tends to bring out intense emotions in people, women's body hair in particular has inspired a wide variety of intense reactions. Years ago, I found a photo of the Italian actress Sophia Loren that I wanted to publish in a book. I wrote to the photographer to request permission to use it in a publication, and he referred me to Loren's agent. Her agent denied my request because he argued that it could cause "personal and reputational damage" to Loren. The idea that a famous European actress—someone with a storied career and many accolades—could somehow be tarnished by her youthful body hair choices seems revealing of how body hair can be emotional. The potential for disgust, revulsion, and even *damage* points toward the ways that body hair gets constructed and built through affect. As such, people's reactions to hair can be especially intense.

The politics of body hair—or, more precisely, the *biopolitics* of body hair (what Foucault has outlined as the relationship between the body and the mechanisms of social and political control over that body)—are chaotic in nature. People will discount the importance of hair and call it trivial and unimportant but will then spend huge amounts of time and energy managing it, thinking about it, worrying about it, and grooming it. Hair informs the core of grooming practices, style decisions, and worries about looking old or unkempt. (Consider that during the early months of the 2020 coronavirus pandemic, hair dye shortages and concerns about women showing gray hair roots dominated public expressions of distress, particularly on social media and in people's "panic buying" behavior.)[2] Because body hair is infused with heightened emotions, bizarre blind spots, and even unfettered anger, it gives a unique window into how power and discourse shape people's experiences with body hair (see chapter 6). It never seems to take much to elicit these reactions, whether intentionally or unintentionally.

Social theorist Sara Ahmed says, "Emotions should not be regarded as psychological states, but as social and cultural practices."[3] Emotions work to perform social functions, regulate our behavior, and put forth clear notions about what kinds of bodies are acceptable and what kinds of bodies are abject, disgusting, and revolting. In essence, emotions pave the way for social and cultural life. If body hair elicits emotional reactions, these emotional reactions also govern and dictate acceptable, attractive, and appealing bodies and, by extension, unacceptable, unattractive, and ugly bodies. As critical theorists Sara Rodrigues and Ela Przybylo have argued, "The process of thinking about abjection, disgust, and revolt is less about thinking ugliness than it is about visceral reactions to ugliness. . . . Thus our visceral responses to dirt, the grotesque, plainness, and/or monstrosity are about maintaining social relations and social margins."[4] Emotions about bodies tend to shape and mold ideas not just about those bodies but about the social status and power of those bodies.

As such, people relate to body hair differently for women and for men, as women's body hair becomes saddled with cultural baggage of disgust and disdain. Women are also taught to attach their value to their bodies, while men get their value from other aspects of their identities (e.g., work, money). Psychologists Marika Tiggemann and Christine Lewis found that people had more negative attitudes toward body hair because they found it disgusting and that women's body hair, but *not* men's, elicited disgust.[5] Other researchers have noted that women's body hair was linked to perceptions of unattractiveness, and that feelings of disgust function to regulate women's bodies in particular.[6] By extension, women of color also had different experiences of their body hair than did white women, as discourses of respectability, dirt, disgust, and social regulation appeared more strongly for women of color and their body hair than for white women and their body hair.[7] The fault lines of the social and political battles around "acceptable" and "ugly" bodies thus appear in full force for the politics of women's body hair.

Still, it remains increasingly difficult to get people to consciously think about, reflect on, see, and challenge the larger structural critiques of power that surround body hair politics. Many different tactics employed by individuals and institutions have worked surprisingly well to suppress serious thinking about women's body hair politics. First, many people—feminists and nonfeminists alike—have argued that things like body hair are trivial and unworthy of serious study or scholarly attention (see introduction). Most often, this has been couched in the framework of imagining women's hair as less important than other more "serious" concerns of women. Historian and activist Roxanne Dunbar-Ortiz writes in her memoir of the early years of women's liberation organizing about how, after a consciousness-raising session about hair and public styles of hair, women reacted in conflicted ways: "The negative reaction by many of the women amazed us. We had done it to raise consciousness and to amuse but had no idea our action would be met with such anger by some. Women gathered around to thank us, but other women told us that they felt we had trivialized women's liberation and reduced it to a matter of style."[8]

Echoes of believing that hair is trivial permeate discussions about hair, feminism, politics, and liberation. Trivialization is a tactic often used by those on the right (and, less commonly, on the left), directed toward feminists and others who seek to undermine practices of body shaming, ageism, and patriarchal control of the body. Taking women and their complaints seriously has not been a strong suit of much of American culture. From asking women to smile more in politics to depicting female athletes as sexy to describing women's anger and rage as purely connected to menstruation, our culture has long forced women to grapple with its tendency to invalidate and diminish their abilities, drives, and passions.[9] Trivialization is a tactic that has long haunted women's lives and women's work. The concerns of women—particularly those connected to the domestic realm and to the body—are often labeled as trivial and silly. A sizable amount of the feminist performance art from the 1970s grappled with these concerns, from Martha Rosler's 1975 *Semiotics of the Kitchen*, where she depicted housework as boring, mind-numbing, and tedious, to Judy

Chicago's 1972 *Womanhouse*, which featured rooms labeled Nurturant Kitchen, Dining Room, Bridal Staircase, Crocheted Environment, Leaf Room, Leah's Room, Personal Space, Painted Room, Red Moon Room. Building on this, Mierle Laderman Ukeles's 1973 performance, *Hartford Wash: Washing, Tracks, Maintenance—Outside* and *Inside,* featured the artist personally mopping and washing the staircases and floors of the art exhibit while viewers walked by.[10]

In tandem with the trivialization of women's body hair as a silly issue, neoliberal claims that people have individual agency and that they can make individually motivated choices outside of a social structure inform the discourses of body hair. These same arguments have been weaponized against fat people as well, saddling them with the burdensome cultural narrative of individual and personal responsibility for body size while erasing the larger structural contexts in which people's bodies exist.[11] Remember that neoliberalism emerged in the 1980s as a mode of rationalizing politics via privatization, deregulation, and disestablishment of governmental power. Its legacy has been an unleashing of a market ethic for *all* aspects of modern life, including gender relations, fashion, beauty, and feminist politics.[12] Neoliberal arguments that hold individuals solely responsible for making "market-driven" choices about their bodies have in part destroyed some of the savvier political and social critiques of how body hair is linked to patriarchy. Instead of imagining pubic hair removal and its widespread increase as a political and highly gendered site of patriarchal fantasy about girlhood and impossibly youthful beauty standards for women,[13] neoliberalism encourages women to remove pubic hair as a matter of individual choice and personal preference without concern for social climate and context. As an illustrative example, a recent *Cosmopolitan* magazine article about pubic hair choices quoted women saying things like, "I love my landing strip and it's completely my choice to have it . . . I like to be able to control the hair. It makes me feel sexy."[14]

Neoliberalism in general has a long history of removing broader social critiques in favor of seeing individuals as making choices as individuals. The fantasy that "feminism is about choice" or that "all choices are possible" and even that "all choices can be chosen" is a concealment technique that distracts people from broader critiques of the relationship between gender and power. Choice—or the idea that people choose things without social context—stands in for power or empowerment, leading to an erasure of patterns or even logic and facts. For example, the link between shaving pubic hair and cleanliness has been flatly refuted by a number of studies, as pubic hair actually facilitates vaginal health and reduces vaginal irritation and infection.[15] Further, removing pubic hair has led to a spike in emergency room visits due to shaving accidents or emergencies, including a rise in staph infections and injuries. Recent data suggests a five-fold increase in shaving-related emergency room visits, with 83 percent of these due to shaving pubic hair with razors.[16] Links between underarm hair removal, the use of antiperspirants, and increased risk for earlier appearance of breast cancer have also been shown in recent studies, again pointing to numerous hazards—some even life-threatening—from shaving body hair.[17] These facts do not, however, coincide with neoliberal notions of choice at the individual level, even when aggregate data suggests that shaving body hair has physical and medical costs to women.

Finally, the notion that women live in a *postfeminist* world that affords them the freedom to do whatever they want with their bodies also lurks at the edges of body hair politics. Postfeminism often takes the form of the nostalgia for a time when women's roles were more distinct and quite conservative, or as a celebration that feminism is over, but it can also appear as a kind of backlash against feminism itself.[18] Feminist scholars Rosalind Gill and Christina Scharff have aptly characterized the way that postfeminism has been deployed to undermine feminist concerns and critiques: "[Backlash discourses] often work by attributing all women's unhappiness to feminism, but may also suggest that 'all battles have been won' or, conversely, that 'you can't have it all—something has to give'; that 'political correctness' has become a new form of tyranny; that (white) men are the real victims, and so on."[19] Building on this, Gill and Scharff draw from Angela McRobbie's work on postfeminism by arguing that "the elision of postfeminism and anti-feminism misses a crucial feature of current media discourses: namely the *entanglement* of feminist and anti-feminist ideas within them."[20]

In this regard, postfeminist ideas about women's body hair might argue that women should return to a state of "just being women" (read: complying with patriarchal norms) reminiscent of the 1950s era of women's grooming and traditional housework duties. Postfeminism might also argue that feminist critiques of body discourses are no longer needed and that women now have access to a wide variety of choices, none of which place them in danger of oppression. Further, postfeminist discourses of body hair might argue that feminism is about choice and being whatever we want to be, and that feminism has paved the way for bodily choices on a wider scale. This tangle of feminist and antifeminist discourses— feminism as a celebration of women's right to choose whatever they want for their bodies without concern for how those choices are made or why they are made—embodies the clever deployment of power disguised as freedom. Exertions of power are still in effect, of course, whether couched as trivializing women's hair conversations as "silly," neoliberal excitement about "choice," or postfeminist dismissal of feminism with "We've already achieved equality." Body hair is thus a sly indicator of—or litmus test of— feminist politics of the body.

BODY POLITICS MEETS FEMINIST RESISTANCE

Recent political events during and after Trump's presidency have engendered new frameworks for thinking about, and seeing the impact of, the intersections of patriarchy, racism, classism, fat phobia, and ageism.[21] As such, it has been much more difficult to erase the structural critiques of patriarchy from public conversations about women and feminism. For many people, this has been a painful period of history, one where the increasingly powerful and public forms of misogyny appear abundantly (e.g., Brett Kavanaugh securing a Supreme Court seat despite his likely sexual assault of Christine Blasey Ford; progressive women in politics labeled as nasty or forced out of view, erosion of abortion rights, and many more).[22] These exertions of patriarchal power, however, have at times been met with more defiant, rebellious, and wonderfully impolite forms of feminism, some of which sprang up from the women's marches and #MeToo activist efforts.[23] Slowly, feminists of this period have recognized a need for a different approach, one less focused on a calm, measured, and welcoming demeanor and more focused on the angry, menacing, and radical visions of feminist resistance.

As Foucault predicted, heavy-handed exertions of power will be met with similar forms of resistance; as power grows and becomes more top-down, resistance, too, meets those challenges by becoming more direct, flagrant, and outlandish. The polite, welcoming, "Feminism is for every-body" version of feminism that featured prominently in the 2000s and 2010s has paved the way for firebrand feminism, full of anger and margins and jagged edges.[24] From Twitter wars about #MeToo to folksingers and hip-hop artists lighting up stages with fiery words to a militant and highly visible Black Lives Matter movement to an angrier and more powerful group of congresswomen ("The Squad") joining the high ranks of federal political office, feminism and its optics have dramatically shifted.[25] Feminists have been up to all sorts of rabble-rousing, from manifesto writing to political organizing to the resurfacing of older radical feminist political groups like WITCH, the Women's International Terrorist Conspiracy from Hell. Recently, in Portland, Oregon, Boston, Massachusetts, and Louisville, Kentucky, WITCH reappeared to lurk in public spaces and protest racist, sexist, homophobic, and transphobic policies and practices.[26]

Body politics scholarship and writing have also grown increasingly defi-ant, edgy, and angry, with a new wave of trans studies scholars taking on trans surgeries and reimagining gender altogether (for example, Andrea Long Chu's wonderfully absurd *Females*) and feminist sexuality scholars making bolder and braver critiques of the patriarchal status quo.[27] Critical feminist work has tackled subjects as diverse as eating disorders, ugliness, memoir, ageism, racial privilege, and madness.[28] Youth studies work has emerged to help people think more deeply about resilience, global networks, families, cyberculture, sexuality, and activism.[29] And feminists have once again linked arms with critical race scholars—past and present—to better under-stand intersectionality, affect studies, structural critiques of institutions, and abject bodies, particularly the work of Audre Lorde, Kimberlé Williams Cren-shaw, Sara Ahmed, bell hooks, Mireille Miller-Young, and James Baldwin.[30]

This work has set the stage for understanding the body as a site of resistance and imagining the body as a social text, a site of protest, and a subject of defiance. Marginalized people have long used the body to enact resistance. Sit-ins and marches have situated bodies to block, impede, show solidarity, arrive en masse to public spaces, or shout down powerful people and institutions. Performance art pieces have also placed the body at center stage (for example, Carolee Schneemann's 1975 *Interior Scroll*, where she pulled a scroll from her vagina and read it aloud, or Patty Chang's 1998 *Shaved (At Loss)*, where she removed her pubic hair while blindfolded and using a Perrier bottle.[31] Other feminist performance artists have dealt with subjects that span a huge range of subjects, time periods, identities, and political contexts, including weight gain, aging, domesticity, racism, silences, and confrontation. VALIE EXPORT, in *Genital Panics: Action Pants* (1969) cut a triangle-shaped hole in her pants, sat in a chair with her legs spread, and aimed a machine gun at people's faces, daring them to objectify her.[32] The body as contested and rebellious, angry and defiant, is a key component of feminist histories and politics, both in the past and today.

THE NORMALIZATION OF WOMEN'S BODY HAIR REMOVAL

Women's bodies have often served as contested terrain in battles over agency, control, power, and identity. The rhetoric of individual choice often appears in debates—feminist or otherwise—about how to critically examine body alterations and modifications, including plastic surgery, reconstructive breast surgery following mastectomies, labiaplasties and vaginal rejuvenation, genital grooming and genital self-image, fashion and technologies of sexiness, and tattoos.[33] Similarly, ideas about, and critical interrogations of, the "disgusting," "mismanaged," or "unkempt" body (what Joan Chrisler calls "leaks, lumps, and lines") often appear in feminist literatures.[34] Alongside discussions of the menstruating body, the "leaky" breastfeeding body, and the childbearing body, conflicts about body hair have become increasingly relevant.[35] Additionally, theories of modern sexism posit that women often ignore or minimize the extent to which practices constrain and influence women in contemporary society.[36] Does removing body hair represent a decision made by individuals who *choose* to do so, or does it reflect larger cultural mandates that require the compliance and obedience of women and their bodies? Can women who have never grown body hair accurately imagine the personal and social consequences of having a hairy body, or must they experience the growth of body hair to understand the kinds of social penalties they might encounter with such "transgressions"? Do different groups of women face different outcomes for body hair, or is the norm of depilation so pervasive that few women remain exempt from the demands for hairlessness?

The pervasiveness and normalization of body hair removal in the Western world—particularly the United States—suggests that body hair removal has transitioned from an optional form of body modification to a relatively universal expectation placed upon women. Recent studies suggest that between 91 and 99 percent of women have removed body hair at some point in their lives.[37] A variety of other countries (e.g., England, Egypt, Greece, France, Uganda, Italy, and Turkey) reported that over 80 percent of women remove their body hair starting at puberty.[38] Pubic hair removal—a practice that largely stopped in the late nineteenth century but restarted in the 1980s—has also shown a dramatic increase in recent years, with younger and partnered women in the United States removing pubic hair at a growing rate and pornography and popular culture idealizing hairless and prepubescent female genitals.[39] Moreover, one recent US study found that although men and women both removed pubic hair, women reported greater frequency of pubic hair removal and described removing pubic hair to achieve sexiness and cleanliness and to feel normative.[40] Women in New Zealand reported removing pubic hair as an issue of choice, privacy, physical attractiveness, cleanliness, and enhanced sexuality.[41] Although older age, feminist identity, and lesbian identity predicted decreased likelihood of body hair removal,[42] these numbers show body hair removal and pubic hair grooming as strikingly commonplace, especially because the 1960s and 1970s bohemian counterculture no longer has much influence on women's body hair practices.

Whenever a body norm becomes this pervasive, questions arise about the reasons for its compulsory status. Across all social identity groups, hairless female bodies have entered the cultural imagination as a compulsory ideal, in part generated by mass media and marketing campaigns that feature Brazilian waxes, eyebrow waxes, permanent hair removal, and body hair removal creams as positive choices for body modification, particularly within industrialized countries.[43] Following the Gillette advertising for women's razors in the 1920s, the 1930s saw advertising campaigns in the United States that featuring flapper girls, photo spreads, and a newfound obsession with physical beauty.[44] Today, both mainstream films and advertisements, as well as pornography, generally promote women's hairlessness as an absolute default (e.g., pornography featuring hair on women's genitals exists now only as a "fetish market"), as women shoulder greater economic and social burdens of making their bodies acceptable via body alterations than do men.[45] The notion that women's hairiness equals dirtiness or even abomination has a firm grip on the contemporary cultural imagination about women's body hair.

These findings on body hair removal signify the extent to which women, including feminists and those who typically rebel against social norms, internalize mechanisms of social control placed upon the body. Women "do gender" both to manage their own (dis)comfort with their bodies and to manage others' anxieties and expectations about their bodies, particularly along racial and sexuality lines.[46] Women learn to pass as heterosexual to escape workplace discrimination, violence, and negative judgments from others; restrict their eating; hide or pathologize their menstruation; straighten and lighten their hair and skin; and medicate their sadness and anger.[47] They also disguise and conceal their natural bodies by "maintaining" their bodies in a way that conforms to social norms. These trends deserve serious empirical and theoretical analysis, for "by refusing to trivialize women's 'beauty' practices, then, we question the narrow definition of 'acceptable' feminine embodiment, which maintains—at the most 'mundane,' and, hence, insidious level—the message that a woman's body is unacceptable if left unaltered."[48]

Clearly, those who resist body hair shaving face social stigma and negative social penalties, particularly because women who refuse to shave have repeatedly described feeling negatively evaluated by others as "dirty" or "gross."[49] Similarly, US women rated other women who retained their body hair as less sexually attractive, intelligent, sociable, happy, and positive compared to hairless women, just as they described hairy women as less friendly, moral, and relaxed, but more aggressive, unsociable, and dominant compared to women who shaved their body hair.[50] Women complied with body hair removal norms in order to achieve femininity and overall attractiveness, as well as to feel cleaner and more confident about themselves.[51] Some women admitted to liking the soft and silky feeling of shaved legs whereas others enjoyed the way hairlessness made them feel sexually attractive for men. In fact, partnered women reported more consistent pubic hair removal than nonpartnered women in both US and Australian studies.[52]

Such compliance with social expectations of hairlessness has not come without a cost for women. Those with negative attitudes toward body hair reported more body disgust, stronger feelings that their bodies were unacceptable and unattractive in their natural state, and more compliance with other restrictive body norms like dieting and cosmetic surgery.[53] Conversely, *not* removing body hair also produced a variety of negative outcomes for women. Lesbian and bisexual women often feared that growing body hair would further out them; some queer women even worried that having visible body hair would provoke hate crimes against them for not complying with compulsory heterosexuality.[54] Compared to white women, women of color and working-class women in the United States described more negative reactions from family members and friends when they resisted removing body hair, as they negotiated narratives of respectability on top of the already racist and classist judgments of others.[55]

Still, rebellions against body hair removal have gained in prominence in recent years. While not much scholarly attention has focused on how women might use body hair to rebel against gender norms, popular media stories have sometimes framed body hair as a prominent public act of rebellion for women—celebrity or otherwise—who have grown tired of body policing and constraints. Consider how hippie women in the 1960s who challenged norms of shaving were criticized and belittled for their hairiness.[56] Links between fashion and rebellion—the body as a social text that reflects the social mores, values, and identity politics of the day—also apply to body hair.[57] With pornography glorifying women's hairless vulvas and magazines emphasizing that women will have great sex if they remove their body hair, women who rebel against body hair norms face steep pressures to conform to sociocultural norms of "appropriate" hair growth.[58] Despite this, a variety of celebrities have espoused body hair growth as a public rebellion, including Miley Cyrus, Sarah Silverman, Scout Willis, Penélope Cruz, Madonna, Gaby Hoffmann, Juliette Lewis, Drew Barrymore, Julia Roberts, and Mo'nique.[59] Dyeing armpit hair has also received attention, with debates online about whether it represents symbolic rebellion, narcissistic calls for attention, or the latest fashionable statement.[60] Young women who identified as "eco-grrrls" also sometimes used body hair growth as the ultimate political act of rejecting gender norms.[61] Thus, body hair is emerging as a key player in gendered rebellions of the body, with new iterations of body hair rebellions appearing each year.

THE BODY HAIR ASSIGNMENT: COMPARING IMAGINED VERSUS LIVED EXPERIENCES

> To maintain their power, dominant groups create and maintain a popular system of "commonsense" ideas that support their right to rule. In the United States, hegemonic ideologies concerning race, class, gender, sexuality, and nation are often so pervasive that it is difficult to conceptualize alternatives to them, let alone ways of resisting the social practices that they justify.
>
> —PATRICIA HILL COLLINS, *BLACK FEMINIST THOUGHT*

Body hair practices highlight sexist, racist, classist, and heterosexist assumptions about women and their bodies because hairiness connotes manly or masculine qualities, whereas hairlessness connotes womanly or feminine qualities.[62] These dichotomies also elicit ideas about the connections between hair, power, and gender norms.[63] Thus, even when men also remove some of their body hair (as 63 percent did in a recent US study), they do this without nearly the same social penalties, particularly from their partners.[64] Women's hair removal has signified a variety of sexist assumptions about women, including their submission, tameness, and differentness from men, as well as the fundamental unacceptability of women's natural state.[65] Women who resist body hair removal negotiate stereotypes that they "cannot get a man," do not care about their bodies, or want to purposefully repel others.[66] Taken together, body hair signifies an intersection of explicitly communicated cultural norms about the body, taken-for-granted assumptions about women's hairlessness, and the dangerous power of a relatively invisible social norm.

Consequently, in this chapter, I ask three central questions:

1. Because women's hairlessness represents an invisible yet compulsory social norm, how do women think about, talk about, and experience violations of that norm?

2. What narrative differences appear when women *imagine* growing their body hair compared with when women actually *grow* their body hair?

3. Finally, how do women conceptualize freedom, agency, and choice when imagining and experiencing body hair norm violations?

IMAGINED EXPERIENCES WITH BODY HAIR GROWTH

To assess women's *imagined* experiences with body hair growth, I utilized qualitative data from a sample of twenty adult women (mean age = 34, standard deviation = 13.35) recruited in 2011 from a large metropolitan southwestern US city. Participants were recruited through local entertainment and arts listings distributed free to the community as well as from the volunteers section of the local online section of Craigslist. The advertisements asked for women ages eighteen to fifty-nine to participate in an interview study about their sexual behaviors, practices, and attitudes. Participants were screened only for their gender, racial/ethnic background, sexual identity, and age; no other prescreening questions were asked. Given that previous research has shown race, class, and sexual identity differences in women's experiences of body hair,[67] a purposive sample was selected to provide greater demographic diversity: sexual minority women and racial/ethnic minority women were intentionally oversampled, and a diverse range of ages was represented (eleven women ages eighteen to thirty-one, five women ages thirty-two to forty-five, and four women ages forty-six to fifty-nine). The sample included eleven white women and nine women of color, including three African American women, four Mexican American women, and two Asian American women. For self-reported sexual identity, the sample included twelve heterosexual women, seven bisexual women, and two lesbian women (though women's reported sexual behavior often indicated far more same-sex eroticism than these self-categorized labels suggest). All participants consented to have their interviews audiotaped and fully transcribed, and all received $20 compensation.

Several of the questions addressed issues relevant to this chapter on women's attitudes about body image and body hair. For example, women were asked four sets of questions about women's body hair:

- "Women describe different feelings about having body hair, particularly leg, armpit, and pubic hair. How have you negotiated your body hair and how do you feel about shaving or not shaving?"
- "Have you ever not shaved during your life? If so, did you face any social punishments? If not, what would it be like to not shave? Is not shaving empowering or disempowering?"
- "Do you feel that shaving is a choice or a requirement?"
- "What do you think of women who do not shave their bodies?"

These questions were scripted but served to open up other conversations and dialogue about related topics because follow-up questions were free-flowing and conversational. Because the questions were broad and open-ended, participants could set the terms of how they would discuss attitudes about body hair and what information they wanted to share.

The community sample of women who imagined body hair growth and discussed their feelings about other women who did not shave described responses that clustered around three themes: (1) belief that body hair removal represented a trivial personal choice rather than a strong social requirement, (2) language of disgust toward other women's choices to grow body hair, and (3) refusal to voluntarily grow their body hair and justification for always removing body hair.

Body Hair Removal as Personal Choice

When I asked women directly whether they felt that shaving represented a choice or a requirement, fifteen of twenty said frankly that body hair removal was a choice, two others said it was a requirement, and the remaining three said that it was both a choice and a requirement. Women overwhelmingly constructed body hair removal as something they, and others, chose to do, even though a few acknowledged the complexity of blending choices and requirements together. Most women unequivocally stated that body hair removal represented a choice for themselves, such as April (twenty-seven/Latina/lesbian), who said, "It's a choice. I don't feel like it's a requirement. I just prefer to shave." Dessa (nineteen/Latina/heterosexual) said, similarly, "It's a choice, yeah, a choice. I do it only out of my own preference." Tania (twenty-five/white/heterosexual) reflected on the way body hair removal felt compulsory by saying, "I think it's a choice that I make a requirement," whereas Keisha (thirty-four/African American/heterosexual) said, only half-jokingly, "It's a choice, but if it gets out of hand it *should* be a requirement to shave, especially if you have body odor. It should be required!"

Some women indicated that they wanted others to accept them without judgment, although they still found body hair disgusting and repulsive. Inga (twenty-four/white/bisexual) admitted that she felt body hair removal was a choice but still struggled with letting her hair grow: "I'd probably feel gross if I grew it out. It's just one more thing I have to try to keep tidy and clean because I'm kind of OCD, and because society doesn't feel it's attractive and my girlfriend doesn't feel it's attractive." Similarly, Kelly (twenty-three/white/heterosexual) firmly believed that body hair removal represented her personal choice, and even although she said she would not judge others, she acknowledged the disgust she felt toward body hair: "If I didn't shave, I don't think my boyfriend would like that, but I don't think I would either. People would be grossed out, and he wouldn't be comfortable with it." When I asked her what she thought of other women who did not shave, she said, "I think it's fine and great. Everyone deserves to live the way they want to live, but if I was their partner, I don't know if I'd be comfortable."

Although women conveyed that removing body hair seemed like a choice in our society—and saw themselves as individual agents who simply decided not to shave for aesthetic reasons, their language often conveyed judgments and negativity toward women who did not shave combined with statements about their acceptance of all bodies. When asked to imagine not removing body hair, Sylvia (twenty-three/white/heterosexual) described conflicts about the kinds of stereotypes it would evoke: "We would just look like we were in a '70s porno. I just don't want to see pubes on my bar of soap or anything. That's the only thing. I don't really care. It's not that big of a deal. I see my mom with hairy legs or armpits sometimes, and I'm like, 'What are you doing?' and she's like, 'I don't care.' She says it doesn't matter, that it's her body and nobody else's. It doesn't bother me." Shantele (thirty/African American/heterosexual) said, frankly, "It's their choice. I don't have to touch you or anything, so I don't care."

Disgust toward Other Women's Choices

Although women mostly discussed depilation as a choice, they overwhelmingly considered not removing body hair an undesirable choice. Disgust toward other women appeared frequently, particularly as women constructed body hair as "dirty" and "unclean." Some women described distaste for hair and judgment of other women who had hair, such as Cris (twenty-two/white/lesbian), who said, "I think women who don't shave are a little gross. Because sometimes, like if people don't shave their entire lives, that's just a little too much to handle for me. I always shave. I don't like hair. I shave everything." Similarly, Abby (twenty-six/white/heterosexual) wanted to accept other women's choices but ultimately found unshaved women disgusting: "I know there are people who choose not to shave. I wouldn't want to subject other people to that. There's kind of a stigma, maybe being unclean or something, and I think people would have those thoughts. I wonder what their partners think about it, whether they are 'hippies.' I guess their partners don't care." Mei (twenty-two/Asian American/heterosexual) showed the vast contradictions in women's narratives about depilation as she simultaneously described some disgust toward women who did not shave, combined with acceptance for not removing body hair, while also admitting that depilation caused her problems: "I had laser hair removal because I had really bad ingrown hairs from shaving and they would get pimply and pus-filled. . . . I feel shaving is a requirement in this society and women should shave everything except for their heads. You don't want to see women with hairs on their fingers or arms. It depends on which culture they're in."

Even when women claimed that they did not judge other women for not removing body hair, their statements often indicated otherwise. For example, Tania (twenty-five/white/heterosexual) described a stereotype of hairy German women by saying, "I think it's a personal preference. I think there's that German stereotype that they don't shave their armpits, and it grosses people out. Typically, if you've got a lot of hair, it looks like a man, and it's not very attractive on women, but I don't think I make total judgments on it. I might just stand ten feet away from them!" Leticia (forty-one/Latina/bisexual), too, said that women could choose not to shave but then added, "Hairy legs and hairy armpits look gross. I just think it's gross. It signifies a woman being lazy and not taking care of herself. Maybe they're not involved with someone, that's just their culture, but it bothers me. Why doesn't she just *shave*? You know what I mean?"

Refusal to Grow Body Hair and Justification for Shaving

Discussions of managing the unruly, smelly, and dirty body appeared frequently in women's narratives about body hair removal. Shantele (thirty/African American/heterosexual) admitted that she always needed to keep her body in control to manage her anxieties: "I never let it get out of control. When I don't shave, I'm not aroused, I'm not turned on. I always do my armpits because of the smell. If I go a few days without shaving, my armpits have a different smell, so you have to use deodorant more often, and that's not good. And then my legs, if it gets too long, it starts to actually hurt, doesn't feel good, so then I'll shave that off too. It doesn't actually get long ever." Tania (twenty-five/white/heterosexual) worried that she would harm others by having body hair: "It's got a lot to do with cleanliness, and you know, there's nothing stuck down there. You can actually hurt the other person, or they get caught in your hair, and it just kind of makes a mess otherwise."

Justifying body hair removal based on attractiveness to men also appeared frequently in women's narratives. Sometimes this appeared more directly, as women said they faced direct social penalties for not removing body hair. For example, Zhang (thirty-six/Asian American/bisexual) noted that her boyfriend "gets upset when I don't shave because it turns him off, and he will get cranky all day." More often, women described this tension more subtly, such as April (twenty-seven/Latina/lesbian), who conflated the notion of personal choice and (heterosexual) social norms when removing her body hair to please her male partner: "I think women are expected to shave, but it's still my choice. I could stop shaving if I wanted, but my boyfriend wouldn't like it. It makes me feel more comfortable, anyway."

Other interviewees also fused personal choice rhetoric with pleasing men. For example, Rhoda (fifty-seven/white/heterosexual), who said earlier in the interview that she "cleaned up" her pubic area but generally thought shaving a bore, described contradictions of both shaving for men and shaving for herself: "When I don't have a man around, I don't shave.

I think it's a personal choice. I feel better if I am shaved. I just think it looks better, feels better. Smooth feels better than stubbly." As another example of accommodating the male gaze, Angelica (thirty-two/Latina/heterosexual) also fused together depilation to please men and removing body hair to please herself: "I choose to do it because I don't feel sexy having sex otherwise. Most men like smoothness. I think that's feminine to me. I know in some countries women don't do all that, but to me it's feminine to be smooth and soft and clean. It's my choice."

Though women often removed body hair, they sometimes reported internal conflicts about the social and technical meanings assigned to hair. Jean (fifty-seven/white/heterosexual) recalled that body hair norms had changed significantly in her lifetime: "When I was younger and first got out into the world, it was free love and all that stuff. I didn't shave much, and I didn't have to. Then I got into the corporate world, and I started shaving. I didn't realize that hair was even bad until then, that it was unattractive, until the times changed. Now I have everything shaved." Patricia (twenty-eight/African American/heterosexual) also described always removing her pubic hair despite having some conflicts about the function of pubic hair and others' treatment of her as a prepubescent girl:

I like the way I look shaved and I hate when it grows back. Even though they'll say keeping your hair keeps stuff from going down in there, at the same time, it can cause moisture, and I don't like that. You don't want to start smelling. It keeps you cool down there in the summer to not have hair. . . . When I started having sex, I was eighteen, but I looked like I was fourteen at the time because I didn't have any hair down there. So guys would be like, "Man, you know you really look like a little girl, like I'm robbing the cradle!" That was frustrating.

Finally, Jane (fifty-nine/white/heterosexual) admitted that, though she admired women who resisted depilation, she could never do it herself: "If I wanted to make a statement, it's not going to be about body hair. I'm going to save my soapbox for something a little more important than about whether I shave or not. I think that women who don't shave are so comfortable in their own skin. They're not trying to be someone else. That's great if they can carry that off and they feel comfortable doing that. I just can't."

Notably, women in these interviews framed body hair primarily within the realm of personal choice, citing it as something that women can or cannot choose to grow. Their narratives often ignored larger social critiques and stories about removing body hair as a social requirement or a mandatory social norm to avoid punishment. The fascinating contradiction between framing body hair as a relatively benign personal choice and then talking about hairy women with strong disgust and rejection reveals the way social norms may embed themselves silently and invisibly in women's lives. In other words, women may find themselves in a familiar quandary: "I feel like I can choose whatever I want, but I still choose to conform." This opens up many new questions, particularly the notion of what would happen if women actually grew out their body hair and faced the social punishments for actually violating the norm rather than merely imagining such a violation. The second group of interviews, then, reveals the experiential facets of growing body hair, giving a stark contrast to the relatively casual assessments portrayed in the first group of interviews.

LIVED EXPERIENCES WITH BODY HAIR GROWTH

To explore women's *lived* experiences with body hair growth, I looked at narratives that emerged from a thematic analysis of the body hair assignment and included the narratives of sixty-two women enrolled in an elective upper-division women's studies course at (129 were enrolled; 79 participated, including 17 men and 62 women).[68] The sample included sixty-two participating women—twenty-three (37 percent) women of color (primarily Latina and African American) and thirty-nine white women. Nearly all participants were under age thirty (only seven students were over age thirty).[69]

Students were asked to participate in an extra credit assignment that asked them to grow out their body hair (underarm, leg, and pubic hair) for a period of ten weeks. Students kept weekly logs of their personal reactions to their body hair, others' reactions to their hair, changes in their own or others' behavior, and thoughts about how changes in body hair affected them. They turned in their logs (averaging five pages in a more "free-flowing" diary format) and a reflection paper (averaging two to three pages in a more formal analysis of the entire assignment) about these issues at the end of the assigned ten weeks. Participation was optional; students were given a small number of points (the equivalent of 1 percent of their overall grade) for successful completion of the assignment. If students terminated the assignment early, they were given one point for turning in a paper about their experiences along with their partially completed logs. No official "checks" were ever completed to confirm whether students were participating; students simply informed me (and often their classmates) of their participation and kept track of their feelings and reactions throughout the semester.

Women who actually grew their body hair discussed these experiences by relating their body hair experiences to the social and cultural expectations placed upon women. Many women reflected on how, although they initially framed body hair as a (sometimes insignificant or casual) personal choice prior to doing the assignment, they changed their views once they grew their body hair. Four themes (sometimes overlapping) appeared in women's discussions: (1) new perspectives on the social meanings of body hair, (2) encounters with homophobia and heterosexism, (3) anger from family members and partners about growing body hair, and (4) internalized feelings of being "disgusting" and "dirty."

Social Meanings of Body Hair

Because most students who undertook the assignment self-identified as feminist, many students initially felt that the assignment would be no big deal and that they had a vast array of personal choices about body hair. At the end of the semester, several women described new perspectives, changes of heart, or more solidified consciousness about the relationship between body hair and social norms. Dee, a white heterosexual woman, reflected on how she wished she could feel more carefree about body hair: "It makes me realize the silly things that we worry about in our society, things that really shouldn't make a difference. I try not to let the media encourage me too much about what's acceptable and what is not, but no matter how hard I try, I still find myself following these trends and not being able to get away from it." Kelci, a white heterosexual woman, reflected on her conflicted feelings about the social meanings of her body hair:

I really did gain a lot from the project. I learned about people and what society has deemed as outcast behavior. I did kind of feel like an outcast when people freaked out about it, but at the same time I felt like a badass because I stuck it out and just kind of accepted my hair as a badge of honor. . . . I love making other people step back and have a good look at real issues, issues that affect the way society has trained us all to believe that shaving is expected of women. I've been asking myself if I feel the need to conform too much to the expectations of society.

Nichole, a Latina bisexual woman, admitted that a dialectic between personal choice and social norms appeared often for her during the assignment: "When this assignment was first given to the class, I thought it was useless. I felt that shaving was entirely my own decision and that regardless of how society plays into my life, I was the one who willingly took razors to my legs and armpits. . . . After completing this assignment, I have realized that having body hair has allowed me to see things through a deeper lens. If the males are content on putting the pressure on us, we should all rise above them and stick it to them—with our hairy legs and armpits."

Encounters with Heterosexism and Homophobia

Women's encounters with homophobia and heterosexism—something that appeared only subtly in the imagined experiences of body hair—typically involved one of two scenarios: either women encountered people who explicitly said that they would not "get a man" or "find a man" if they grew body hair (heterosexism) or they encountered negative comments that body hair had directly signaled a lesbian or nonheterosexual identity (homophobia). As an example of the former, Leila, a bisexual white woman, wrote about a Facebook interaction with a male acquaintance after she posted about growing body hair:

HIM: Good thing you're single right now. GULP.
ME: That is so fucking insensitive and offensive.
HIM: Why offensive? Mainly my thoughts were that any girl wanting to take part in that project would be tough. Most guys don't like their girls all hairy.

ME: Body hair is not gross, first of all. It's HAIR. I'm not covering myself with leeches or refusing to use toilet paper.

HIM: It's part of a daily personal care routine, like saying don't take a shower for X days.

ME: Body hair doesn't smell. I'm still showering!

HIM: I and the rest of the world have this viewpoint. It's an inconvenience for you and your boyfriend or any other couple.

As an example of direct homophobia, Noelle, a white bisexual woman, described her boss's negative reaction to her body hair: "My supervisor made some lesbian jokes. He knows I am pretty vocal about feminism and gay rights, so he makes lots of jokes about my body hair, saying, 'Are you trying to tell me something?'" Or, as Hilary, a white lesbian, said after describing the homophobic statements she heard from others: "Never underestimate the difficulty of going against social norms. It is certainly not as easy as it seems, even for 'radicals.' It is not easy to be different in a world that masquerades behind the face of individuality, but in reality thrives off of the conformity and the predictable and sheepish nature of people."

Anger from Family and Partners about Body Hair

Several women recounted horror stories of their partners and families reacting with anger, disgust, and outrage about the body hair assignment. In particular, women sometimes felt pressured to seek permission from partners (especially male partners), which elicited a variety of responses. For example, Marina, a white bisexual woman, recounted her boyfriend's adamant resistance to the assignment:

When I brought up the idea of doing the project, he was automatically opposed. First I got, "Ew, no. I won't let you do that." Then I got a joking but upsetting "I will not engage in any sexual acts with you until you shave." Obviously upset and hurt that my partner would put my shaved body on such a pedestal, I decided right away that I *would* be taking part in this project. After this verbal assault on my womanhood, he went on to say how "it was pointless" and "women can do whatever they want now because it is 2011." Outraged again, I had a hard time deciding not to be a lesbian separatist and put my inner radical feminist back in her place to clarify the project. I explained that there was obviously an issue with women's body hair and that he had just qualified it in his mini panic attack over my wanting to stop shaving.

As another example of negative partner reactions, Liz, a white heterosexual woman, recalled that her boyfriend became angry and hostile when she first mentioned the assignment: "My boyfriend started yelling when I first told him, not at me, but he was upset that my teacher was trying to interfere with my life in this way. He is really attracted to legs, and that is a big part of our sex life. His anger made me cry."

Still, both women proceeded with the assignment and noted that it served a pivotal role in helping them decide whether to stay in a relationship with a man who would not accept their hairy bodies. By the end of the semester, Marina was still with her boyfriend, whereas Liz had left the relationship.

Family reactions also revealed the powerful ways that parents and siblings monitored and controlled women's choices about their bodies. As found in previous research, women of color received particularly harsh judgments from their families when growing body hair.[70] Lola, a Latina heterosexual woman, recalled how her mother found it amusing when the project was temporary, but when Lola threatened to do it forever, her mother became enraged: "Her voice changed from content and happy to shocked and appalled. She told [me] how underarm hair is 'for men only' and how it makes girls look 'sloppy' and how she 'did not raise a sloppy daughter.'" Rosa, also a Latina heterosexual woman, had a similar encounter with her mother, who fused concerns about respectability with ideas about compulsory heterosexuality: "She was absolutely opposed to the fact that I haven't shaved. She said it was gross, dirty, and not right. She asked if I had a problem or if I was too broke to buy more razors. She told my grandmother that I was letting myself go after my recent four-year relationship had ended, that I'd never find a boyfriend now." As an unexpected twist on family rejection, Michelle, also Latina and heterosexual, noted that her daughters (both tweens) also conveyed these same messages of respectability: "My eldest daughter said it was gross of me not to shave for that long. She rubs my hairy legs. I heard her calling her sister names and [referring] to her as being disgusting like my legs."

Internalized Feelings about Being "Disgusting" and "Dirty"

Many women struggled with feeling disgusting, dirty, and sexually unattractive, even when others did not provide that direct feedback. Anika, a white heterosexual woman who admitted that she would readily take a pill to stop all hair growth on her body, recalled feeling preoccupied with how "gross" she felt: "My legs looked ugly and fat with their hair on. I constantly thought about my gross hair, especially at the gym. Every time I was taking a shower, every time I changed my clothes, it was always on my mind. I couldn't believe how much time I spent thinking about my hair. It was insane!" Rosa, too, felt disgusted by her armpit hair, such that the mere disclosure of having it upset her: "I will never ever show anyone my pit hair. I really don't want anyone else to ever know that I ever had pit hair. Ever."

Some women also reflected on how they wanted to feel more confidence about growing body hair but nevertheless caught themselves with feelings of doubt, anxiety, and self-directed disgust. Rux, a biracial bisexual woman, admitted that she wanted to feel freer than she did: "I feel like women are trained to oppress themselves, that we're brainwashed to a point that even when we question, there is still something inside us which recoils from that questioning. That's the way I felt. Even though I knew what I was doing was supposed to be freeing, and it *was* to a point, mostly I felt embarrassed and ill-defined." Lola wrote about her conflicted anxieties at the start of the assignment: "I'll admit that I was sure to shave entirely before I started this assignment. Halfway through the process of my meticulous shaving of my body, I remember thinking how pathetic I felt. It was as if I was preparing for battle and that my hairlessness before the war would help give me an advantage for my courageous task of overcoming my judgmental enemies." Cat, a white bisexual woman, also expressed similar conflicts, noting that she fluctuated between feeling attractive and unattractive with body hair, even while ultimately seeing it as rebellious: "Since I am not heterosexual and somewhat actively looking for a girlfriend, will my hair growth appeal or repulse another? Today I saw some women walk by, and every single one of them had their legs shaved. My initial reaction was, 'Eww.' That kinda took me by surprise and I laughed a bit. Kinda cool that I had that reaction." As a final example, Leila did some soul searching after some particularly difficult encounters with coworkers: "It's hard. My coworker told me I was 'brave,' and she said she'd never have the courage to do that. People act like I'm standing up to Hitler! Another guy said that I should tell the teacher to go fuck herself. I'm still deciding what I want my form of resistance to be. To what extent am I going to 'play by the rules'? Will I pretend to be a good member of society while actually revolting against it? My body hair remains a work in progress."

Women who faced the challenges of actually growing their body hair had new perspectives about the meaning of body hair, particularly the compulsory aspects of needing to remove it. Women faced heterosexism and homophobia, as well as anger from family members and partners about growing body hair, and they internalized feelings of disgust and dirtiness about themselves. In contrast to women who only imagined body hair growth, the women who grew their body hair discussed their violation of body hair norms as having severe consequences for them. In addition to the affective responses it provoked in others, it clearly challenged their own comfort with, and agency around, their bodily choices. In particular, it made visible the intersections between social identities like sexual identity, race, and class, while also provoking them to assess their own comfort with pushing back against social norms about women's bodies.

CONCLUDING THOUGHTS: THE FUTURE IS (HAIRY) FEMALE

Reflecting now on the body hair assignment and its impact on students' understandings of personal choice, structures of power, and the intricate webs and networks of power that control and evaluate their bodily decisions, I return to the notion that *imagining* resistance is not enough. Foucault's great contribution to understanding and challenging power is his claim that resistance mimics the transmission of power, and as such, because power is exerted in many (often invisible) ways, resistance too is forever multiplied, always-already present in our lives. He writes,

Hence there is no single locus of great Refusal, no soul of revolt, source of all rebellions, or pure law of the revolutionary. Instead there is a plurality of resistances, each of them a special case: resistances that are possible, necessary, improbable; others that are spontaneous, savage, solitary, concerted, rampant, or violent; still others that are quick to compromise, interested, or sacrificial; by definition, they can only exist in the strategic field of power relations. . . . And it is doubtless the strategic codification of these points of resistance that makes a revolution possible, somewhat similar to the way in which the state relies on the institutional integration of power relationships.[71]

People must move beyond mere imagination of resistance and instead *enact such resistance in public and in private.* Clearly, the body can be utilized for such resistance in order to understand the controlling apparatuses of families, friends, coworkers, and partners.

The body hair narratives described in this chapter reveal that people remain tangled in power, at times unaware of its operation while at other times keenly aware of and impacted by the workings of power. The conflicted, ambivalent feelings so many students had when doing this assignment—wanting to rebel but facing the limits of what they could tolerate, enjoying aspects of using their bodies to resist but facing severe negative feedback, taking delight in provoking others and suffering through shame and anxiety about their bodies—reveal the very dynamics Foucault describes for the nature of power and resistance. More hopefully, he argues that resistances need not be total or singular or even fully effective in order to matter; the body hair assignment serves as testament to this. Every tiny, covert, and hidden resistance contributes to the "plurality of resistances" necessary to combat patriarchy, racism, ageism, and homophobia.

Building on this, Foucault argues, "Power is everywhere; not because it embraces everything, but because it comes from everywhere. . . . Discourse transmits and produces power; it reinforces it, but also undermines and exposes it, renders it fragile and makes it possible to thwart it. In like manner, silence and secrecy are a shelter for power, anchoring its prohibitions."[72] Beneath the veneer of cultural encouragement for women to comply with gender roles and social norms is a kind of sustained, forceful pressure that relays punishments—big and small—for refusing to conform. Talking about the body as a mechanism for resistance works to undermine the mechanisms of power, upending the ways that secrecy allows power to go unchecked. My ultimate claim in designing such an assignment is this: Taking seriously the power of breaking silences and violating social norms will only make the feminist movement stronger and smarter.

I hope that we can continue to use our bodies to defy and rebel against all sorts of norms that restrict, harm, and limit people's movements, options, and possibilities. Whether individually or collectively, the body vividly reveals the intersections of self and culture, control and chaos, person and group, power and resistance. These tensions underscore the possibilities of the body as a social and political text and the potential for the body to serve as a guide in imagining and creating something new. Our job is to use the body to render fragile the discourses and practices that seem impossibly strong and powerful—of misogyny, racism, unbridled wealth, and homophobia—and to refuse silence and secrecy at all costs. In essence, we must see in the mundane something extraordinary.

2

Body Hair Battlegrounds

The Dangers and Promises of Nonnormativity

Soft and sweet and shaped like a triangle
Some girls want no shape and they shave it all
That's so whack, it hurts with the stubble
Walking 'round and look like an eight-year-old
I say grow that shit like a jungle
Give 'em something strong to hold onto
Let it fly in the open wind
If it get too bushy, you can trim

—AMANDA PALMER, "Map of Tasmania"

I OFTEN REMARK TO STUDENTS AND COLLEAGUES ALIKE THAT hair is "crazy making." Perhaps because we spend such an enormous amount of time managing and containing our hair—making sure it does not get too unruly or wild; trimming and shaving and plucking it into submission; cutting, dyeing, waxing, and styling our hair—it becomes impossible to truly assess how strongly we cling to ideas about "proper" and attractive hair and, by association, "proper" femininity and masculinity. Hair brings out deeply personal notions of morality, cleanliness, beauty, attractiveness, and status. In my career as a women and gender studies professor and a practicing clinical psychologist, I have spent a rather large amount of time thinking about, studying, exploring, and provoking others to experiment with their body hair. This has offered me many insights into "doing gender" but has often come at great cost to me both professionally (as it is easy to dismiss work on hair as frivolous) and personally (as my work on hair has inspired others to act in irrational ways toward me). And yet, each time that these reactions unfold, and each time the price of the work becomes clear, I feel renewed inspiration about the importance of these body hair battlegrounds.

In this chapter, I argue that hair makes us dangerously crazy, wildly incapable of direct and self-reflexive conversation, infused with the most panicky and anxiety-ridden sense of danger. Feminist scholars should approach the study of hair with the most seriousness we can muster, seeing it as a vehicle for social control, displaced anxiety, intense emotional energy, and cultural distress. Hair is at once a marker of social class and respectability, a highly racialized site of inequality and difference, a deeply gendered signifier of beauty and gender (non)conformity, and a form of artistic and cultural expression; it is messy and complex and always-already laden with stories about power.

This chapter extends my earlier work on a pedagogical exercise about body hair, in which I outline the ways that women college students characterized the temporary experience of growing out their body hair, by revisiting the question, What do women's overt body hair rebellions provoke in others?[1] Drawing from the extra credit assignment I give to students that asks them to engage in nonnormative body hair behavior (women grow hair on their legs, underarms, and pubis while men shave hair from these areas) and write about the experience, I revisit the question of what this assignment teaches students and the sorts of things that they learn from challenging traditional gender roles. Instead of only looking at the specific individual experiences of students in my courses who have chosen to grow out their body hair, in this chapter I also examine the ongoing public media attention (most intense in 2014 but repeated in subsequent years) that this assignment received in the mostly conservative news media.

In order to imagine what women's body hair rebellions have provoked—individually, collectively, and, now, culturally—I first trace the most common findings from the body hair assignment during the span of 2007–20, followed by an analysis of some of the changes that happened over time and the new and emerging areas of focus for the body hair assignment. I conclude by examining the chaotic experience of watching my work "go viral"—often with negative consequences for me and this work—as an example of why hair deserves the utmost attention in times of social stress and of why body hair rebellions matter. I conclude by reflecting on gender nonnormativity, along with the backlash against embodied choices that rebel against gender norms, as way to imagine the future of embodied resistance and body hair rebellion.

KEY FINDINGS FROM THIRTEEN YEARS OF THE BODY HAIR ASSIGNMENT

Initially, when this assignment began in 2007 with a small group of women in an upper-division sexuality course, it was a way to stop merely talking abstractly about body hair—as we often did in women and gender studies courses—and instead have a more physical, corporeal experience with hair. The students had jokingly said that they should all grow out their body hair and write about it. I agreed to try it and asked them to keep a weekly log and write about it at the end of the semester. The results of this first semester were staggering; students reported a huge variety of people who had an interest in, or felt they could comment upon, their body hair choices, including partners/boyfriends, parents, siblings, coworkers, friends, and acquaintances. Student narratives also showed an intense level of internalized sexism and homophobia, as well as personal fears and reservations about violating gender roles, even for self-identified feminists in an upper-division critical feminist course.

This first semester then inspired the next thirteen years of work with this assignment, and it has proven to be as powerful now as it was back in 2007. Students express their feelings and reactions to this assignment not only through their written work sent to me but also in their informal conversations with other students at the start of class or after class. Most students (almost without exception) find the assignment to be more dif-ficult and intense than they anticipated; some expect it to be hard but are surprised at how difficult it is for them to tolerate their own feelings about being "unclean" in their hairy bodies. Some imagine it to be easy and find out that others have a lot to say about their bodies. Some expect that it will be hard internally but that others will support them in their choices, only to find out that the opposite is true—it often proves harder to gain support from family and friends than to give oneself that support. Students often begin to see how many people want to "have a say" in their choices about their bodies even during the first week of the assignment when they go home to discuss it with their partners and their families. (For example, women partnered with men consistently report that one of the first family/friend reactions to disclosing that they are participating in this assignment is "What does your *boyfriend* think?" and "Is he OK with this?")

Reflecting on the last thirteen years of doing this assignment, I highlight here the six most significant findings of asking students to resist the social norm of body hair across the hundreds of students who have participated. These findings both reflect and extend upon the previous writing I have done on the body hair assignment, and they show why pedagogical work around body hair deserves a place in women and gender studies pedagogy. Experiential learning—the combination of feminist theory and practice ("praxis")—is crucial to drive different kinds of student learning that prioritize activism, greater insights about daily interactions, embodiment, and a reconfiguration of self/other relationships.[2] Students often report coming away with deeper and more meaningful understandings of course content based on participating in this assignment. Further, they understand both the fragility of power and its invisible strength; grappling with such contradictions has given new depth to understanding the body as a social and political text.

Internalized versus Externalized Oppression

The body hair assignment puts on vivid display the ways that oppression can appear either as an externally imposed entity (e.g., women hearing negative feedback about their hairy bodies from friends, family, coworkers, and partners) and as an internalized part of their psyches (e.g., feeling disgust and loathing toward their own hairy bodies, feeling dirty and gross). This latter form of oppression—where women internalized the messages they heard and saw in the more public parts of their lives—was captured in especially vivid ways in women's narratives about the body hair assignment. One of the students, Esperanza, wrote of this dialectic between external and internal oppression, "My sister said it was absolutely gross and out of this world. My biggest problem I had was not shaving my pubic hair. I hated my body during my period. Hygiene wise, it was the worst experience I ever had. I would not stop shaving my pubic hair unless I had a medical impediment that forced me to do it."

Examples of externalized negative social feedback appeared frequently in students' narratives about their body hair experiences. For example, Ana described her mother's negative and hostile reaction to her new body hair: "My mom said it was unsanitary and disgusting and that I needed to stay away from her because the look of it grossed her out, and if my leg or underarm hair touched her, she'd have to take a shower." Cecilia described a bevy of reactions of disgust and horror from a variety of people in her life: "My sister called me a women's studies lesbian and said I needed to change my major because it was messing with my mind and turning me into a man. My male relatives were name-calling me lesbian, he-she, ape, mud flaps, and they were laughing. My partner explained that I had been doing it for a school experiment. They could not understand why I would even do something like this for school or why my partner would allow it." Samantha also described intense ridicule for growing her body hair related to her supposed lack of femininity: "My boyfriend made a joke about how I might as well go as a werewolf for Halloween because I already have a costume. I feel like a man."

Sometimes women recognized that this external feedback had consequences for women's own internal feelings about their bodies and sexuality. Samantha described a process of becoming increasingly uncomfortable with her boyfriend after growing her hair: "I was fine with the whole idea of not shaving until my partner started making comments. He was very supportive at first, but he had a hard time with it later. He joked a lot about it being gross. I felt gross during sex. I would get distracted, and I could not reach orgasm. My boyfriend would ask me every day to shave my pubic hair and say that the teacher would never know anyways. I think it might be because he thinks he has some control over my sex organs." This sense that boyfriends have control over women's choices was ubiquitous throughout the narratives of women partnered with men. Caroline, too, struggled with her boyfriend's negative judgments and how they impacted her internal feelings about body hair: "My boyfriend told me that he could "tolerate" my body hair and claimed that he did not find me less attractive for it, yet he said that he was not attracted to hair on women. He feels that hair on women makes them appear somewhat masculine and threatens their femininity. He wants to know that the person he is in a sexual relationship with is strictly 'female' in appearance, and not 'in between.' I did feel less attractive after he insinuated that my natural bodily hair was lesser than his." One striking feature of the body hair assignment was its ability to reveal modes of control that often stay hidden in plain sight; though women may have sensed that their boyfriends wanted to control or manage how women looked physically, this assignment seemed to reveal that tendency in more detail.

Women's internalized narratives of feeling "dirty" and "gross" also showed the intensely emotional and affective implications of body hair. Women often reacted to the assignment by arguing that body hair—especially armpit hair—was inherently dirty (sometimes even "bug-laden"), prone to excessive bacterial growth, resistant to deodorant and antiperspirant, smellier than shaved armpits, and fundamentally unnatural and unsanitary. At least half of women's responses included direct references to body hair as "gross," revealing how body hair provokes visceral reactions of disgust for many women. Elaine could not shake the feeling that her unshaved body felt dirty: "I personally had a difficult time with the constant feeling of being unclean. I didn't mind how I physically looked, but I mentally felt dirty. Even after I showered I would still feel unclean simply because I hadn't shaved. This consistent feeling of being unclean—which I knew was inaccurate—is still what I had the most trouble with."

Consequently, women changed their behaviors in order to avoid negative social penalties and to ease their shame about body hair. The substantial list of behavioral changes women made included refusing to wear certain kinds of clothes (e.g., dresses, bathing suits, shorts, tank tops, Capri pants), hiding in their houses rather than going out with friends, avoiding exercise at the gym, having sex less often or not at all, not going on job interviews, putting on more moisturizing lotion, taking more showers, wearing what they called "excessive" amounts of deodorant, and adopting "men's" deodorant (apparently perceiving it as stronger and more effective for underarm hair). Women also discussed situations of hyper-femininity and bodily exposure as particularly shaming, such as attending a wedding while they had armpit hair, visiting the gynecologist, wearing tank tops and shorts around the house in front of roommates, or engaging in oral sex where they worried about their genitals being "unclean." Elaine noted that body norms became visible during the assignment: "Oftentimes body norms don't warrant a response unless we are not doing them."

Respectability, Race, and Class

Reactions to body hair carried raced and classed elements, particularly connected to respectability and cleanliness narratives. This was particularly true for women of color and/or working-class women, who reported more familial regulation of body hair and far more social penalties for growing out their hair than did white or middle/upper-class women. For example, women of color often expressed that body hair exacerbated their "differentness" from white or middle/upper-class women in the course. For example, Ana compared the quality of her body hair with her white classmates: "When I compared my hair to the hair of the other girls in class, there was an obvious difference. My hair grew in thick and coarse. The other Latina women in the class understand that the white girls had it easier because their hair was thinner. I felt like people would think I was a 'dirty Mexican' because of the hair, that I was doing something nasty, and people would connect my body hair to my being lesbian or Mexican." Body hair for some women of color became a marker of racial status, which made it harder to assimilate into what they perceived as white middle-class educational settings.

White students also frequently commented that the assignment demanded less of them because of their lighter hair color. Elaine noticed a marked difference between herself as a white woman and the women of color in the class: "When looking at some of the legs and underarms of other girls participating in the assignment, I did realize that my leg hair is significantly lighter than theirs, which may be why my reactions were so minimal." Women of color also experienced more policing of sexual identity and gender expression, as being "good women" meant conforming to particular boundaries of gendered expression. For example, Cecilia talked about her relationship to her mother and respectability politics: "My mother was so upset that she scolded me and asked if I needed money to purchase razors or if something was wrong. She thought she did not teach me the proper way to clean myself. My mom could not look at me and asked that I cover up. She called me a lesbian and wanted me to stop my women's studies classes because they were corrupting my mind, my beliefs, and my identity." Lupe also felt that respectability politics loomed large in her body hair decisions: "I come from a family that didn't have much money, and to let yourself go is going against everything I have been taught. I'm always careful about coming across as respectable and clean, just so I don't confirm all of those stereotypes people have of me as dirty and low class." These comments reflect the association of body hair with both a lack of femininity and a lack of respectability, as women of color implicitly faced judgments about how their bodies circulated in public spaces as indicators of their racial or classed statuses. Women of color constructed their bodies as having more at stake in this perceived loss of respectability.

Confronting stereotypes about women of color and poor women as "dirty" also appeared in women's narratives about body hair. Dorothy confronted her feelings about class and respectability with regards to body hair: "I also thought, like most people, that women who did not keep up on their appearance through body hair removal were lazy, dirty, and kind of crazy. . . . I never thought that it could be a choice." Sharon, who could not finish the assignment because she found it intolerable, described her fear of dirtiness as a raced dimension: "As a Black woman, I know what it's like to be looked down upon by white people. I don't need to be made aware of that any more than I already am." Ana similarly commented on her body hair by noting its raced and classed dimensions: "I found myself wearing makeup more often, at first unconsciously. Before I'd stopped shaving, I hardly ever wore makeup. I started because I didn't want anyone to think that I didn't 'take care of myself' and I'm always aware of the fact that, as a Mexican, I have to go that extra mile. I'm not a college professor, and I don't live and work with other feminists like some of my girlfriends do. I'm a waitress, and my coworkers would think I was a freak."

Patriarchal Control of Women's Bodies

Links between body hair removal and patriarchal control of women's bodies also appeared in students' narratives, coming mostly from boyfriends but also from family members and friends. Cecilia wrote of her boyfriend's intense reactions to her body hair:

> My partner noticed for the first time and was appalled by the sight of my pit hair being so long. He requested that I shave and would laugh at me. He boycotted sex with me, saying it was too hairy or a jungle down there. He asked that I not put my arms up while sleeping because it troubled him, just the sight of it. He stopped rubbing my legs or showing me any affection. He made a decision not to be in the same room while I changed clothes or when I got out of the shower. He would compare me to an ape or a man.

She later reflected that his resistance to her body hair made her question the relationship with him altogether.

Most women faced concerns about, and patrolling of, their femininity from others. As women surrendered some currency of femininity, others suggested they could not "get a man." Cherise faced this concern from her sister and grandmother, who believed body hair would repel potential husbands (yet another fusion of sexism and heterosexism) and construct her as promiscuous: "My sister asked me, 'What if guys saw it?' I told her, 'Then they'd see it.' She told me I should be glad I wasn't dating anyone right now because if I were, I wouldn't be able to go through with it. I didn't say it out loud to her, but to myself I admitted she was probably right." She added, "My grandmother almost had a heart attack on top of her dinner plate when I told her I was growing my body hair. She told me I'd never find a husband if I carried myself like a tramp. She said it was bad and unladylike."

Interestingly, even women who embraced the assignment—and whose partners embraced their body hair—often faced social punishments from extended networks of men outside of their families (e.g., coworkers, male partners' friends, and so on). Deena articulated the shaming she experienced by her boyfriend's friends, who "ask him about it all the time. They wanted to 'know what it was like' and one specifically asked him if I was 'beastly.' Once he told me about what they were asking, I felt like they were thinking I wasn't good enough for him, or that they felt sorry for him that his girlfriend was now manly. Even though he laughed about the situation, it made me feel unwanted and not as feminine as a girlfriend 'should' be." Kelly faced critiques from male coworkers even while she resisted such criticisms and embraced the assignment: "I was asked a question by a male coworker if my husband and I have sex during my body hair growth. I replied by saying yes. He asked if my husband thought he was having sex with a 'dude.' I told him, 'Why would he think that? The rest of my body is still there. I still have boobs and a vagina. I'm still the same person as before. I just have some hair.' I have really enjoyed making the guys at work cringe." The enforcement of gender here—shadowing fears of trans identity, gender bending, and crossing lines of femininity—speaks to the networks of power that enforce heterosexuality, cisnormativity, and femininity. Kelly must reassure others of her femininity as anything representing blurred gender lines becomes too threatening to those around her.

As an even more direct indicator of patriarchal control of women's bodies, nearly all women partnered with men said that the first comment they received upon describing the body hair experiment to others involved some notion of whether not depilating was "OK" with their boyfriends/husbands. Lynn described a confrontation with her future father-in-law: "My fiancé told his father about the body hair thing I'm doing. He was very offended by it. The first thing he asked was, 'Did she ask for your permission first?' I was so offended by this. As if my fiancé is in control of what I do to my body! I don't need anyone's permission for anything I want to do with my body." Laura also heard that she should seek her boyfriend's approval before going forward with the assignment: "They'd say, 'Is he alright with that?' That was from my best friend! This was the first thing she said after I informed her that I was officially doing the body hair assignment. She wanted to know if I had received permission from the person I was dating. It was just a smack in the face." Cindy relayed a similar story, noting that people were more concerned with her husband's feelings than with her own: "If someone asks anything about my hair, it is usually about how my husband feels. I specifically say husband because people are concerned about a man dealing with a hairy woman. People don't really seem to believe that my partner doesn't care about the hair and that he actually thinks it's normal and kinda funny."

Tatu also communicated that her family expressed concerns about her husband's reactions to not shaving, even insisting that he would leave her if she continued not removing body hair: "My family said that I needed to start grooming myself. What does your husband say when you let yourself go like that! Men like well-groomed women! Even when I told them my husband doesn't mind, they still insisted that he does mind and that he was just being polite to not hurt my feelings. They told me if I continued like this he would go out looking for a good-looking woman."

Women also worried about how their male partners would react to the assignment, noting their reliance upon their partners' assessments in order to gauge their own feelings. At times, women's boyfriends and husbands reacted with extreme negativity and disgust; for example, Kim wrote, "My partner said, 'I'm not going to wipe my ass until you shave,' as if that was the same thing!" Even those male partners who claimed to support women often did not. Cris's partner, who allegedly supported her in the assignment, reacted with aggressive humor: "My partner jokes about how many rolls of duct tape he was going to need, or sharpening up the chainsaw."

Sarah described the paradox of her boyfriend's acceptance combined with implicit prohibition: "The assignment did, however, make me wonder how my boyfriend would react. . . . I explained the assignment and asked him if he thought he would still be attracted to me if I had hairy armpits and legs. He told me that he would always be attracted to me no matter what. He did add, however, that if I had just stopped shaving on my own he probably would think I was crazy but since it was for an extra credit assignment then it was okay." Mona admitted that her partner helped her to buffer the negative reactions of others: "I think that without having my partner to put things in perspective for me, I most definitely would have felt ashamed and disgusted about my body, as my mom kept implying, and as society in general silently states with its classification of 'natural' body hair as taboo." Laura felt dismayed by her reliance on her boyfriend's opinion about the assignment, writing, "This would

FIGURE 2.1. Students at Arizona State University upon finishing the body hair assignment, fall 2018.

reaffirm the notion that if a male validates a woman's 'practice or behavior,' that then and only then is it acceptable." Even when women felt uneasy or angry about the tangled web of heterosexual permission about their body hair, they often did not see an obvious way out from it.

Homophobia and Heterosexism Linked Together

Heterosexism, compulsory heterosexuality, and gender policing (that is, behavior designed to ensure traditional gender role behavior) occurred both subtly, as women students heard accusations that they could not "get a man" with body hair, and in more direct ways, as students heard accusations about their alleged (and "deviant") queerness. For example, Beth relayed a story about her brother's insistence that body hair would lead to celibacy or lesbianism: "He asked me if this was some kind of sign that my women's studies degree was corrupting me and turning me into a big lesbian. He said that any woman with body hair certainly couldn't get a man, so I'd have to start dating women if I wanted to ever have sex." As a more direct example of homophobia and the pervasiveness of compulsory heterosexuality, Paula communicated fear of being physically harmed because of others' homophobic reactions: "I had read that a lot of women were afraid of growing their hair because they have heard of women getting beat up by homophobes or whatever. I had considered this possibility, but nothing has happened. Yet." Interestingly, Elaine's friend suggested that her leg hair would protect her from being violated in a parking lot, supposedly because she surrendered some of her vulnerable femininity: "He said, 'You'll be fine. If anyone tries anything they'll just see your legs and conclude you're one of those tough chicks.'"

Students who already identified as queer also experienced intensified homophobia and transphobia from others. Mona, a bisexual woman who had recently come out, offered a story about how her mother's homophobic fears ballooned into fears of her becoming transgender:

I have never been a "girly girl" by any means, and one of my
mom's main hang-ups has always been that I never really
conformed to traditional female roles. I always played football
with the boys and refused to wear pink or dresses. About a year
ago, my mom found out that I am a bisexual and that I am in a
relationship with another woman. This made her even more
sensitive about my gender identity. Upon talking in class about
this assignment, many women that were participating made the
remark that someone asked them if they were turning into
lesbians. I guess since my mom cannot be worried about me
being a lesbian, she just jumped to the next step and asked me if
this assignment was really just an excuse because I wanted to get
a sex change. In actuality, I am very comfortable being a female,
and I even had to show her the paper for the assignment to
reassure her that I was not just making something up so I could
prep for a sex change operation that I do not want. Her horrible
comments throughout this entire period made me feel very
uncomfortable about my body. It seemed like she wanted me to
feel ashamed of my lack of normality.

Mona's response reveals the panic that many women's social networks expressed surrounding their body hair, as they saw it not only as a marker of Otherness but also as a symbol of gendered upheavals.

For women who felt shamed by growing their body hair (over two-thirds felt this way), these gender policing moments enhanced their embarrassment and self-loathing, as women often felt they were treated as "circus animals." Women encountered severe negativity like gagging noises, disgust, eye rolling, and metaphors that likened body hair to things like "the juice in the bottom of a garbage can" (Zoe). Others wanted to pet and sniff their body hair, treating it with curiosity and/or overt repulsion. Lynn noted a story about a family gathering where she felt uncomfortably on display: "I came downstairs and everyone was looking at me funny. When I was halfway to the table, my nineteen-year-old sister lifted up my arm for everyone to see and said, 'Look!' I was so embarrassed. I got at least ten 'Ewww's' and lots of 'Why?' and 'That's so gross!' 'You look like a man.' My sister put me on the spot in front of everyone. I was so mortified." She later described a similar event with her friends, noting that they made her feel ashamed and publicly humiliated: "My friends took a picture of us all lifting one arm in the air, with me (and my hairy armpit) in the middle. They all used me as some kind of tourist attraction. I laughed it off, but I'm still a little uneasy about how uncomfortable women are with body hair. I was the same way. Body hair is so rare, no one has it! And when someone does, they become a circus act!"

Men and Anxiety about Masculinizing Their Body Hair Removal

While the men who shaved their body hair had some experiences that were similar to the women's—particularly surrounding homophobic reactions, policing of gender, and belief that body hair removal was "unnatural"—they also worried far less about their partners' reactions and more often embraced the assignment as something that represented their personal agency. This could reflect greater permissiveness from partners or the reality that men cared less about partners' reactions. Regardless, men prioritized and cared more about how their bodies would be judged by other men (nonpartners) rather than how their bodies created a sense of shame, negative reactions from (women) partners, or concerns for respectability. The general notion that men had more social and cultural permission to make a wider range of choices about their bodies was clearly evident.

Most men complained about the difficulty of body hair removal, as they found it labor-intensive, time-consuming, and often quite useless and meaningless. Eli relayed his surprise at the difficulty of shaving his awkwardly shaped underarms: "The pit is an exquisite body part. It is literally a PIT! Have you tried to shave inside of a pit? It is so hard to get it flat or to even look inside of it for long amounts of time!" Sergio expressed his difficulty with body hair removal combined with a newfound respect for women's labor of depilation: "I had difficulties for the plain and simple reason that [shaving] is alien to me. I found myself spending about ten to fifteen minutes shaving, thinking I did a good job, just to step out of the shower, put on my glasses, and realize that I did not do so well. I would then stop and go back and try to do it again, which was very frustrating. I slowly began to realize what women go through just to fit in." Tom also directly confronted the sexist double standards inherent in the shaving/ not shaving assignment, noting, "I mentioned the assignment to a group of guys, and they said it was fine for men to shave but disgusting for women not to shave. Just the look in their eyes about it made me feel bad for the women who weren't shaving."

Men did express a variety of social penalties from other men, particularly related to sexual identity. For example, Max expressed anticipatory fear of his coworkers' reactions: "What will the guys at work think? I usually wear shorts when I'm out on runs but not anymore. They'll tease the shit out of me." Chris conveyed a need both to fit in and to rebel against social norms, noting his need for male approval in particular: "I usually think of myself as a rebel and an outcast but I still want to be liked and appreciated by other dudes. I guess hair matters. I'm not gay, but I like their approval." Ben experienced more direct homophobia and policing of his sexual identity during the experiment:

> Initially, I felt that shaving my legs and armpits would be a very
> emasculating experience. I feared facing difficulties from my
> family especially, since they are very conservative/ex-Catholic. I
> was raised to be afraid of catching the gay, or becoming gay, and
> my dad did his best to involve me in programs that would

reinforce masculinity and stave off homosexuality. . . . My fears were not without at least some basis in reality. My father started off on rants about homosexuality, and my mother kept bothering me about it, her concern over me shaving quite palpable. . . . My dad kept using the gay comment. I really hate it when he assumes shit. I keep telling him that it's nothing big. I'm JUST shaving my body.

On the other hand, gay and bisexual men more often found the assignment liberating and, at times, a boost to their self-esteem. Spencer wrote, "The people at Walgreens would probably think I'm gay or really weird or getting in touch with my feminine side. This is precisely what I am doing. I'm getting in touch with my creative, free-bird, feminine side." Eli encountered more sexual attention from a friend, which then led to feelings of liberation from gender norms: "My friend who is gay has a fetish for hairless men. For a while he kept texting me and eventually propositioned me to have sex. I was in a bit of a shock. . . . I am proud to have fought back against the social norm and even get positive reactions for doing it. I feel times are changing and all it takes is one person to show everyone that it is OK to break the norm, and eventually, people will follow."

Not all men viewed the assignment as a way to express their "feminine side"; many men found ways to "masculinize" the experience of depilation to remain macho, at times creatively reconfiguring it as manly and powerful. For example, Jason admitted that his shaved body itched but he felt no qualms about scratching himself while in public: "I found myself scratching my genitals, armpits, and buttocks in public, which generated stares from people, and at times I found it embarrassing. On the other hand, I was uncomfortable, so when it came time to scratch, I did it without any reservations." Michael resisted shaving creams, labeling them as too feminine: "I just shave dry now. It's bad enough to do this assignment in the first place, so I'm definitely not using lady creams and pink razors and stuff." Rick managed to sexualize the experience with his partner: "For me, the shaving of my body parts charged our sexual performance in a more sensual way." As a more extreme example of masculinizing the assignment, Ben resisted razors entirely, preferring more "manly" methods of depilation that he did publicly and in front of strangers and classmates: "My use of the buck knife [a folding hunting knife] and box cutter made me feel even more intimidating and masculine. I caught many people's attention by shaving in public at my convenience. That part of was kind of fun."

Men's perceived bodily agency allowed them to engage in body modifications without nearly the same array of social penalties and disciplinary practices that women faced (a finding echoed in recent research as well).[3] Men's relationships with their bodies were largely dictated by their acceptance from other men (whereas women factor in both acceptance from other women and, to a greater degree, acceptance from men). Consider this statement from Max, where he claims agency by asserting his masculinity: "As long as I could blame it on you, I enjoyed it. I would never do this otherwise, but halfway through I started wondering why I kept repeating that it was for a class assignment to people who asked me about it. Why couldn't I just say that I did it because I felt like it? I'm a man. I don't need a reason."

Postexperiential Reflections

Most students who attempted the assignment reported that they learned a great deal about their bodies, social constructions, and the deep investment others had in controlling and patrolling their bodies. Jason noted his surprise that the assignment taught him as much as it did about power and sexuality: "I want to be seen as attractive by social standards for men. I think we as men are conditioned by society to have these needs. To be looked upon by other men with envy and desired by women. . . . I never thought such a simple assignment would have this effect on me. This was totally unexpected. I now understand that I must take social construction very seriously, because our very lives are based upon it."

Several students commented that they wished everyone could try the assignment and that it had more value than they originally expected it would have. Zoe felt jolted into a new understanding of her body not only in an abstract way but also in a tangible manner:

This experiment was a healing process in a way. If anything, it
greatly made me more aware of my body. Often girls start
shaving before their hair fully grows in and darkens, so in a way

this is a part of ourselves (myself) that we never know, that we are fragmented from in some way. To watch my hair grow in was a journey in and of itself; to see my hair pattern as my hair fully grew in, to feel it in different stages of growth, from prickly to rather soft and long—it was all part of the experience. I definitely feel more in tune with my body, its patterns and textures. I formed this weird attachment to my hair and I felt like "we" really bonded. I don't think I would consider myself more masculine or feminine (non-feminine) throughout the duration of this experiment, but I felt more "me," or at least aware of me.

Many women confronted their feminist attitudes and challenged their belief that they choose what they do with their bodies. Eva described the assignment as a wake-up call and a source of greater reflection: "This experience was more painful than freeing because it made me realize that I have a lot of soul searching to do. Although I am always the first to reject many of our society's norms, they never quite affect me as directly as this assignment did. I can't yet deal with the backlash of others when resisting social norms about looking good. This assignment did help me get one step closer to who I aspire to be. I want to accept myself." Layla wondered about the evolution of her feminist identity: "I thought I had an in-your-face attitude about everything until it came to raising my hand with a hairy armpit in class. My feminism has a long way to go, but I'm working on it."

Women also expressed a heightened awareness of gender norms and expectations in general. Lauren wrote of her broader reflections on women's power:

This makes me think, when will it end? Are women worse off or better off now? We don't have to stay at home and wear pearls while vacuuming and cooking all day for our husbands. We have more rights and choices, but in a way we have only added to the expectations of women rather than fully changed them. Now we wear pearls, heels, shave, wear makeup, have styled hair, are thin—the look of today's most desired women. Combined with this, we're supposed to have an education, a successful career, a social life, and a happy (traditional) family life. I feel like now that I know these things I have a responsibility to myself as well as others. I am not at all a radical, not the kind of person to speak out or act out, but I can keep myself informed, think more critically, and change my actions if need be.

Students also changed their behavior in a more long-term sense, as over half of those who responded to a follow-up email one year later indicated long-term changes. For example, some chose sexual partners differently based on their reactions to body hair (as body hair became a litmus test for a partner's attitudes toward women's agency and choice about their bodies), broke up with partners who had criticized body hair or constructed it as disgusting, removed body hair less often (for women) or more often (for men), thought deeply about the friends and family they listen to for advice about relationships and sexuality, and felt more confident about their bodies in general. Angela said that growing body hair would be a test for a future partner: "When looking for a soul mate, when the time comes, I am definitely going to see if he's okay with me not shaving all the time or if he would still find me attractive. . . . We should live our lives by our own standards." Some reported no changes or a deep relief that they could now revert back to their old ways, and some felt that the assignment was a "fun thing to try in college" but nothing more. Still, the majority expressed that the assignment had a lasting attitudinal and behavioral impact on their lives.

CHANGES IN THE BODY HAIR ASSIGNMENT

One of the gifts of doing this assignment for thirteen years is that I have been able to watch students change and adapt to the cultural contexts of their time. The body hair assignment has evolved in new and interesting ways, as each semester differs, and each group has its own dynamic unique to those students. That said, with remarkable consistency, new nodes of learning, understanding, and growth have happened with the body hair assignment, as students learn how their social networks control, comment upon, limit, punish, or restrict their bodily choices. Many students prior to this assignment imagine that they have nearly unlimited choices with their bodies; after doing this assignment, their viewpoints on the patrolling of gender norms vastly change. (They also, of course, often feel far more rebellious and brave about asserting their right to their own bodily choices, which sometimes means they break up with boyfriends who admonished their body hair, or they rebel against coworkers or family members who labeled their bodies as "gross" or "disgusting.")

In looking at the body hair assignment with an eye for what has changed over time, I want to highlight six themes that have emerged since the body hair assignment began in 2007. I look at a group of fifty-nine women from diverse backgrounds to illustrate these changes over time: (1) stronger awareness of underarm, leg, and pubic hair as *differently* attached to gender and sexuality norms; (2) internal conflicts about body hair disgust; (3) stronger barriers at many workplaces to having body hair; (4) contradictions between growing body hair as a rebellion and women's body hair being seen as "sexy"; (5) body hair as a way to explore trans and nonbinary identities; and (6) women of color feeling that white (especially blond) women cannot understand their body hair experiences (a racial consciousness gap).

Different Meanings to Leg, Underarm, and Pubic Hair

During the last four semesters of the body hair assignment, students have indicated that they attach different meanings to their leg, underarm, and pubic hair, a finding seen again in chapter 6 when I conducted interviews with body hair rebels in the broader community. Typically, legs have represented the site with the most freedom and flexibility regarding hair. For example, Evelyn (nineteen/Latina/heterosexual) said, "My leg hair wasn't as big of a deal as my armpit hair. I sometimes have let my legs grow out before, but I would *never* do that with my armpit hair." Pubic hair, by contrast, seemed more private compared to armpit hair, as pubic hair was discussed only with partners and elicited no "public" responses. Leila (twenty-two/Latina/lesbian) described her relationship with her pubic hair in intensely private terms, noting a reversal in how she expected to feel about growing pubic hair: "Having pubic hair made me realize how uncomfortable I actually felt before, when I didn't have it. I felt like a thirteen-year-old girl before, and shameful feelings came up. I used to avoid looking at my hairless vulva, so I definitely felt refreshed when I stopped shaving."

Underarm hair has elicited the strongest and most intense reactions both internally (from women reflecting on the assignment) and externally (from people in women's lives who evaluate and judge their hairy bodies). This may connect to its more public status—others can see underarm hair more easily than leg or pubic hair—or it may connect to its status as more abject or more connected to masculinity than other kinds of hair. Cat (twenty-two/white/heterosexual) noticed a difference in how her friend reacted to leg and armpit hair: "I have a friend who hates my armpit hair along with everyone else's armpit hair. She refuses to even look at mine. She has seen my hairy legs many times, and she does not even take a second glance at them at this point, but armpits are apparently a whole other beast." Suzanna (twenty-three/Latina/bisexual) felt triumphant when purposefully making others uncomfortable with her armpit hair: "Whenever I was at the grocery store and someone was by me, I made it a point to lift my arm near their face and pretend like I was grabbing something from a top shelf. The face reactions that I got were priceless. One lady literally gasped and left her cart full of stuff in the middle of the aisle as she walked away." This sense that different regions of the body have different meanings attached to gender and sexuality—with armpit hair symbolizing the most defiant and panic-inducing region—shows how meanings of body hair inspired different sorts of reactions in others and carry different symbolic weight.

Internal Conflicts about Body Hair Disgust

Women often described their body hair as "gross" and deeply repulsive to others, using language that reflected visceral disgust. While women in earlier semesters talked about self-consciousness and social penalties with their body hair, women in later semesters reported more conflicts about feeling disgust than did women in earlier semesters. This persisted, notably, even while women recognized the inherent value of the assignment. Vivian (twenty-six/white/lesbian) said, "I thought I would be fine with this and others would be disgusted. Unfortunately, I found that other people were not as bothered by the body hair as I was. This was a

FIGURE 2.2. Advertisement for Schick Hydro Silk Trimmer (2015), still image from television.

disappointing discovery for me as a feminist. I felt dirty and unkempt. The hair made me feel ugly." Desiree (twenty-two/Latina/heterosexual), too, noted that she felt tremendous anxiety about body hair and that she felt repulsive to others: "My body hair gave me anxiety. I had to actively remind myself that it was okay to let the hair grow and that there was absolutely nothing wrong with it. I was tempted to shave it every day. I felt dirty. I avoided sexual acts which required me to remove clothing. I definitely tried to keep my armpits hidden." These descriptions of feeling repulsed by body hair reveal the ways that women experienced conflict between how they *should* feel and how they *did* feel.

Workplace Barriers to Having Body Hair

As increasing numbers of my students have secured full-time jobs while going to school—many of which are in professional settings rather than in minimum-wage and more casual settings—the pressures to equate hairlessness with both femininity and professionalism have increased. Amy (twenty-five/biracial/heterosexual) noted that she was uncomfortable at work when she wore her normal work attire: "Mostly I felt self-conscious, especially at work, as body hair on women is generally considered unprofessional and I wear a dress almost every day. When I wore short sleeves,

I was hyper vigilant to keep my arms at my sides or to watch other people to see if they noticed my hairy underarms and what their reactions would be." Ashleigh (twenty-three/white/heterosexual) endured her colleagues continually asking, "You're still showering, right?" Carrie (twenty-six/white/bisexual) described workplace harassment around her body hair: "My boss wanted to discuss it with me every single day. He came up to me and told me how gross it looked, how unprofessional I was for having it, and how disgusting my legs looked in skirts. I tried to reason with him and explain what this assignment was for, but he didn't buy it. Other coworkers supported him in humiliating me in this way. I wanted to be brave, but mostly I just felt ashamed of my body." This sense that body hair does not belong in the workplace was difficult for women to challenge.

Body Hair as Rebellious versus Erotic

One unexpected finding of the last several years was that some students reported tensions between seeing body hair as a form of rebellion and, for some, feeling disappointed when others saw body hair as sexy. Ashleigh (twenty-three/white/heterosexual) wrote of her boyfriend's reversal of feelings about body hair and how this diminished the feeling of rebellion for her: "I was so happy when he finally conceded that body hair norms for women were wrong and that my body hair was just as normal as his. However, recently he has started to find it sexy. I see a smile on his face when I raise my arms, for example, and that pisses me off because my armpit hair was supposed to be a way for me to subvert gender norms." Lena (twenty-one/white/heterosexual) also discovered this reversal from rebellion to eroticism with her boyfriend: "Having body hair made me feel like a feminist warrior. I didn't want my boyfriend to like it. I wanted him to be grossed out. But when he wasn't grossed out, it was because he thought it was 'hot' and not because I was a feminist warrior." This conflict between hair as rebellion and hair as "sexy" showed how body norms can shift in meaning rapidly and in directions women do not want.

Other women described a stronger sense that body hair represented *only* rebellion. Cat (twenty-two/white/heterosexual) described her refusal to care about pressures to remove body hair: "I simply do not have the energy to care if my legs are baby smooth when wearing shorts. I cannot be bothered to spend time with men who think they have a say in my armpits. In fact, I just really cannot be bothered with pressure to fit into any gender norm, hair or otherwise." Similarly, Leila (twenty-two/Latina/lesbian) felt better about herself while growing body hair, sensing that she gained her partner's approval: "Growing my body hair made me feel good about myself, or at least part of myself again. I felt empowered as a badass feminist again. My partner was excited that I was growing my body hair out. She didn't understand why I shaved in the first place." Finally, Anjelica (twenty-one/Latina/lesbian) described growing body hair as a true feminist statement for her: "I am happy that I am able to use my body as a metaphor for protest against patriarchy. We seem to forget that body hair is a natural occurrence, and we only attribute it to certain demographics, cultures, or historical periods. I believe this is our way of alienating or distancing ourselves from body hair in order to negatively criticize it."

Body Hair as a Way to Explore Trans and Nonbinary Identities

In recent years I have also had many more trans and nonbinary students who tried the body hair assignment, particularly as students become more aware of the link between gender and body hair norms. In recent semesters, two trans students and one nonbinary student wrote about their experiences (all were assigned female at birth, and all had never grown body hair before). For them, the assignment mapped onto their anticipated transitions and gave them a window into the way that hair and gender overlap. Collin (twenty-one/Latinx/queer) described an experience where newly grown body hair helped him to feel more manly: "We went to Walmart this week, and I did get weird stares, and some people had a hard time figuring out if I was a girl or a guy. A lady walked by as I reached for something and said, 'Excuse me, sir,' and took three looks at me, up to down, 'Uh, excuse me, miss?' and walked by. I tried to see how many more people would question my gender." He went on to say, "It makes me mad in a way because now that I have body hair, people automatically think I'm male. I feel like it's stupid to think that! I mean, I may be a bit androgynous sometimes, but having body hair shouldn't put me in the man category right away." Chance (twenty/white/heterosexual) described the body hair assignment as a first step in gauging others' responses to his gender identity: "Growing body hair helped my mom to finally imagine me as a male for the first time. She even started using the male pronouns and my male name when she had resisted that before. She still thought the hair was disgusting, but it helped her to see me as a man. My brother liked the hair too and said I 'looked like a dude.'" Jackson (nineteen/Latinx/bisexual) wrote about their experiences with growing body hair as affirming their nonbinary identity: "When I first came out as nonbinary, I still kept shaving my legs and underarms maybe because I wasn't ready to be seen as gross. During this assignment, I let myself grow hair and realized that I felt more like myself. My body hair was coarse and dark. The hair was neither masculine nor feminine. It was just me." These students helped to further broaden the potential scope of what the body hair assignment can do in teaching students about how their bodies are policed or controlled by others (and how gender identity and hair are deeply intertwined). Their stories also point to the ways that nonbinary people may simultaneously be more able to push back against traditional gender norms of the body while also struggling to navigate the constricting qualities of binary spaces.[4]

Racial Consciousness Gap

In earlier years of the assignment, women of color mentioned self-consciousness about their hair and the difficulty of hiding their hair in comparison to white or lighter-haired women. Recent years have seen a shift in this rhetoric, as women of color expressed a more direct racial consciousness gap in that white women did not *understand* their experiences. Women of color with dark hair repeatedly wrote in their papers that white (especially blond) women could not understand them and that white women did not experience the same stigma. This seemed like a layered comment both about the technical differences in body hair but also about the sense of social penalty or punishment they faced in comparison to women with lighter hair. For example, Alma (twenty/Latina/heterosexual) described her body hair in comparison to the blond women in class as difficult for her in part because she had a long history of being compared to white women: "I have dark hair, so of course I was going to have dark body hair. I felt envious of all the girls who had light body hair. White girls always had blond body hair so even during my childhood, I grew to hate my dark body hair, which made me lack confidence with my body. They didn't." Sasha (twenty-two/African American/heterosexual) felt that white women did not understand the difficulty of having dark, visible hair for a woman of color: "I listened to the white women in the class complain about their boyfriends and how their boyfriends didn't like their hair, how hard it was to tell their mothers. They don't know anything about hard. Being Black means I always have to worry about others thinking less of me, not just my boyfriend. I wouldn't dare tell my mother that I grew armpit hair. It's not even an option for me like it is for the white women in class." This sense of a racial consciousness gap seemed notable in that darker-skinned women of color wrestled with notions of respectability, stigma, and social punishment differently than did white and lighter-skinned women.

FIGURE 2.3. Students at Arizona State University participate in the body hair assignment, spring 2019.

As the body hair assignment has continued to grow and evolve—with students rebelling in new ways, recruiting others to join them in doing the project, confronting new challenges (workplaces, expressions of femininity), and redefining gender roles—this has meant the assignment has gotten new kinds of attention from the public sphere when I share the results in journals, conferences, and media outlets. One of the pedagogical strengths of the assignment is its ability to rapidly ignite conversations about body hair among women and their social networks. Hair has much salience in people's lives and represents an easy access point for tougher discussions around hegemonic masculinity, social control, compulsory heterosexuality, and intersectionality. People *love* to talk about body hair; it somehow is just provocative enough that conversation is allowable about the subject, while still being taboo enough that debates, strong feelings, defiant actions, and healthy banter can easily ensue. As a sex researcher, I have published on a variety of topics I wish people would talk more about—for example, the rapid growth in numbers of teenage girls having unprotected anal sex with teenage boys, or the specific sorts of power imbalances that exist in mainstream pornography these days—but it seems that none of my work has inspired more conversation and media attention than body hair. This may reflect how people have to choose and manage aspects of their hair every day: shaving, plucking, waxing, grooming, washing, styling, presenting, controlling, et cetera. Hair is wholly relatable because everyone deals with it in their lives. (Sexuality, on the other hand, can alienate certain audiences fairly quickly and has fewer nearly universal entry points into conversation.)

While feminist researchers often worry that their work goes unread or that they do not engage enough in the public sphere as public intellectuals, my unanticipated jump into the media spotlight proved to be a harrowing experience that underscored the difficulty of having such exposure. In the summer of 2014, I had just published my most recent piece on body hair in *Psychology of Women Quarterly*, a respected journal that publishes mostly empirical psychological pieces about women and gender. In June, my university (Arizona State University) had published a short online story about the body hair assignment and how I had won the Mary Roth

Walsh teaching award from the American Psychological Association for designing the assignment. This short online article got picked up by a conservative journalism student (and member of the superconservative Campus Reform organization) who sent it to some ultra-conservative media outlets like the *Drudge Report* and Fox News. Soon, the body hair assignment had gone viral, with over one thousand news outlets running stories about it within weeks. The story morphed in fascinating ways, with a number of false details circulating wildly: I routinely "checked" students' pubic hair; I was running a Communist training camp; I was giving enormous amounts of extra credit; I was handing out A grades for armpit hair (notably, leg hair disappeared from most of these stories, and armpit hair loomed large); and I was "ruining America" by giving this "pointless" assignment. I learned quickly that nearly every major media outlet that ran the story had not researched a single original detail. Instead, they reprinted (and reprinted and reprinted) the same quotes, ideas, and information as the original story, often selectively leaving out information about the potential value of the assignment, without bothering to fact-check or even to gather new pieces of information.

Soon, the hate mail started pouring in. Hundreds of emails were sent to me, the university, the dean, and my program about my body hair assignment. Angry parents wrote the school. Outraged conservatives from all over the country sent hotheaded, vitriolic letters calling me every profane name imaginable (of course centering on sexual identity, gender, fatness, and in some cases, race). Fox News speculated on national television about my own body hair practices and "analyzed" my eyebrows for clues. Rush Limbaugh talked angrily about the assignment to his listeners. Eventually, emails started to arrive that outlined for me in vivid detail how I should die. People posted comments about bringing guns to my university or defecating on my desk. These various grotesque forms of hatred bombarded my life. I had to get emergency training in speaking (or not) to the media, and I underwent a security evaluation by local police for monitoring my home. My emails were reviewed by a team of experts (it compounds the assault on your dignity when hateful things about your body and your imagined identities circulate to the higher-ups at your place of work), and I consoled myself by clinging to the occasional message of support sent from fellow psychologists and sociologists. Body hair had gone wild, or at least it seemed that way. Such a serious attempt to silence and degrade an extra credit assignment about body hair may even signify the success of that assignment, given that countermovements are most vitriolic when traditional foundations are challenged.[5]

I recount these events not to again dive headlong into the drama of that situation but to emphasize the importance of embodied resistance. Such resistance is not merely abstract, theoretical, irrelevant, or pointless; resistance based in the body is fundamental to the understanding of how power operates, how power is deployed, and how people can grapple with power or lack thereof. Body-hair-gone-viral shows a deep insecurity about the status of gender and the maintenance of gender roles today. And while I understand that people emailing me and telling me I should die because of this body hair assignment could be a form of cultural hyperbole, exaggeration, or insanity—something I should brush off as worthless and insignificant—I am not entirely certain I agree. My students' experiences with body hair show a kind of pervasive, now over a decade-long freakout about women growing body hair. By combining visceral disgust, conflicts about race and class, confusion about what constitutes rebellion, and various phobias and isms (homophobia, sexism, racism, and transphobia, in particular), body hair is, I think, of paramount importance. The hatred toward women for rebelling *is real*. The hatred toward me for assigning this *is real*. The hatred toward gender rebels, punks, and freaks *is real*.

Notes on Body Hair and Resistance

Looking ahead, I conclude with a few points I want to reiterate to readers: (1) We must imagine why our own (body) hair matters and what sorts of social meanings it has in our lives. (2) After careful consideration, I have good reason to believe that women can far better see, feel, and understand the networks of social control and policing that exist around their bodies when they use their bodies to engage in nonnormative gender behavior. Simply imagining such resistance is not enough (see chapter 1). The body must be utilized for such resistance in order to understand the controlling apparatuses of our families, friends, coworkers, and partners. (3) Beneath the veneer of cultural "encouragement" for women to comply with gender roles and social norms is a kind of cultural terrorism (that is, the enforcement of gender norms and deep hostility and even violence toward those who do not conform) that can emerge randomly and without warning. Taking seriously the potential chaos of such resistances will only make the feminist movement stronger and smarter. (4) Finally, I hope we can continue to use our bodies to defy and rebel against all sorts of norms that restrict, harm, and limit women's movements, options, and possibilities. Whether individually or collectively, the body vividly reveals the intersections of self/culture, control/chaos, person/group, conservative/progressive, and cynicism/hope. These tensions underscore the possibilities of the (hairy) body and the potential of using it as a tool of feminist resistance.

PART 2 |

ART AND ACTIVISM

3

Hairy, Not So Scary

Body Hair Zines and Drawings as Activism

My little beast, my eyes, my favorite stolen egg. Listen. To live is to be marked. To live is to change, to acquire the words of a story, and that is the only celebration we mortals really know. In perfect stillness, frankly, I've only found sorrow.

—BARBARA KINGSOLVER, *The Poisonwood Bible*

BODY POLITICS HAVE OFTEN FOUND A HOME IN SELF-PUBLISHED zines, particularly for aspects of the body considered to be abject, countercultural, out of bounds, or taboo. Too often, people cannot find representations of themselves in the world of mainstream media, as manicured bodies, plastic surgery, and a compulsive investment in thinness dominate the majority of television, magazines, social media, and movies.[1] Zines, on the other hand, in creating homemade, do-it-yourself, low tech pamphlets and booklets, can invent new worlds for the bodies rarely seen in mainstream media. Zine historian Red Chidgey situates zines as a medium especially relevant to those working as permanent outsiders, saying, "Zine writers are often 'resisting subjects' writing against the mainstream, using a fringe method of publication, and documenting lives which are often under-represented in the public record (for example, young women, women of colour, working class youths, queer and transsexuals, young feminists). Zine writers, writing their lives and the lives and circumstances of their families and communities, can also be seen as 'resisting subjects' in terms of being a postmodern autobiographical subject."[2]

Certainly, the zines that focus on body hair draw from a fusion of the personal and political, the whimsical and the serious, the creative and the analytic.

This chapter examines fifteen recently published (2015–20) body hair zines and a series of drawings about body hair by Pakistani American artist Ayqa Khan in order to situate these creative works as *activist* efforts. By seeing them as a mechanism to normalize women's body hair and bring body hair into the public conversation about feminism, choices about the body, and resistance to patriarchy, I recast these zines and drawings as politicized and distinctly feminist. Drawing from the diverse work of these zine writers, I theorize these zines and drawings of hairy bodies as an integral part of contemporary feminist politics and activism. This chapter also extends the existing parameters of how artists imagine body politics by including art that is often marginalized or ignored as "trivial" or "silly." In doing so, I reimagine body hair zines and drawings as a contemporary reflection on marginalized bodies and, more importantly, *resistance* to the sidelining of marginalized bodies.

A BRIEF HISTORY OF ZINES AS ACTIVISM

> Dear Body Hair, At first, I didn't like you. Then, you made me itch. And now, you are starting to grow on me.
>
> —GINA MCMILLEN, *DEAR BODY HAIR*

The history of zines belies their contemporary use as a genre of do-it-yourself artistic and political resistance. As menstrual activist and scholar Chris Bobel writes,

> According to zine historian Stephen Duncombe, these modest but mighty periodicals were born in the 1930s when fans of science fiction began producing "fanzines" to communicate with each other as consumers, critics, and producers of science fiction. In the 1970s, fans of punk rock music started producing zines in which they discussed the genre and culture unique to punk. In the 1980s, when zine making was taken up by fans of myriad

other cultural genres, alienated self-publishers ignored by the mainstream, and political dissenters from the 1960s and 1970s, the current generation of zines was born (and the "fan" was dropped).[3]

In all, Duncombe has identified a number of different types of zines that make up the body of work produced in the past ninety years: fanzines, political zines, personal zines, scene zines, network zines, fringe culture zines, religious zines, vocational zines, health zines, sex zines, travel zines, comics, literary zines, art zines, and "the rest."[4] Body hair zines work at an intersection of personal, health, and art zines, thus bleeding the genre's boundaries.

Zine historian Jennifer Bleyer gives an elegant definition of zines as "the intersection of art, protest, confession, and theory."[5] As such, zines serve as a way for people to circumvent the narrow and often restrictive world of mainstream publishing. As feminist scholar Ann Cvetkovich writes, "Using the photocopy machine and the power of self-distribution, the zine maker does not need a publisher to get her word out. Feminist intellectuals waiting for the media to come calling might take a lesson here."[6] In their interviews with forty zine makers, Dawn Bates and Maureen McHugh found that zines were particularly compelling to young women and served as "a method of feminist empowerment and resistance."[7] The need for such alternative modes of creative expression has been overwhelming, as zine researchers have cited between ten thousand and fifty thousand zines in circulation, with an estimated readership of one million to three million, though it is impossible to track whether this has increased or decreased more recently.[8]

Young women often use zines to express their voices, particularly as they have often been stripped of representation and voice in mainstream publications and mainstream media. Chris Bobel describes this as a kind of radical self-determination embodied in the feminist zine: "The model of politics they embrace is a discourse of the individual. Expanding what counts as political, they personalize politics by filtering issues through daily lived experiences."[9] Social movement scholar Michelle Kempson notes that zines often represent the bumpy and jagged connections between third-wave feminism and do-it-yourself culture, as they embody the subjectivities of those feminisms in ascendancy during the period of time in which they were written.[10] Elke Zobl notes that feminist artists, often excluded from male-dominated gallery spaces, have used zines to show their work, circulate their ideas, and reclaim space in the patriarchal art world.[11] For feminist artists and writers, zines serve as a way to reclaim space, upend glossy and fancy depictions of feminist work, and put forth new narratives of individual and collective creativity.

Zines often feature the embodied personal rather than the disembodied statistical or empirical, and they celebrate the value of individual narratives, grammatical and typographical creativity, splashy outsider art, agitprop poetry, and the necessity for self-representation. Zines can move between the deeply personal—particularly narratives that dive deeply into the individual (tormented) psyche—and the collective, as groups of writers and thinkers come together to make art, poetry, and essays in a scrappy, homespun manner. They can, as Red Chidgey argues, serve as spaces of feminist *memory*.[12] Scholar Kimberly Creasap also notes that they can serve as a tool of feminist pedagogy, inviting feminist students to imagine themselves as creators of knowledge and participants in the feminist archive.[13] Zines thus have a logical place in the spheres of feminism, activism, and body politics, all of which rely on countercultural narratives that eschew corporate and pharmaceutical stories about health, bodies, and morality. Moreover, zines might, as scholar Adela Licona argues, represent a crossing of borders—between academic and nonacademic, practice and representation, activism and scholarship.[14]

AN ANALYSIS OF BODY HAIR ZINES

because this body hair it is—
calligraphy written all over me,
a letter to you, a letter to me
it is lace, waves, eternal softness
it is an invitation to another way to be
on the other side of shame,
BODY HAIR IS BEAUTIFUL

—@ALOKVMENON

For this chapter, I selected and analyzed fifteen contemporary zines on body hair, all created between 2015 and 2020.[15] The zines were found at independent bookstores and through the Etsy website, which emphasizes DIY art, zines, and homemade projects. The body hair zines in this chapter include the following:

Hairy Femme Mother, volume 1, by Jen Venegas (n.d.)

Hairy Femme Mother, volume 2, by Jen Venegas (compilation of others' work) (n.d.)

Hairy Femme Mother, volume 3, by Jen Venegas (compilation of others' work) (n.d.)

Why Does Society Care So Much about My Body Hair by Crash Reynolds and Edd Castillo (June 2019)

Hairy & Happy by Jamie Squire (n.d.)

Hairy, Not So Scary by Janice Quiles-Reyes (2018)

Frida at My Table by Janice Quiles-Reyes (issue 1, 2016; issue 2, 2019)

Body Hair: A Love/Hate Story by Olga Alexandru (n.d.)

A Journey into Body Hair by Maryam Adib (n.d.)

Hairy Hair by Dayanita Ramesh (July 2015)

Static Zine: A DIY Magazine by Jessica Lewis (Body Issue, May 2015)

a lil zine about shaving and me not doing it by Bitter Tooth (n.d.)

Affirmations by Lubadalu (2020)

Dear Body Hair by Gina McMillen (n.d.)

Hairy: A Zine Braiding Personal + Public Strands of Hair by Dena Lake (2020)

While body hair zines might typically be overlooked as a form of activism, these zines provide unique insights into the ways in which body hair is situated as a form of resistance. Notably, this resistance is often first couched in the normalization of body hair shame and distress, helping readers who might feel more ambivalent about body hair to better understand their own conflicted feelings about hair. These zines are both intensely personal and highly political, filled with anecdotes, stories, and a wide range of emotional expressions, particularly angst, anger, and anxiety. Zine writers include aesthetically interesting choices—for example, drawings and photos of body hair, gorgeous watercolors and paintings,

Statistics show, the average woman spends 72 days, or 1728 hours of her life shaving

Most women also report it being their most hated 'beauty ritual.'

Life is short, why waste time trying to live up to patriarchal standards when hair grows back within a couple days?

Imagine what you could do instead...

a semester of school, a few vacations, working towards your goals.
Time not worrying about shaving!!

Time not feeling uncomfortable from razor bumps!!
A world of possibilities!!!

What would you do with 10 extra weeks?

FIGURE 3.1. Image from the zine *A Journey into Body Hair* by Maryam Adib (n.d.). Courtesy of Maryam Adib, Instagram: @thrifted_underwear.

marginalia and sketches—to communicate a powerful retelling of body hair stories. In doing so, these body hair zines challenge notions of health and beauty for women, pushing back against body shaming but also including the authors' own stories about body hair (the good, the bad, the ambivalent) for readers to explore. They are joyful and powerful, strange and peculiar, silly and serious.

While these fifteen zines took different approaches to critiquing beauty norms and the double standards that operate for women and men, some patterns emerged in them. After doing a qualitative content analysis of the language in the fifteen zines,[16] I noted six different themes threaded through these documents: (1) reminiscing about adolescent shame, (2) normalizing and resisting body shaming and anxiety, (3) anger at gendered double standards, (4) positive feelings toward body hair, (5) racial consciousness and body hair, and (6) resistance and fighting back.

Reminiscing about Adolescent Shame

First, many zines included narratives about childhood and adolescence, with writers reminiscing about their youth and having to face choices about shaving early in their lives. Eddie Jude writes poetically of their shame about body hair and the typical mishaps that happen when adolescents try to shave without instruction about how to do so: "You don't think to shave your legs or underarms in grade school so the boys make fun of you and the girls look at you with pity. You don't feel the desire to shave but you learn early on that it's never a good idea to stray from what the others do. So you steal your mother's razor and try to shave in the bathtub alone. The water stains red."[17] Similarly, Janice Quiles-Reyes writes in *Frida at My Table* about being caught shaving early on and getting in trouble for this: "My mom caught me shaving my legs once. I was 13. She was upset and told me NOT to shave anything else. I've only shaved my pubes once or twice in my life. I typically rock a full bush and I've never shaved my underarms. I tend to get more negative comments from women regarding the hair on my body. Men have said that they can't remember the last time they were with a woman who had much body hair. That's made me realize how out of the ordinary it is."[18]

Adolescent shame stories seemed to have a powerful impact on women's experiences of their bodies, with some writers acknowledging that early experiences of body shaming led to a lifetime of struggle with wanting—and then not wanting—to remove hair. Crash Reynolds and Edd Castillo write in *Why Does Society Care So Much about My Body Hair,* "If I ever think about being ashamed of my body hair, specifically my legs, I remember gym class. In grades 6–9. And always feeling embarrassed and ashamed of my hairy legs. Super pale white skin with super dark brown hair. There is (and was) no hiding it. At least not in my gym shorts. And my dad refused to let me shave my legs. If I wanted to remove the hair I had to wax it off myself. 11 year old me was horrified of that."[19] Similarly, in *Body Hair: A Love/Hate Story,* Olga Alexandru writes about an early experience of body shaming about her facial hair, linking it to broader observations about gender and power: "When I was in grade 8 a shithead named Michael yelled out 'Olga has a mustache!' to the entire class . . . I do remember feeling ashamed and embarrassed. As if I was somehow personally responsible for having a mustache. As if there was something abnormal about me. . . . After that moment I made sure I was always plucked, waxed and shaved within an inch of my life. Lest anyone know that I had body hair. Because body hair meant ugly. Meant masculine. Meant not going to ever have a boyfriend."[20]

Normalizing and Resisting Body Shaming and Anxiety

Even though most of the body hair zines ultimately celebrated women's body hair, they often couched these body positive messages in the language of normalizing shame and anxiety and, ultimately, working to overcome those emotions. In *Affirmations*, Lubadalu writes a series of statements about how body shame gets normalized: "We are taught to be ashamed of and discontent with our bodies," and, "The way society defines me for being a woman is not how i define myself, nor what i actually am."[21] In *Why Does Society Care So Much about My Body Hair*, Crash Reynolds and Edd Castillo describe feeling scared of people's judgments but ultimately finding power in not shaving: "I am desperately terrified of having people look at my hairy legs now. To try and overcome my fear I've been wearing half see-through mesh pants. IN PUBLIC! And no one has noticed my hairy legs! MAYBE NO ONE CARES AS MUCH AS I WAS BRAINWASHED TO BELIEVE. Stop brainwashing people."[22]

Some of the zines also functioned as a kind of consciousness-raising and educational outlet about hair, communicating to readers about key findings from studies combined with personal anecdotes and stories about their own experiences. An emphasis on how gender norms can harm women and girls permeated these zines. Dena Lake writes, in *Hairy*, of her first experiences with shaving as a negative initiation into the consumerist frameworks for womanhood: "These instructions ushered me into an imagined community of Western women; into a tangible consumerism designed to take my time, devour my cash, create an ideal object, consume my Self."[23] Janice Quiles-Reyes writes in *Frida at My Table* about the shaming of women's bodies: "In recent dialog with women ranging in ages from 13–65, the following words were most repeated regarding their feelings on BODY HAIR: disgusting, dirty & smelly. The word used most when relating stories of how they were made to feel about their body hair;

FIGURE 3.2. Image from the zine *Hairy & Happy* by Jamie Squire (n.d.). Image courtesy of the artist.

shamed. Many women have memories of someone talking about facial hair and hair on their arms and legs as early as age 9; concern about pubic hair growth, around age 16."[24] In the next issue, she follows this up by thinking about how these messages impacted her: "I absorbed tons of negative feedback from media, even porn. I always knew in the back of my mind that body hair shouldn't define your cleanliness or grooming habits. So what if you had underarm hair? It's natural to have hair there. But as a teen and young adult I felt pressure to conform to certain ideals when it came to 'unwanted' hair."[25]

Ambivalence and Personal Conflicts about Body Hair

Several zines also included content about their creators' ambivalence and personal conflicts about body hair, particularly how they at times stopped shaving and at times did not. Janice Quiles-Reyes writes in *Hairy, Not So Scary* about her struggles with managing body hair and sometimes removing it despite her best efforts not to do so: "I dig deep into my own discomforts with my body hair. I write out every memory of being shamed for having a thick connecting brow, upper lip hair, hairy toes, hairy legs and hairy fingers. I stop using self deprecating body talk. I create body balms to soften and care for my new skin. It takes only two days for me to thoughtlessly find a pair of tweezers and pull out a couple of hairs that continually bother me."[26] Along these lines, Olga Alexandru writes, in *Body Hair: A Love/Hate Story*, about the way she justified continuing to wax her pubic hair: "When I got my Brazilians I convinced myself that I liked it. That it wasn't as painful as everyone said it was. It fucking was. That it made me sexier. That it was necessary."[27]

Conflicted reasons for not shaving also appear frequently in body hair zines. Bitter Tooth writes in *a lil zine about shaving and me not doing it* that she did not stop shaving only as an overtly political gesture: "I didn't stop shaving to be different or go against the flow, or that's not the only reason. I wanted to because yes I was reading up on feminism and yes it was partly political. But mostly I just wanted to see what it was like and I just didn't see the point in doing it when boys didn't have to."[28]

Zine writers also expressed envy at those who were able to resist in more bold or direct ways. Alexandru writes of these conflicts: "I didn't question why I shaved, waxed or plucked. I just took it as a given that it's what women did. Sometimes I would see women on the bus holding onto a bar with hairy armpits. I used to roll my eyes and think 'fucking hippies.' Maybe I was just jealous they weren't conforming and that I felt forced to. Though I didn't know that at the time."[29] Jen Venegas poignantly admires femmes with facial hair, noting her own jealousy of their bravery: "When I see other femmes with facial hair, my heart swells with love and admiration. And sometimes, jealousy. But I know it's not always a freedom, that it can come with shaming, violence, harm. I know if I were to grow mine, the freedom from shaving can come with shaming, violence, and harm. And so I can grow facial hair. And so it takes from me time and intimacy. And so I shave every day, hate it every day, hide it every day."[30]

Anger at Gendered Double Standards

As a tool of consciousness-raising, body hair zines frequently included narratives about anger toward double standards of beauty for men and women. This formed a key part of the zine writers' intervention, as they flagged for readers the impossible double standards of hairiness and hairlessness, powerfulness and powerlessness, that are pushed onto men and women. At times, zine writers talked about their own horror at realizing these double standards, as when Bitter Tooth writes, "I remember being 12 years old and seeing a boy with hairy armpits and I said 'youre gunna have to shave those' AND his mum said 'why' and I said 'because youre supposed to, aren't you?' And she told me 'Only girls shave their armpits' I asked why. She said 'that's just how it is.'"[31] Dena Lake writes of her anger when realizing that growing hair made her simultaneously revolting and eroticized: "There was something simultaneously empowering and infuriating about my body as a site of revulsion and desire for people I had not invited to have a look in the first place. But, what does it mean to invite visual access? Had my body created a convoluted memory, opened itself to critique by sprouting black hairs and breasts, and housing a loud, confident voice?"[32]

Other zines focused on the double standards in a more feminist educational mode. In *Why Does Society Care So Much about My Body Hair* by Crash Reynolds and Edd Castillo, they discuss these double standards directly: "Girls are told they need to be thin, tanned with no body hair to be considered 'beautiful' by the media. Boys are told they need to be muscular hairy men in order to be considered a 'man.' What's the point?"[33] Similarly, Quiles-Reyes writes in *Hairy, Not So Scary* about the double standards that informed her body hair politics: "Typical Explicit Messages: Facial hair/beards/lots of body hair: manhood, philosophical wisdom, strength, worthiness, bravery, strong will and motivation. Implicit messages: Hairless face/body: feminine, weak, timid, fragile, powerless and feeble."[34] Maryam Adib, in *A Journey into Body Hair*, touts the freedoms women could enjoy by not shaving: "Statistics show, the average woman spends 72 days, or 1728 hours of her life shaving. Most women also report it being their most hated 'beauty ritual.' Life is short, why waste time trying to live up to patriarchal standards when hair grows back within a couple days? Imagine what you could do instead . . . a semester of school, a few vacations. working toward your goals. Time not worrying about shaving!! Time not feeling uncomfortable from razor bumps!! A world full of possibilities!! What would you do with 10 extra weeks?"[35]

A few body hair zines also included explicit descriptions of how trans and gender-nonconforming people might differently experience body hair removal or growth and how this could link to potential risks of mockery, violence, and discrimination. In *Hairy Femme Mother*, Jen Venegas writes,

> Femmes with visible body hair, particularly femme trans people, can signal gender-nonconformity. To say this makes people uncomfortable is an understatement but it can also incite incredible violence and a lack of safety. Visible body hair on a trans femme can mean being "outed" or failing to pass. There is political resistance in this but it can come at a heavy cost, especially for trans femmes of color and black trans femmes. So while I am trying to celebrate and embrace my body hair, I am also honoring those that choose to remove it for safety, for passing, for however they may choose to perform and embody femme. For me, femme has room for it all, but it also acknowledges the ways that body hair can be fucking dangerous and how we can protect and uplift our trans and gender non-conforming people with visible (and even sometimes not immediately visible) body hair.[36]

Awareness of these double standards about gender and beauty norms was also depicted in body hair zines with direct, unabashed anger from women across ages and identity categories. Alexandru writes of her intense outrage at the different standards expected of men and women:

> I was angry that I had been fed the lie that shaving was natural but having body hair was not. I was even more angry that I had believed it for so long. I was angry at how I didn't feel

comfortable leaving the house if I hadn't waxed my upper lip or plucked my eyebrows. How I would feel physically uncomfortable if I had visible armpit hair because I was 100 percent convinced that that's all anyone else could see. That my body, and by extension my whole self, would be deemed disgusting. Hairy. Not beautiful. Unfuckable. I was angry that men didn't have to do anything to appear normal. Male stubble was a sign of sexiness and style. I was angry I had to shave in order to feel comfortable or sexy during sex. I was angry that I didn't know how to change it.[37]

Jen Venegas indignantly rants about the strict expectations of femininity and hairlessness expected of women and girls: "There are a lot of things I could say about how the patriarchy shows men a femininity that is hairless (among A LOT of other things) and therefore 'clean' and how expressions that fall outside of that are seen as 'dirty.' Or how women or femme-presenting people need to present that femme or femininity a certain way in order to be validated by the male gaze which dominates our culture and dictates safety and respect and visibility (among LOTS of other things)."[38]

Positive Feelings toward Body Hair

As a key intervention of body hair zines, the direct expression of liking body hair, finding it appealing, discovering it positively for the first time, and embracing hairiness worked to upend patriarchal expectations of women's hairlessness. These positive body hair narratives appeared in nearly every body hair zine. Bitter Tooth writes of seeing her body hair as normal and appealing: "I like my hair. I like bodies with detail. Like when a make up artist takes off a full face, Like I like someones freckles or moles or tattoos."[39] She went on to write of the reasons she appreciated her body hair: "Shaving takes too much time and energy. I like the feeling of the air and water on my legs. I want to be normal. I don't want my body to become the topic of conversation. The only way to make the 'weird' and 'different' normal is by doing it. Regardless of what anyone else says. Yes. I have had enough of being told what I should look like. And above all I do it to make myself happy."[40]

Some of the zines described the sensual and physical experiences of body hair in glowing terms. Jen Venegas talks affectionately about her body hair: "Feeling the wind rustle my leg hairs for the first time was an experience I gladly welcomed while acknowledging the fact that this experience was one that typically only one gender gets to experience. Here I was, a cis queer femme, feeling the air hit my legs in a way I had yet to know. Knowing this feeling . . . what a gift. Seasons of shorts, skirts and bare arms since then and I still can't get over how the air tickles my body hair in the most delicious way."[41] She writes in an earlier volume about learning to embrace the smell and eroticism of hairy armpits: "I struggled with it at first but now I love my pit hair. I love how my pits don't itch anymore like they used to from shaving. I love how they smell, even on those days when I don't use deodorant & they are a little ripe. I love getting naked for someone and letting them see my pits for the first time. I love wearing sleeveless tops and feeling the summer breeze make my pit hair dance away. My pit hair makes me happy. So does a lot of my other hair. And the ones that don't, well, I'm working on that too."[42]

Racial Consciousness and Body Hair

As a key example of content largely missing from the scholarly journals, body hair zines also talked frankly about the racial aspects of body hair, both from their own personal experiences and through a broader framework of racial politics. Olivia M. writes of growing body hair as a Latina and how this connects to dehumanizing racial stereotypes:

> As a mestiza Latina, I tend to have thick hair, wherever on my body it happens to be. Not necessarily super hairy, but dark, thick and noticeable. There's baggage that comes along with being a hairy Latina. Latinx people are stereotyped as being more emotional and animalistic, which is often associated with hairiness. Body hair, especially on women, is also seen as being gross and dirty, the product of laziness, which only piles up on top of stereotypes about lazy, dirty Mexicans. All of these characterizations stand in opposition to white, skinny, hetero, capitalist ideas of femininity. A racist worldview doesn't have room for femmes like me.[43]

Jen Venegas echoes these claims in her personal narrative about the extra cost of growing body hair as a Latina adolescent in school: "At my small co-ed Catholic school, other girls had started shaving their legs too, including my sixth grade best friend . . . she asked me how often I shaved my legs. I didn't want to tell her that in order to keep them smooth, I had to shave my legs every single day. Feeling ashamed, I instead sheepishly replied, 'every other day.' I sensed a hint of jealousy, probably because she too was a hairy Latina. I immediately regretted lying but I still wasn't ready to embrace any sort of hair pride that solidarity with her would bring."[44]

At times, narratives about race and body hair targeted white women's blind spots about the social costs of body hair. Dayanita Ramesh, in *Hairy Hair*, writes as an Indian American of feeling erased from dominant narratives about women's body hair: "Part of policing the female body includes expectations of hair removal—in particular from the legs, pubic area and armpits. The rest of the body is excluded from the conversation on body hair and as a woman of color, western third wave feminism does not care about my hair, which is thick, coarse and dark."[45] She also admonishes white women for not recognizing the racial double standards between women: "When white women decide not to shave, pluck or when they dye their armpit hair—it's seen as liberating and revolutionary. It's weird, because for WOC, we are told our entire lives to ascribe to white/western ideals of beauty and now they wanna look like us, but it's still wrong for us to be ourselves."[46]

Feelings about "dirtiness" and negative social judgments by strangers also appear in body hair zines when women of color describe their experiences of growing their hair: "I still grow wide eyed when I see people catch a look at my hairy legs on BART [public transit]. I am still aware that all of the white girls' arm and leg and armpit hair around me combined could not amount to the undesirability I feel just from a two-inch gap between my skirt and Doc Martens that reveals my unruly leg hair. I am still aware that my blackness will always impact my ability to take part in 'body revolutions.' I hope one day, I and all my lovers and friends will bask in my body hair."[47] Jen Venegas also describes similar feelings of anger about her hair being perceived as dirty: "There are a lot of things I could say about how femmes of color are already seen as 'unclean' and to have socially unacceptable or gender nonconforming body hair has us seen as even 'dirtier.' Yeah, there are a lot of fucking things I can say about this."[48]

Ethnicity also appeared as a subject of interest, particularly as hairy white women with darker body hair reflected on their differences with blonder, lighter-skinned women. Alexandru writes of her ethnic background and her adolescent experiences with body hair: "I'm Romanian and Hungarian and, as a result, hairy. . . . I used to blame my heritage for my hairiness. I used to curse whatever gods were giving out perfectly smooth skin the day I was born for sleeping on the job. Growing up in a predominantly Indian neighborhood I had lots of Indian female friends. We used to bond over the loss of the genetic lottery when it came to body hair."[49]

Women of color also expressed ferocious anger at the colonialist, racist, imperialist, and patriarchal framing of their hairy bodies. Nancy Aragon writes, in "Open Letter to: White Supremacist, Capitalist, Hetero Patriarchal Hairless America,"

> You think I don't see you? I fucking see you destroying families
> Incarcerating racialized hairy bodies
> Telling us to go back to where we came from
> But what you don't get is that
> You are the outsider. We are standing in indigenous lands that are
>   stained by colonization
> We are tired.
> We are angry.
> We are hurt.
> WE ARE HAIRY!
> You need to know we are resilient and we are powerful and you will
>   no longer silence us.
> Porque somos semillas y seguiremos creciendo![50]

Resistance and Fighting Back

Nearly every body hair zine included content on resistance to gender rules, ranging from the more mild and individual-level resistance to ambitious cultural and societal-level forms of resistance. For example, a more individual-level reading of resistance was Jamie Squire's *Hairy & Happy*, where she writes of her reasons for not shaving: "I decided to stop shaving my body because I hated the maintenance and I don't think that being shaven should be a qualifier for feeling beautiful. When I made art about my hairy legs and posted it online, the response I received was shocking. I couldn't believe how many people still feel so repulsed by something as natural as body hair, and this only amplified my determination to normalize it."[51]

Women describe growing their body hair as a way to model for their daughters how to embrace body affirmations, resist capitalism, and fight back against social norms that restrict women's bodily expressions. For example, Quiles-Reyes writes of wanting her daughter to normalize women's body hair from an early age: "I stopped all hair removal because I didn't want my daughter to grow up thinking it was necessary or even normative for women to remove the hair that marks them out as adult. The rest of society will be modeling the alternative, so I feel I have to show her what the other option is!"[52] Adib writes of the environmental impact of shaving and how not shaving can be a more responsible choice: "Disposable razors are one of the highest waste contributors when it comes to bathroom products. An estimated 2 BILLION are tossed per year! Recycling razors can be done, however it is a lengthy process that most aren't willing to do! The steel in razors [is] recyclable, however they must be removed from the plastic cast before doing so."[53] Riffing on this, Quiles-Reyes describes not shaving as a way to resist patriarchal beauty standards and practices: "How do we begin to normalize the idea that body hair on women is okay? We need to stop shaming the hair off our bodies. And I'm not talking about never shaving or waxing or plucking or going for laser treatments again. I'm talking about having the freedom from feeling that we MUST defur before going to the beach, playing sports, before going to the gym or before going on a date or before having sex."[54]

Body hair zines also included material that encouraged readers to picture an alternate reality, one where women are less saddled with baggage around their bodies and beauty routines. Quiles-Reyes, in *Hairy, Not So Scary*, imagines a different future for girls: "WHAT IF there were no more comparisons of breast sizes, waistlines, hair & skin textures, body shapes and types? WHAT IF all little girls had the opportunity to experience puberty, free from the shame that comes with all of the change?"[55] Dena

Lake writes of not shaving as a way to regain power and autonomy: "Rather than providing 'increased visual access' to a normative object-of-sensory-access, I refused to remove my arm or facial hair, which produced an intentional mindfuck/barrier in interactions with men I was not actually sexually attracted to."[56] Adib writes about the necessity of fighting back against beauty norms: "Natural occurrences in our bodies should never debilitate us from living our lives. Don't feel trapped inside your body on the account of society's expectations! We as women constantly have our bodies and general appearances policed. We are more than our external beauty! Fight back against these outdated silly standards, try embracing your body even just for a week to challenge yourself and how the world sees you. You may be pleasantly surprised at how easy it is."[57]

The defiant and imaginative character of body hair zines, embodied in both the writing and the imagery, also worked to push resistance as a key theme. Venegas writes of how resisting body hair norms can upend capitalism and the stranglehold that the beauty industry has over women: "Body hair can also be used as a form of political resistance in terms of capitalism. It is a direct confrontation against all hair removing products in the beauty industry. Fuck depilatory creams. Fuck razors. Fuck hair bleach kits. Fuck waxing. Fuck tweezing. Fuck that whole industry that tells us we need to conform and be bare, hairless and 'clean' to be accepted."[58] Finally, Squire calls for a defiant posture when reimagining women's body hair, saying that women can and will resist norms of hairlessness: "It turns out women are ready to embrace their body hair. And a lot of them already are. And this changes the rules . . . because if women want to be hairy, THEY WILL BE HAIRY. And when women choose to have body hair . . . It is feminine. It is womanly and it is right. And it won't matter if you call them gross or disgusting or ugly, because they're not listening."[59]

AYQA KHAN'S BODY HAIR DRAWINGS

In tandem with analyzing body hair zines, the work of Ayqa Khan, an emerging Pakistani American Muslim artist based in New York, also serves as a unique kind of body hair activism. Khan's work focuses on the South Asian diasporic experience, particularly the ways that bodies become politicized and trapped within systems that imagine certain

FIGURE 3.3. "Brows(e) through the Ages: An Embarrassingly Hairy Journey," by Bhairavi Thanki, from *Static Zine: A DIY Magazine* (Body Issue, May 2015).

bodies as beautiful and other bodies as abject. As a self-taught, multidisciplinary artist with no formal art degree, she uses mediums that include digital image, video, painting, digital illustration, and writing. In her description of her artistic identity, she wrote that she "is interested in exploring the psychological lenses in which we view our own selves and others."[60] She draws on the experiences of body hair to explore the boundary line between our own and others' bodies, particularly as body hair becomes a metaphor for borders themselves.

In the last few years, Khan's work has garnered more mainstream recognition for its compelling exploration of race and abjection. In an interview with Khan, Nat Brut describes her work as grappling "with the notion of *taking up space*—occupying space, moving in space, imagining a future in space—which is timely. . . . There is no way to look into Muslim space without acknowledging the female Muslim 'other.' To enter the private space of Ayqa Khan is to come into contact with her body. Throughout her Insta-oeuvre, shadows and skins of living bodies have a way of inconveniencing the voyeuristic gaze and interrupting the silent interiors decorated with breezy curtains and oriental rugs." Brut goes on to focus on Khan's body hair work and its connection to South Asian diaspora:

> Khan's work is drawn from her own experience as a brown woman negotiating diaspora through excessive body hair. According to many South Asian and North American beauty standards, the appearance of excessive body hair on cis-gendered women elicits an abject response. The unaesthetic abject is located at the border between the beautiful and the ugly. When the border appears, the subject experiences, 'an acute crisis of self-preservation,' and is unable to cross borders easily. . . . Khan's body hair invokes a feeling of being on the opposite side of the border, with one side looking in and the other side growing.[61]

Famously targeted on Tumblr by reactionary trolls calling her work "gross," Khan reflected on these criticisms and her reason for making art that features women's body hair: "I think some of the funniest comments I have read are ones that range along the lines of 'she'll never get married' and 'removing body hair is hygienic and respectable' and 'why doesn't she preach about actual woman's issues?' What has bothered me the most is not people's narrow-mindedness, but more so the idea that this isn't a big deal or issue. If this wasn't a big deal, there would be no hate. When a FEMALE is attacking another FEMALE on what to do with her body, that is an issue to me."[62] She described the purpose of her work in an interview with Huffington Post, saying, "My intentions are to normalize [body hair] . . . because it is something that shouldn't be a huge deal considering body hair is natural and the removal of it is a social construct."[63] Added to this, Khan wanted to expand visibility for South Asian women, telling reporters, "South Asian woman do not get enough representation in most spaces and I feel the need to express this in an organic way."[64]

Khan went on to write about her own family experiences growing up and how those stigmatizing experiences impacted her decision to make art about body hair: "My mother owns a beauty salon where she has made me get waxed ever since I was about 11 because she thought that the hair that was given to my body was 'unfeminine.' What bothered me the most was not the pain of getting waxed, but the idea that she thought something natural about me was 'gross.' I felt looked at as an object, rather than a HUMAN. People from my school would stare at my thick arm hair in disgust really. And yes, this made me feel really insecure and unworthy."[65] Given this painful adolescent history, Khan has created an entirely different world, one where women's body hair is assumed and expected, glorious and beautiful. She moves between subject and object, with her characters experiencing ordinary aspects of life (e.g., watching television, swimming in the pool) while being obviously hairy.

Khan has explored body hair in her art and drawings through multiple mediums, though her first collection of body hair drawings—playful, colorful, splashing with light and optimism—stand out as uniquely edgy and provocative. In this work, Khan inverts subject/object in the women she depicts, and she presents women's body hair as both mundane (that is, in the background, entirely ordinary) and on display (featured, homed in on, centered on). In one image, two women sit waiting for the New York City subway, surrounded by images of Donald Trump's face as a dartboard, ads for online dating, and posters about anxiety, decolonization, and self-help. Their body hair is both foregrounded and placed in the background in this busy scene. Similarly, *Day Off* portrays two characters sitting on a couch in front of a large Persian rug surrounded by empty juice boxes and a laptop, hair poking through the tiny openings at their ankles and midriffs. This contrast—between hair as the focus and hair as a subtle presence—permeates Khan's body of work.

The fact that she layers her body hair work with racial, ethnic, and religious themes also gives her drawings a distinctly political edge. At times this appears as an overtly politicized embrace of queerness and brownness, as depicted in *I'm Out*. Here the hairy nude brown body drives wildly through a dreamscape where, instead of queer rainbows, patterns of colors and textures that reference Islamic art appear while tapestries form moons and suns in the sky. Freedom here is layered on as multiple entities: the hairy body, the freedom of outness, the disregard for social convention, and the playful reference points of cultural and ethnic heritage, cut up and reassembled as the universe.

In her work, Khan combines unexpected pairings and contrasts, at times leaving the viewer with arresting images that command attention and redefine how women—especially Muslim women—appear in the American cultural imagination. In *Disco Baby*, she depicts two women dancing, one with underarm and leg hair exposed and one wearing a full, colorful burka, crouched on the ground. Importantly, though, we do not read these as opposites per se, but rather as the embodiment of a similar kind of freedom. *Both* are disco dancing, *both* embrace color and wild red eyes, *both* are roller skating to their own groove. Perhaps these pairings of women—or trios of women, as she sometimes chooses instead—represent fragments of Khan's imagined intimacies with herself, with women she knows and loves, or with the general emotional register of joy she experiences through defiance.

Khan understands hair as a boundary, a symbol of the body, something that can fall into the background and push to the foreground. Take *What's on TV* and her image of hairy legs in sneakers as examples of each of these. In the first, two hairy adolescent girls watch a soap opera, surrounded in the room by a framed portrait of their parents (or grandparents), a stack of religious books, plates of snacks, an algebra book, pencils, and a hairbrush. Their mother peeks in, unobtrusively, framing the piece as a study in beauty norms and how they are expressed (television, internalized beauty practices, motherly advice and guidance, etc.). We are meant to reflect on body hair as a product of institutions, influences, and the oppressive omnipresence of the beauty industry. Another image, by contrast, foregrounds body hair, in a racially diverse portrait of women's legs and colorful sneakers. Here the body as joyful, moving, jumping, and

FIGURE 3.4. Ayqa Khan, *Disco Baby* (2016). Image courtesy of the artist.

embracing hair—particularly the similarity of the hair and the difference of the skin colors—works to upend notions of body shame, covering up the body, or saturating the body with narratives of hairlessness-as-good.

Khan often presents women in various states of playful intimacy, whether sitting on a park bench together (as in *Furry Ladies*), embracing or snuggling (*Mama's Day*), playing games with each other, or relaxing in a swimming pool (*Summer's Over*). These images of relationality—the intimacies created by simply *being* in the body without anxiety and sharing space with other hairy women's bodies—are themselves conjuring a world we often do not experience or even imagine. What would it be like, for example, if women could lazily float in swimming pools with full armpit hair, relax together, or lie next to a mother entirely disinterested in taming or managing her daughter's leg hair? These images make a powerful intervention, one that viewers immediately experience as a kind of longing for another world rather than a marker of abject status.

Much of Khan's work, however, also focuses on the individual woman as she moves through life as the embodiment of contrasts. In *Stressed*, she depicts a woman plucking her chin hairs—an oft-done activity rarely seen in art or photography. This image of the everyday hair removal throws together contradictions and contrasts. She is "done up" with lipstick and nail polish and yet hairy on her chin, hands, and arms. She is tattooed yet traditional, hairy yet smooth, dainty yet masculine, beautiful yet working with the abject. In another image, Khan depicts a sexualized hairy dominatrix lying on what we can imagine might be Persian rugs (or patterned clouds). Here, the contrasts—between the erotic dominatrix and the passive sitting stance, between the hairy, whip-yielding woman and the soft and sensual rugs/clouds—are striking. As an even more complex example, one Khan drawing shows a hairy-legged brown woman sitting in a relaxed yet powerful position on a chair, surrounded by a dildo, coconut oil, a book on existentialism, a painting of two Muslim women, handcuffs, a *Playboy* poster, a burka, tarot cards, and a box of pastries. She smokes a cigarette in this space of contrasts and contradictions, as objects of taboo and comfort keep her company.

Khan's work also moves between spaces, spheres, and worlds. As a self-taught artist, she also sold her work herself, marketing it on her website and—at least initially—selling it for remarkably inexpensive prices. She has called herself an "artist from the internet."[66] Her work is meant—like body hair zines—to be accessible and resists the stuffy and classist mechanisms of the traditional art world. She has reproduced her images online, given interviews at a variety of blogs and magazines (e.g., Huffington Post, BuzzFeed, *Vice*, *Teen Vogue*), and has worked to depict,

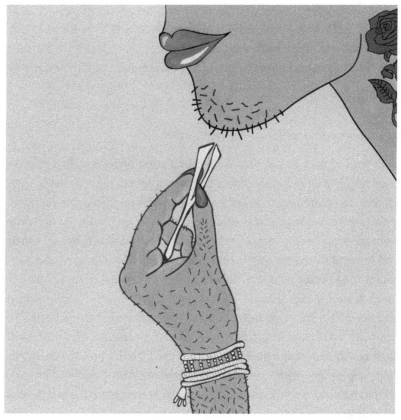

FIGURE 3.5. Ayqa Khan, *Stressed* (n.d.). Image courtesy of the artist.

and speak about, hairy Muslim women in a way that draws in audiences from disparate parts of the art and activist worlds.[67]

Writer Alison Roberts captures some of these wild contradictions Khan so effortlessly embodies in her work: "Evoking strong sentiments of nostalgia, there is a longing in these images, a longing for place and time. The connection to Pakistani and South Indian culture is celebrated. Khan's series are filled with images of niqabs, ornamental jewelry, and various Pakistani food items. Her illustrations are set in classic American diners and retro rollerblading rinks, while her photography is hued with muted tones and pastel palettes. It is within this duality of culture that her protagonists rest both comfortably and uncomfortably."[68] She thus works with abject bodies, situates herself between different artistic spheres, and images hybridity—in culture, bodies, and mediums—with remarkable ease. The work she creates and her identity as an artist subvert traditional notions of beauty and position her work as activist in nature.

ZINES AND DRAWINGS AS ACTIVISM

Body hair zines contain a unique combination of seemingly disparate aspects of body politics, as evidenced by the fusion in these works of playfulness, complex emotions, and political resistance. These zines serve as tools of feminist consciousness-raising, drawing together a range of claims from the more basic and straightforward (double standards between men and women) to the notably radical and complex (risks to trans and nonconforming people who grow hair, conflicts about capitalism, reflections on adolescent brainwashing). In this regard, they work to both embrace and normalize abject bodies, situating women's body hair as beautiful, desirable, and something to have affection for. In essence, they push back against a system that values women and their bodies only to the extent that they comply with traditional gender roles. This happens alongside the more nuanced political work of normalizing women's body hair in spite of its abject status as "dirty," "gross," or "disgusting."

Writers of body hair zines also wonderfully embrace their own shortcomings, ambivalences, and hesitations about the shameless acceptance of body hair. They talk about how body hair is often a painful story for them, how they have struggled to love it and not internalize patriarchal beauty standards that dictate hairlessness as the only kind of beauty, and they discuss the huge range of ambivalent feelings they have about using body hair to resist. Some zine makers even went as far as discussing the deep shame they have felt (and sometimes still feel) about body hair, conjuring a nearly fanatic array of behaviors they have engaged in to eradicate hair from their bodies, faces, nipples, legs, underarms, and pubic regions. This bringing together of messy personal narratives—not always linear or hopeful or perfectly consistent—expands the readership and normalizes the struggle of abjection rather than merely the end point of arriving at a "happy & hairy" existence.

Further, these body hair zines and drawings poignantly describe and depict forms of resistance that are creative, multiple, and wildly different from each other. Some forms of resistance emphasize visibility and seeing women's body hair (especially the drawings of Khan), while others focus on directing anger and rage at patriarchal beauty standards. Some are playful and silly, while still others are reflective and straightforward. Some forms of resistance embrace a sweeping critique of capitalism, while other kinds of resistance look to the feminist work of mentoring and mothering as sites of activist intervention. Some forms of resistance emphasize difference—especially the racial differences between women and the importance of taking those seriously—while others look at women (and humans in general) as engaged in shared experiences and understandings of gender oppression. This diversity of perspectives and approaches shows the necessity of having, as Michel Foucault has argued, "a plurality of resistances."[69]

Such a plurality of resistances embodied in these body hair zines and drawings shows a playful and down-to-earth version of feminist activism that is too often excluded from more scholarly accounts of feminism. This version of feminist resistance is full of humor and fun, typos and scribbles, do-it-yourself ethos rather than externally validated (and cited) writing, and radical self-reflection. Khan's powerful and impactful drawings center hairy women of color and draw upon bodies that are too often sidelined in feminist work on bodies. Muslim women roller-skating, hairy women swimming in pools, and various scenes of bodily proximity and hairy body intimacy embody a new and distinct contemporary feminism that has largely freed itself from the weighty baggage of third-wave identity politics while putting forth a playful vision of feminism that centers women of color, abject bodies, and women's solidarity with each other. Khan's work reveals that feminism can connect to many other parts of its identity as a social movement, integrating marginal bodies and perspectives, upending visibility of its key players, and moving toward an embrace of its jagged edges and its emotional and fiery contrasts, while celebrating its wonderfully diverse bodies.

4

Expanding the Body Hair Imaginary

Photography as Social Intervention

> That work is never complete: the very boundaries of our bodies, to
> say nothing of the limits of empathy and political action, are, and
> may be, continually remade. Perhaps it is this openness, this
> fragility, that has for so long animated hair, that made it a matter of
> concern to presidents and protestors, scientists and theologians,
> artists and pornographers: the fundamental unruliness of life.
>
> —REBECCA M. HERZIG, *Plucked*

WOMEN'S BODY HAIR OFTEN EXISTS WITHOUT A VISUAL NARRA-
tive to animate it; consequently, it is commonly imagined as a nuisance
or an irritant, an invisible part of the body without a history in images. It
is worth remembering that the mere act of *seeing* women's body hair can
be jarring, unsettling, and, perhaps, politically fruitful. This chapter positions art photography that features women with visible body hair as an
emerging mode of artistic expression. Given that widespread body hair
removal, for women, largely began in response to the development and
circulation of fashion photography between 1915 and 1919, the relationship
between women, body hair, and photography is fraught and significant.[1]
As photographers grapple with abjection, discourses of the natural body,
and the visually arresting possibilities of women's body hair, they also
visually document the powerful social norms of women's hairlessness,
both by rebelling against them and by, in some ways, reinforcing them. I
specifically argue in this chapter that body hair photography is itself a

social intervention, working against the operations of making body hair invisible, silent, and secret. Body hair photography expands and nuances ideas about women's body hair by exposing tensions between the "natural" and "unnatural" and by asserting a different relationship to women's body hair and the concept of beauty. Notably, though women's body hair *is* in many ways natural, it also appears in these photographs as shocking, abject, strange, peculiar, and perhaps erotic.

In this chapter, I examine three contemporary photographers whose work captures the complexities and contradictions of visually documenting women's body hair, particularly as it draws together personal identities, social identities, and the political contexts in which artists live and work. In particular, I look at British photographer Ben Hopper's series called *Natural Beauty*, in which he contrasts the highly stylized traditions of fashion models and fashion modeling with the natural, makeup-free, diverse bodies of women with body hair. I then examine Oaxacan artist Zuly Garcia's series called *The Valentine's Day Series*, in which she photographs Mexican American and Sikh women showing their body hair against a backdrop of traditional, campy femininity. I also look at photographer Marilyn Minter's images of pubic hair in *Plush*, where she features an array of slick, textured, humid, explicitly erotic photos of women's pubic hair. To conclude, I look at historical and contemporary feminist performance art—in particular, Eleanor Antin's 2017 reimagining of her classic 1972 piece, *Carving*—to consider how the notion of the natural is an inadequate framing to capture the subversive qualities of body hair photography. Ultimately, I argue in this chapter that photography of the body can serve as a social intervention, one that embraces rather than erases contradictions while better understanding the time and context of its subjects.

PHOTOGRAPHY AND ABJECTION

Photography has long been used as a medium to explore the relationship between bodies and abjection; that is, "themes that transgress and threaten our sense of cleanliness and propriety particularly referencing the body and bodily functions."[2] The term *abjection* literally means "the state of being cast off" and is derived from the work of French intellectual

Julia Kristeva, whose book, *Powers of Horror*, provides an elaborate philosophical analysis linking together abjection, death, and women's bodies through a feminist analysis of maternity and identity (see introduction).[3] The subversive French writer Georges Bataille, who wrote *The Story of the Eye* and *Blue of Noon*, also helped to define and describe the character of abjection through his vivid and raunchy work on the erotics of death.[4] Both of these writers have highlighted the ways that abjection has become linked to women's bodies, as women's bodies are "abjected" by the patriarchal social order.[5] Thus, all aspects of bodily spaces deemed impure and gross, or which become linked with disgust, horror, and repulsion, can be characterized as abject.

Many feminist artists and photographers have played with and referenced abjection in their work, often in order to make various kinds of social commentaries about the relationship between women's bodies and patriarchal power. In particular, Cindy Sherman, whose photographs of herself in various 1950s and 1960s Hollywood and film noir stereotypes and as an unhappy housewife, an aristocrat, a jilted lover, or a milkmaid, has captured the essence of, and created a well-known body of work around, abjection.[6] Feminist performance artist Carolee Schneemann has also created works grappling with abjection, particularly *Meat Joy* (1964), where a group of people play with raw chicken, uncooked sausage, wet paint, and scraps of paper in a tangled, abject mess. She also created *Interior Scroll* (1975), where she pulled a scroll of writing from her vagina and read it aloud to audiences while standing nude in front of them.[7] Other artists known for imagining and dealing with abjection include Louise Bourgeois, Helen Chadwick, Sarah Lucas, and Kiki Smith.[8]

Most famously, photographer Diane Arbus—whose work captured marginalized, forgotten, and discarded people and peculiar and emotive expressions on people's faces—aimed to humanize and empathize with abjection, giving life and humanity to characters often stripped of their subjective perspectives. Though she died young (of suicide, at age forty-eight), Arbus built a body of work now recognized as singular in its approach to understanding and capturing the conditions of abjection and marginality.[9] She famously photographed what "gnawed" at her, drawing in subjects considered too damaged, racy, or problematic to be taken seriously. In doing so, she laid the groundwork for generations of photographers who came after her to document and observe the interplay between emotions, interiority, marginalization, and abjection, particularly as it played out on the body.

THE OPTICS OF WOMEN'S BODY HAIR

Beyond the art world, women's body hair has had a long and strange history, seen at once as a symbol of women's independence and rebelliousness and as emblematic of being old-fashioned and backward. Rebecca Herzig traced this history of early twentieth-century body hair removal and found that the 1910s brought about "the rapid growth of print advertising and newly revealing fashions in clothing but also changing gender and sexual roles and intensifying emphasis on racial ideals of hygiene. As ever, body hair was a ready repository for wider social and political concerns."[10] With the widespread circulation of fashion photography—which increasingly featured hairless models—combined with fears of women's growing independence and changes in women's fashion, pressures for women to remove body hair by any means necessary became widespread. Women were encouraged to use anything at their disposal, from low technology to more high-tech medical procedures: diathermy, fine-grained pumice stones, sandpaper depilatories, sodium sulfide depilatories, chemical hair removal, razors, shoemaker waxes, and X-ray hair removal.[11] The pain involved in enacting many of those procedures speaks to the desperate and labored attempts women made to conform to expectations of hairlessness.

The new exposure of skin in visual images, and fears of women being seen as rebellious and powerful, led to pressures for hair removal. Whereas thick stockings had once hidden women's leg hair, as hemlines rose, women internalized a greater fear of revealing their leg hair. Similarly, as clothing started to reveal women's underarms more readily, a newfound self-consciousness was born around women's hairy armpits. Thus, women's body hair and its presence or absence became a "multivalent symbol." Herzig writes of the link between women's body hair and their social rights: "For critics of changing social roles, visible body hair on women served as tangible evidence of a surfeit of manliness. As women who pushed for voting rights and access to jobs and education were depicted as sexually inverted, so, too, were they depicted as hairy."[12] In this context, a cultural aversion to women's body hair spread rapidly, layered with an overtly racialized idea of health, hygiene, and fitness. To be morally good and hygienically clean, women had to maintain a state of hairlessness.

The omnipresence of hairless women in photography and advertisements came to mark this period of early twentieth-century history, as cleanliness and modernity became linked with incessant hair removal from all areas of the body. As Herzig argues, "This preoccupation with spotlessness was made manifest in period advertisements: voluptuous flesh and visible hair yielded to clean, athletic figures, whose smooth, sanitized whiteness was crucial to their virtue."[13] The magazine *Harper's Bazaar* had a fivefold increase in the number of advertisements for hair removal products during the period from 1915 to 1919, far outpacing any other personal hygiene product. The message was clear: to be stylish and fashionable, one must be hairless.

Embedded within these prescriptive notions of gender lurked the specter of the scary, hairy, manly, powerful woman. An advertisement for the De Miracle Chemical Company from 1912 warned that, without hair removal products, America "May Become a Nation of Bearded Women."[14] Advice columns, popular beauty books, and magazines all promoted hair removal for women as a necessity, even (ironically) as women gained more freedom in so many other areas of their lives during this period of time. Body hair on women became vilified as unnatural, excessive, and disgusting, and hair removal became a way, as Herzig writes, "to separate oneself from cruder people, lower class and immigrant."[15] Even the advertisements started to have racialized undertones, with one advertisement claiming, "Whatever you do—wherever you go—you need to have your skin CLEARED from this dark shadow."[16] Women's body hair was more than a nuisance or a hassle; it symbolized, for many, the ultimate in racialized, classed, and gendered social status.

The social control mechanisms of body hair have thus persisted for over a hundred years, largely hiding the problematic history carried within the seemingly benign, trivial, and simple act of women removing body hair. The convergence, then, of the feminist art world—often eager to grapple with women's abject status—and the fashion world—often repulsed by deviations to gender and body norms—is thus embodied in the realm of body hair photography. I consider here three examples of recent body hair photography series, including the artist's own ideas about the work, the critical reception, and my interpretation of the work's meaning and impact, followed by a reconsideration of feminist performance artist Eleanor Antin's self-photography in *Carving* from 1972 and 2017. This is designed to show body hair photography in its current iteration as connected to a longer history of the photography of abjection and to the history of hair removal inscribed as a "moral" and social action.

BEN HOPPER, *NATURAL BEAUTY* (2007–20)

Starting in 2007 through to 2020, London-based British photographer Ben Hopper photographed women with underarm hair for a series he called *Natural Beauty*. In this series, all of the models went without makeup and many were featured in plain white tank tops; most of the images feature women staring straight into the camera. While the series has been widely embraced as exposing the problematically narrow standards of beauty imposed onto women, Hopper himself had different intentions for the series. He told *Cosmopolitan* magazine, "It started as a joke about contemporary art and how a lot of artists create a body of repetitive work only to be treated seriously by overwhelmed audiences. I thought photographing a lot of really beautiful women with armpit hair would make a similar effect."[17] He ran into some unexpected issues with the models' own feelings about body hair while doing the shoots, saying that one of his models was so repulsed by her own armpit hair that she chose not to go through with it.[18] When asked how he got access to so many models with armpit hair, he told reporters, "It's a varied collection of women. Most simply open-minded individuals. Some I know from previous work, some I get introduced to, some contact me. Some grew the hair especially for the pictures, some contacted me when they already had fully grown hair."[19]

Hopper intended the work to expose the contrasts between the largely hairless fashion world and hairy female bodies. This effect is immediately felt when looking at the images; many of the women are conventionally attractive, and many have traditional features of models

FIGURE 4.1. Cassia Chloe posing for Ben Hopper, *Natural Beauty* (2014). From Ben Hopper's *Natural Beauty* project (2007–ongoing). Find more info on http://therealbenhopper.com.

(e.g., overwhelmingly thin, young, symmetrical faces). The images feel arresting to look at, in part because of the collisions between stereotypes of fashion and stereotypes of hairy women. He told the *Daily Mail*, "The whole point is contrast between fashionable female beauty and the raw unconventional look of female armpit hair. . . . I expect [the photos] will surprise a lot of people and I guess, in a way, that is one of my intentions."[20] He explained to the *Telegraph* why he chose a conventional model lineup: "Because if I asked 'who would you expect to have armpit hair?' you'd never imagine a fashion model or a very beautiful hygienic looking female. . . . That's the stereotype and I'm trying to use it to intrigue a stronger reaction."[21] (Clearly, Hopper's equation of beauty with hygiene reinforces the problematic assumption that body hair is dirty.)

The women in these images also pose by taking up space and looking powerful rather than looking meek or powerless. They have fierce, stern faces rather than the vapid or sullen expressions that characterize so

FIGURE 4.2. Charlot Conway posing for Ben Hopper, *Natural Beauty* (2018). Photo courtesy of the artist.

much of the contemporary fashion world.[22] When the viewer engages with these photos, the sensation is one of awe, intrigue, and power, like a contemporary twist on the iconography of Rosie the Riveter and/or the mythical story of Medusa. The photos play with stories of women's bodies and with the viewer's own relationship to looking at women's bodies.

Hopper's choice to use conventionally attractive models has also attracted some negative attention. One review notes, "Frankly I'm not sure why the focus on thin attractive women with brushes of armpit hair is particularly more provocative or contemplative of what comes under the ambit of natural beauty as promoted by the beauty and fashion industry. In both instances, attractive thin women are de rigueur. One just now has hair under her armpits. Or perhaps she always had hair but now some of us dare admit it."[23] Hopper said that he intended the work to serve as a protest against beauty norms: "Although armpit hair is a natural state it has become a statement. Why is that? . . . For almost a century we have been brainwashed by the beauty industry, encouraging hair removal. *Natural Beauty* could be classified as a type of protest.

By creating a contrast between common 'fashionable' female beauty and the raw unconventional look of female armpit hair, thoughts are intrigued and a discussion is made."[24] Hopper did successfully engage the media in writing about these images, with coverage in publications as diverse as Huffington Post, *Bust*, *Cosmopolitan*, the *Telegraph*, the *Daily Mail*, and *Elle* (among others).[25]

Perhaps more importantly, Hopper captures the notion that those women who have noticeable underarm hair have certain personality qualities of defiance and bravery. He told the *Telegraph*, "Under the circumstances, armpit hair can be empowering and sexy. You need an attitude to be a female with hairy armpits nowadays."[26] This construct has also permeated the critical reviews of the series; one reviewer of his work writes, "It's just body hair, but seen through Hopper's lens, grooming habits and the refusal to shave is seen as an act of social defiance."[27] Like many other visible markers of women's body hair, this photography series has also attracted quite a lot of negative attention from the lay public, with comments about the models as "nasty" and "gross" and social media comments like, "Shave under arms bitch your [sic] not a man."[28] One review chides feminism itself for Hopper's images, saying, "No strides for feminism are made by women who are willing to give up their sweet-smelling armpit super powers in order to rail against beauty standards that women have been quietly resisting all along."[29] The review goes on to say, "Instead of trying to reduce women to the odorous and hairy ways of men, feminists would do more for women, and the world, if they got men to start shaving their pits to strive to be hygienic as we are."[30] Again, this strident reinforcement of hairlessness and cleanliness, morality, and achievement speaks to the difficulty of imagining these images outside of the existing frameworks of women's compulsory hairlessness.

Clearly, the women in Hopper's photographs struck a nerve, particularly as they posed with many of the traditional markers of fashion photography stripped away. In one of the images, visible scars line one of the model's arms; in another, tattoos are visible. These images feature a stripping away of the layers of *hiding* women's bodies, instead offering a relatively diverse array of bodies, expressions, ornamentation, hairstyles, muscles, and body hair that grounds the viewer in women's material bodies. As such, they work as a screen onto which viewers project themselves and their

notions of defiant, hairy women. For some, this brings out excitement, envy, awe, and a recognition of beauty in many forms. For others, these images seem to provoke outrage, anger, disgust, and bafflement. In this regard, Hopper captures some of the ambivalence and tensions that women's body hair evokes, particularly in this bold and "in your face" style of photography.

ZULY GARCIA, *BODY HAIR POSITIVE SERIES* (2018)

While the reimagining of fashion photography in Hopper's work plays with the conventions of stereotypical beauty found in modeling, Hopper still relies on the norms of fashion photography, and the beauty of thin and attractive models, to make his statement. In contrast, Zuly Garcia's work inverts the scripts of conventional beauty standards and instead reimagines the faces of modeling while preserving a traditional, campy, ultrafeminine background. As a Los Angeles–based Oaxacan indigenous artist, Zuly Garcia made quite a splash with her work depicting women of color and their body hair. Garcia identifies herself as a portrait photographer and set designer with a social consciousness. Doing mostly occasional pop-up art shows in Los Angeles, she has started to gain a following for her work's body positivity, body consciousness, and intersectional depictions of women confronting beauty standards. Garcia told *Voyage LA* that her work aims to fuse together art and social commentary: "Although I am mainly focused on art-photography, my work is inspired by sociology theory to discuss social constructs and how to dismantle a socially constructed perspective of beauty, gender norms/expectations, toxic masculinity, and more."[31] She sees her art as a way to "heal and educate marginalized communities on how to love yourself and others," going on to say, "My artwork creates a safe space for all folks from all identities, backgrounds, and bodies to come together in solidarity to honor their 'flaws.'"[32]

Feeling pushed out of academia and excluded from media representation—particularly as an indigenous Mexican American woman—Garcia was (in her words) colonized by ideas about her lack of worth. She said of her work, "When I flip through magazines I don't see Oaxaqueñas. It's such a difficult era that we're in, where we kinda push them aside to the shadows. I'm doing this by the people and for the people."[33] Her first large-scale project, *Flores Politicos*, focused on dismantling beauty standards and gender expectations through the burning of blond Barbie dolls (a symbol of "European beauty standard/mindset of beauty that has been sold to kids throughout the globe").[34] She said of this first series, which was part of a one-night-only show called the Politics of Womanhood, "In media we lack representation of folks with different cultures, identities, disabilities, backgrounds, body types, etc. *Flores Politicos* seeks to dismantle our socially constructed mindsets by challenging gender expectations, body shaming, and gender policing through photography. *Flores Politicos* wants to give a voice to those who have felt neglected by society, and we do it like no other by including non-binary folks, queer individuals, culture, body positivity, indigenous people, and more."[35]

Since this project finished, Garcia has completed a number of other major projects, including a series of photographs of Chicano men engaged in nonromantic affection toward each other called *Soft*. The series again plays on gender norms and expectations, particularly as they intersect with racial stereotypes of machismo. Garcia has also worked to directly confront Eurocentric beauty norms, normative beauty regimes, gentrification in Los Angeles, and other Chicanx/Latinx social justice issues like farm work, immigration, and appropriation.

More recently, Garcia went on to create *The Valentine's Day Series* as part of her *Body Hair Positive Series*, a collection of photographs depicting women and their body hair against the backdrop of traditionally (albeit campy) beautiful and highly feminine set designs. The idea came from her own experiences with body hair and her desire for body hair to operate as a space of solidarity with other women. She told HipLatina, "I was starting to grow out my hair more than I ever did before and I was just really inspired by other women of color that were just like always on body positivity."[36] Garcia herself struggled with a family that had quite narrow definitions of beauty and worth, particularly lighter skin color and light eyes.[37] She wanted to send a clear message to viewers: "Love your armpit hair, your hairy legs, stretch marks, scars, your nose, skin color, curves,

FIGURE 4.4. Zuly Garcia, Image from *The Valentine's Day Series* (2018). Photo courtesy of the artist. "Our bodies don't have flaws, they tell stories."—Zuly Garcia, a.k.a. Crenshaw Proletariat. Visual sociology photographer and educator. Instagram: @zulydelarose. Website: http://crenshawproletariat .com.

and the list goes on. We were sold on an idea of beauty to not just colonize your mind but to capitalize off you."[38]

Garcia released the series on Valentine's Day, a holiday she called "so heteronormative and capitalistic."[39] The series includes intimate and candid scenes of sisterhood and visual images of a variety of women of color—Chicanas, African American women, and Sikh women—revealing their body hair. She described the recruitment of models as "exhausting," saying that she was "getting requests every single day."[40] Women's interest in subverting traditional ideas about beauty in photography was overwhelming. Similarly, critical reception to the series was enthusiastic and positive; Garcia felt that her message was well received by those seeing the photographs (though "I did have people unfollow me after that").[41]

The series presents an arresting array of unexpected contrasts: the women sit instead of stand; the backgrounds are traditionally feminine and evocative of a set design; the flowers look unnatural and stilted, while the women laugh or smile comfortably; and the bodies feel both familiar and strange. The work also includes a variety of details that merge together tropes of campy American beauty photography (e.g., endless roses, posed chair) with traditional Oaxaqueña details (e.g., blanket around the neck, shawl, tiered skirt). Body hair stands out as a symbol of freedom from the constraints of beauty culture, but it also exists as a mundane part of the body, something viewers simultaneously notice and forget. Garcia captures that tension wonderfully, giving viewers a busy background, lots of textural detail, and hairy women of color smiling, laughing, or defiantly meeting their gaze.

The work also figures the bodies of women of color as playful, uplifted, joyous, and defiant, while never seeing them *only* as bodies. This infusion of subjectivity into her subjects, of interiority and emotionality, of beauty and grace, of posing and also moving the body naturally, presents viewers with an unresolved tension. The photographs clearly have an emotionally provocative element, while being stylized through the texture of campiness. Most notably, Garcia ascribes to her subjects the *right* to be shamelessly and proudly hairy, boldly undermining the conventions of beauty photography and femininity and instead offering one version of a decolonized way of seeing these women and their bodies.

MARILYN MINTER, *PLUSH* (2014)

As a third example of body hair photography that makes a social intervention, New York–based artist Marilyn Minter's work on pubic hair fuses together the techniques of fashion photography with the gritty sensuality of oily pubic hair. The images conjure a contrast between glamour and grunge, high fashion and seedy pornography. Given Minter's biography, we can assume this tension is one she has intentionally created for her entire career. In an interview with *Playboy*, Minter described her upbringing in the American South—from her birth in Shreveport, Louisiana, to her childhood in South Florida—as painful. She referred to her childhood as the "land of no parents," noting that her poor and drug-addicted mother would "pass out and never get out of bed and always wear nightgowns and float around. . . . It was all this kind of bastardized glamour."[42] Minter has infused her work with some of that edginess, rawness, and unflinching shamelessness, never seeming to look away from the imprint of her early life. She honed her techniques early on, shooting images of her mother in 1969 and later building a fifty-year career out of the contrasts between beauty and abjection, telling reporters, "Nobody has politically correct fantasies."[43]

Her award-winning body of work is impressive in its scope, style, and ability to provoke. She has portrayed subjects as diverse as pop art blow jobs (*Porn Grid*, 1989), models in snakeskin stilettos kicking up mud (*Shit Kicker*, 2006), and tongues pressed to frozen glass (*Deep Frost*, 2016); she has shot images of Pamela Anderson, Lady Gaga, and Miley Cyrus for advertisements (2007–9); she has even danced in a Jay-Z music video.[44] Minter exhibited work at the feminist gallery Gracie Mansion in the 1980s, received a Guggenheim Fellowship in 1998, became the first person to advertise artistic work on late-night television, had a 2016 museum retrospective, and had her work selected for the prestigious 2006 Whitney Biennial.[45] Critical reception of her work has highlighted its controversial nature; one critic writes, "Few other visual artists are so committed to the erotics of the everyday or to the sticky sweetness of what it means to be alive."[46]

Minter herself has struggled with feminist tensions surrounding pornography, pitting herself against the "giant anti-porn movement" by saying, "They really wanted to ban any sexual imagery whatsoever, and I love porn."[47] She instead has tried to reimagine pornography away from heterosexual men's desires and fantasies and instead push viewers to redefine pleasure, sexual desire, and beauty norms on their own terms. A strong believer in anticensorship and in the creation of new images and practices no matter how controversial or uncomfortable, she told *Vice*, "The answer is to *create* in response to something you don't like. Repression leads to distortion. Shaming is disastrous. Shame is the worst thing you can put on other people."[48] Of her 1989 hardcore porn series, which garnered controversial reactions, she said, "I tried to reclaim sexual imagery from an abusive history. Why shouldn't women have images for their own pleasure?"[49] Thus, Minter's recent interest in pubic hair photography stems from a lifetime of trying to grapple with sexualized and eroticized bodies, prescriptive and rebellious ideas about women's sexuality, and the human need to project fantasy onto bodies.

Minter's *Plush* series stands out as exceptional, even in a body of work devoted to jarring contrasts, uneasy feminist readings of sexuality, and overtly erotic imagery. *Plush* was derived from a series of photos she did for Neville Wakefield (the original name of the series was *Bush*) where models were paid to grow out their pubic hair and then model for Minter.[50] She then developed a book called *Plush* based on some of these images. In this book, she wanted to break from the constant erasure of women's pubic hair from public consciousness, saying, "There's nothing wrong with pubic hair, and it's been totally erased in art history. We all know Courbet's *L'Origine du Monde* and that's it."[51] She told the *Observer*, "The idea was to create beautiful images of pubic hair, a subject matter that seems to be disappearing from popular discourse."[52] To do so, she collaborated with underground publisher Fulton Ryder and chose the evocative name *Plush*.[53] Minter said that Fabiola Alondra came up with this choice: "The word itself is lush in its sound and the images and feelings it provokes are charged with power. The term dates back to the 16th-century French word *Pluche & Peluche*, a smooth or shaggy/hairy fabric. In the 19th-century, plush was used as the term to refer to pubic hair."[54]

The result was a compendium of photographs and hyperrealistic paintings, all embossed in a glossy, contradictory aesthetic. Some of the pubic hair is dressed in gold chains or obscured behind glass. Some of the images focus on the interplay between manicured fingernails with bright polish and the wild textures of long pubic hair. (She has emphasized that none of the pubic hair is dyed and is entirely natural.)[55] She said of the critical reception of *Plush*: "I tried to make the images so beautiful that they could be in any house, gallery or museum, but as soon as people realize what they're looking at, they don't want them anymore. I don't care. I'm still making paintings and shooting different people."[56] In part, Minter has formed her identity around an embrace of the abject, telling *Artforum*, "I'm interested in making the kinds of images that are sidelined or erased in our culture, and I like to push them a little further. When I'm shooting I look for that one errant hair, or the spit strands that form when you open your mouth, or hair on the top of your lip. I like freckles, sweat, pubic hair, pimples, and wrinkles, but these attributes are erased in magazines."[57]

The images in *Plush* feature curly and stylized pubic hair, often from the model's point of view. She wanted viewers to engage with women as subjects, seeing their own pubic hair in these images, rather than looking at them as objects.[58] This inversion plays with the typical way that pornography situates women's bodies, with women being erased as subjects and instead being merely consumed or looked at. Minter wanted something different, where women's own perspective is centered and the viewer enters the women's subjective position. Minter also wants women to embrace their natural bodies and their pubic hair: "I just want to show that it's really beautiful stuff! That it is a beautiful thing and fashion changes. Don't laser it off!"[59] She added, "The glamour industry has created such distortion in young girls. I know young girls who are [lasering] all the hair off their bodies! And for pubic hair to look disgusting to young boys, that's not healthy. I wanted to make beautiful images of pubic hair so that women have more choices."[60]

Pubic hair has been seen, especially in the art world, as tainting, low-culture, and rather gross, even among those who often dabble in cutting-edge extremes and avant-garde mentalities. As writer Chelsea Summers says of the history of pubic hair in art, "Indeed, what was most shocking about the Goya, the Courbet, and the Modigliani was their eliding high and low art. A chick's pubic hair will do that to an otherwise respectable painting."[61] This politicization of pubic hair photography represents, in part, Minter's own political activist priorities; she considers herself a strong left-wing activist for reproductive rights and bodily autonomy and has spoken widely about her abortion experience and her efforts to promote Planned Parenthood.[62]

A fan of the "feminine grotesque" and the work of Sandy Kim and Petra Collins, Minter wants her work to reject double standards, to symbolize women's freedom, and to reimagine pubic hair as both fashionable and desirable. As one of the reviews of *Plush* notes, "Hair is big. Hair attracts. Hair is what adults have. But hair, women are told, is unsightly. In pubic hair's [aestheticization], then, lies the rhetorical rebuff to the ideology underlying censorship."[63]

More significantly, Minter layers onto pubic hair a sense of *subjective* desire, insisting on wetness and slickness of the pubic hair to evoke the viewer's sensation of *feeling* wet. This clearly conjures notions of wetness, desire, slipperiness, and arousal—all largely missing from most artistic depictions of pubic hair. Even in the images where the perspective changes to that of the viewer instead of that of the subject, as many of the images of pubic hair behind glass do, the viewer still understands the images as full of heat and moisture. These are not "inactive" pubic hairs but rather erotically charged tufts of hair. Perhaps this, too, is a feminist victory, accomplishing the daunting task of depicting pubic hair as both a subjective experience *and* an objective experience, an internal experience of sexuality and desires *and* an implied sense of arousal when looking from the outside. This playful back-and-forth—self and other, felt and seen—gives us a distinctly feminist reading of how we might see pubic hair differently.

A LOOK BACK AT ELEANOR ANTIN, *CARVING* (1972, 2017)

Contemporary versions of body hair photography feature subversive and bold ways of reclaiming women's bodies as diverse, subjective, rebellious, and visually arresting. That said, I also want to briefly rewind to an earlier iteration of feminist performance art that has beautifully documented the elusive and rebellious nature of body politics and body hair photography. In 1972, then thirty-seven-year-old feminist artist Eleanor Antin staged a piece called *Carving*, in which she photographed herself in black-and-white nude images 148 times over the course of a thirty-seven-day weight loss and forced starvation project. To sharply critique the concept of women "carving themselves" through dieting, Antin photographed herself from four repeated angles—front, back, right side, and left side—in what she called a "dieting performance."[64] Antin imagined this piece as drawing from the traditions of Greek sculptors of marble, where she carved away her own body in, as one observer called it, "flesh falling away daily in subtle and magical ways, like a stone block cut down slowly to an idealized figure."[65] Starving herself intentionally and choosing to dramatically refuse food, Antin documented her disappearing body. She performed an elaborate, painful ritual that critiqued women's objectification and the labor of weight loss expected of women in order to conform to thin-obsessed normative gender roles.

FIGURE 4.5. Eleanor Antin, *Carving: A Traditional Sculpture*, detail (1972), 148 silver gelatin prints and text, 7 × 5 inches each. From the collection of the Art Institute of Chicago. Courtesy of the artist and Ronald Feldman Gallery, New York.

Feminist art scholars have long admired this piece, seeing it as the epitome of the agonizing labor women put into their bodies as they work toward the impossibility of precise and idealized thinness. Feminist scholar Clare Johnson writes that Antin captures the way that women work toward the illusion of perfection while trying desperately to ward off feelings of bodily failure, stating, "Here femininity consists of a developmental, teleological aspiration to an identity that is, ultimately, never achieved. Antin shows us the already-failed character of femininity as an effect of a naturalizing gaze and an experience marked by displeasure, monotony and inadequacy. When the grid of photographs is read left to right very little difference in body shape is discernable and what emerges is the inevitability of the failure of the exercise."[66] Antin subjected herself to rigorous documentation and control, a process that viewers can viscerally feel (and perhaps recoil at) when seeing these photographs.

Witnessing these self-portraits is an exercise in provocation, in digesting the layer upon layer of meaning displayed in the sharp contrasts and powerful symmetries of Antin's body. Antin had initially imagined this piece as drawing from conceptual art performance, photography, and sculpture, and the work was considered so shocking and outrageous that it was excluded from the 1970–71 Whitney Annual when she proposed it to them. She considered it a fusion of sculpture and performance art, perfect for the annual show featuring sculptural work, but the Whitney Museum rejected it. Forty-five years later, at age eighty-two, Antin decided to restage the performance using the exact same techniques and photographic choices and using her own body, this time significantly older than the body photographed for her 1972 version.

This 2017 version—where Antin's body as an octogenarian appears as shocking, larger, more crooked, and weathered with time—captures the transience of time, the process of aging, and the way that Antin manages, even while directly positioning herself to be objectified and looked at, to embody the spirit of feminist defiance. Staging the show at the Los Angeles County Museum of Art (LACMA) and the Art Institute of Chicago, she told writer Alice Butler, "The idea of growing older doesn't have to be some horror. I've always found older faces with life on them really interesting. There's experience on the body, which I realized as I was working on my own body."[67] A reviewer of the later work notes, "Carving: 45 Years

Later is even larger, with five rows of over 100 images each. In both, the female form seems to strain against the rigid framework—the flesh resists the grid."[68] In essence, Antin uncovers many of the anxieties women had, and continue to have, about their bodies as they age, gain weight, sag, and change. She documents, perhaps unwittingly, the way that pubic hair thins and slowly disappears over time in the processes of aging. In this way, her later piece beautifully features the lesser-explored intersection of aging and hair, the inevitability of losing the thickness of body hair, and the movement of hair from the foreground of the nude body for her younger self to the background for her older self. Antin suggests, through these visual works, that body hair gets more soft and subtle with aging, that fertility and fecundity are in many ways attached to the robustness of hair.

Art scholars have celebrated Antin's choice to restage the performance in a much older body, one that showcases the impacts of aging and the interplay between women's bodies as subject and object. As Butler notes, "The politics of representation that made the first *CARVING* so disruptive emerges with renewed energy in the later version, as the 1970s is remembered in the present moment, where women's bodies—in all their intersectional differences, including the aged body—continue to experience violence, oppression and shame."[69] Antin purposefully confronts viewers with aging, not as a horror show but as the careful markings of

FIGURE 4.6. Eleanor Antin, *Carving: 45 Years Later*, detail (2017), 6¾ × 4¾ inches, five images per day, one hundred days, starting March 8, 2017. Courtesy of the artist and Ronald Feldman Gallery, New York.

time, maturation, womanhood, grief, and self. Staging the piece shortly after the death of her husband of fifty-six years, she imagined the piece as a meditation on losing parts of herself. She told the Art Newspaper, "It's basically about loss. The loss of my flesh, the loss of my lover and partner of 56 years, the loss of the body I used to know and lived with for so long."[70]

The work also serves as a meditation on the ways that time, particularly in feminist work, operates in nonlinear ways (what queer theorist Elizabeth Freeman has called "temporal drag").[71] As Johnson writes, "The work describes a never-ending, but nevertheless measured, movement towards an unobtainable goal, which is, in turn, always shifting its terrain. Carving functions as a denaturalizing critique where femininity is understood as a future-oriented project in which the goal is not, in fact, to lose weight, but to consent to a perpetual state of 'becoming feminine.'"[72] Certainly, Antin's work provokes thinking about the mundane qualities of bodies, the impact of trauma and time on them, and how seemingly small details—particularly hair—resonate with powerful stories about our own choices and impacts on our bodies. Johnson concludes, "My suggestion is that Carving calls forth a complexity of times and tenses, which complicates any simplistic division between a feminist past and a post-feminist present."[73]

In particular, Antin's work forces a deep consideration of how the *natural* is an inadequate framing to capture the subversive qualities of body photography—including body hair photography. There is a temptation to see body hair photography—including Hopper's, Garcia's, and Minter's work—as about the exposure of the natural and the celebration of the natural, but Antin animates many of the other components at play in such work. The power of Antin's work is not in the exposure of her natural body but in the revealing of how narratives of gender, power, and time get layered onto her body. The body exposed in these ways does not illuminate the natural but rather the complex interplay between the body and its interpreters, the subject herself and the many observers and witnesses to the body. Antin's body, in essence, serves as a marker of how bodies do not belong to us as individuals but rather to the time and context in which we live and exist. We can read the 1972 version of *Carving* as a lesson in Antin's suffering or discipline but also in the cultural context of diet culture, idealization of thinness, and embrace of full-bush pubic hair. As Butler writes of Antin's work, "Antin shoots arrows through and across time. She creates, desires, an alternative mode of time that coughs up the past in the present, belatedly; that brings death into life and life into death; that carves away flesh to carve the future."[74]

In this way, Antin's body is never natural and always natural, both her own and belonging to the world, weighed down with stories about aging and beauty but also full of independence, outrageousness, defiance. Her body is a story and a testament, captured and framed and yet embodying a freedom all too uncommon in women's experiences of their own bodies. Her quest to carve herself out marks her own self-determination and shines a light on how painfully we adapt our bodies to suit the norms of the time. In this way, her "carvings" reach out in conversation to the other bodies of work considered in this chapter, asking questions about what it means to photograph the body, to imagine it as a form of resistance, and to situate the body as a living subject rather than a consumed object.

Antin's work is thus a proper meditation for ending this reflection on body hair photography. Though her images provide a stark contrast to the models of Ben Hopper's work, the young women of color in Zuly Garcia's images, and the hotly erotic subjects of Marilyn Minter's photographs, they all point toward the powerful ways that photographs of the body capture the essence of that time and place. Antin perfectly encapsulates the power of what body hair art photography can do, as it reveals bodies we have never seen and gives a visual narrative to previously unspoken stories. The work makes a social intervention, pushing against the erasure of bodies marked as abject, upending notions of the "natural," and changing the optics of how viewers see women and their bodies. Whether striving toward cultural ideals, boldly rejecting social norms, or embodying the wonderfully complex dance between compliance and rebellion, the body and its hair, wrinkles, lines, textures, and colors can mark and shape time.

5

China's Armpit Hair Contest

Body Hair Resistance as Global Contagion

The freedom of our people lies bound up with the freedom of women—The freedom of women lies bound up with the freedom of our people.

—South African National Women's Day slogan

WHILE BODY HAIR HAS MOSTLY BEEN USED AS AN INFORMAL mode of gender resistance and expression—rendering the rebellious character of these actions as largely individual and personal—body hair has also become a tool of collective and organized forms of resistance for women across the globe. Body hair has played a role in visible and public forms of feminist resistance, from collective efforts like Armpits4August to protests that showcase public shaving to social media campaigns that raise money based on women growing their body hair.[1] The sociopolitical meanings of women's body hair vary across society and nations. Body hair politics link together everyday expressions of feminism and collective efforts to use the body as a site of revolt. The potential for public and collective forms of body hair resistance appeared in startling and notable ways during the 2014–15 explosion of body hair activism in China. The impact of this activism on political conversations about Chinese feminism during that period demonstrates how body hair can ignite a politics of revolt and tie in to broader stories about gender, power, and protest.

In this chapter, I examine the cultural context of China's gender politics, particularly surrounding the conflicted messages around the

Communist Party gender equity claims as contrasted with newer pressures for Chinese women to embrace traditional gender roles, marriage, and child-rearing—largely a consequence of China's one-child policy and the population imbalances of men and women that resulted from this. I then look closely at the political protests and performance art activism that occurred in response to these changing gender role norms from 2012 to 2015, focusing heavily on the work of feminist activist and women's rights advocate Xiao Meili (real name Xiao Yue) and her colleagues. I examine the rationale for, and consequences of, the 2015 "armpit hair contest" in China started by Xiao Meili on the social media website Sina Weibo. Subsequently, I consider the movement between the polarities in which this contest operated, as it shifted between the silly/campy and the serious/impactful. In tandem with this, I focus on the March 2015 arrest of five Chinese women activists called the Feminist Five (three of whom participated in the contest) and the international impact of these arrests on Chinese feminist activism in the subsequent months and years. By looking at the frenzied media coverage of both the armpit hair contest and the arrest and detention of the Feminist Five, I explore the ways that feminist resistance, especially around body hair, can move across geographical and cultural spaces with remarkable speed and impact. I also consider the value of performance art activism around body hair, particularly as these protests posed a threat to the status quo both in China and throughout the world. Ultimately, the work in this chapter demonstrates how Chinese feminists offer shrewd and innovative tactics for using the body as a framework to provoke and unsettle expectations about, and policies around, gender.

"LEFTOVER WOMEN," POLITICAL REVOLT, AND CHANGING GENDER NORMS

The status of Chinese feminism has a long and tumultuous history, one steeped in the neo-Confucian culture that practiced female foot binding and the contradictory histories of Communist revolutionary history.[2] Communist ideologies under Mao Zedong largely pushed for women as equal, encouraging women to wear haircuts and army uniforms that minimized gender differences from men.[3] That said, recent shifts toward idealizing traditional gender norms and domesticity have interpreted this "equality" in the direction of reproductive labor mandates. In a dramatic reversal of previous policies and pressures, recent years have found Chinese women leaving the labor force, experiencing an increase in domestic abuse and violence, and turning toward traditional values in full force.[4] These shifts underlie what feminist scholar Leta Hong Fincher calls "the patriarchal underpinnings of [China's Communist Party's] authoritarianism."[5] Mao Zedong advocated for equality between men and women ("what men can do, women can do"), with the Communist Party celebrating female tractor drivers and locomotive operators as national icons. Consequently, the tensions rooted in sexism now experienced by contemporary Chinese women, especially around feminism and liberation politics, have become painful and consequential.

The specific challenges and pressures faced by Chinese women stem in part from the gender imbalances in the population following China's one-child policy and subsequent illegal sex-selective abortions, which has left China with twenty million more men than women. This imbalance has left single women under thirty, particularly those residing in urban centers, facing new pressures to marry and forgo their economic and romantic independence. Notions that women should marry in order to better support society, and that they should bear children and surrender their personal happiness, appear frequently among male writers, commentators, and governmental bodies.[6] Highly educated career women without children are derided for being unpatriotic, and the romanticizing of children and marriage has become omnipresent.[7] Women who are not married and pregnant before thirty years old are often chastised as "leftover" women who serve no purpose in Chinese society.[8] In a marriage registration office in Beijing's Xicheng District, for example, a poster tells women, "Being a good housewife and mother is the greatest skill of a woman. Why do you insist on competing like crazy with men, taking their place and resources?"[9] This rhetoric is supported by data that finds few traces of gender equality, as Chinese wives took on nearly twice the domestic responsibilities of their husbands.[10] (Remember, too, that women who refuse marriage are all too often barred from owning homes if they do not have a husband, as most residential property in China is solely owned by men.)[11]

Notably, in the era after the 1989 Tiananmen Square protests, women's relative earnings compared to men's *dropped* between 1990 and 2010, with women earning 77.5 percent of what men earned in 1990 and earning just 67.3 percent of what men earned in 2010.[12] In essence, women miss out on building wealth, as Fincher notes: "Chinese women—including highly educated, upper-middle-class women—largely missed out on the biggest accumulation of residential real-estate wealth in history (worth over $30 trillion according to an analysis of figures provided by HSBC Bank) because of gendered factors, such as intense pressure on women to leave their names off property deeds and new regulatory barriers to women's property ownership."[13] Moreover, bizarre suggestions that women take *two or three* husbands—and care for them sexually and domestically— circulated throughout the world media in 2020. Professor Yew-Kwang Ng suggested, outrageously, "It's common for prostitutes to serve more than 10 clients in a day. . . . Making meals for three husbands won't take much more time than for two husbands."[14]

This pressure on women to surrender economic independence and power in service of traditional norms of marriage and child-rearing has infuriated many Chinese feminists. In recent years, Chinese feminists have derided the Chinese government for their complicity in women's oppression and second-class status. As activist Xiao Ban has suggested, there are

> just two different types of women within the women's rights discourse. One side is just happy that she was never aborted or given away as a child, that she no longer needs to bind her feet, has enjoyed education and has the ability to work. All the rest is not important, "a bit of sexism" is not worth complaining about, and certainly no reason to interrupt China's "harmonious society." Then there is the other side: women who think about all those girls that actually were aborted, given away, and cut off from education or work, and then want to do their best to fight for their rights.

She went on to add, "If we try hard enough, and are courageous enough, awake enough, we can maybe become the first generation of Chinese feminists."[15]

Chinese feminist and women's rights activist Xiao Meili wrote an op-ed for the *New York Times* in which she summarizes some of the contradictions faced by contemporary Chinese feminists:

> When I was growing up in the 1990s in Sichuan Province, I found many cultural traditions and practices puzzling. At home, I addressed my mothers' parents as "waipo" and "waigong," or "outside grandma" and "outside grandpa," because I was told that my father's family mattered more. In school, my teachers held higher academic expectations for boys than they did for girls because they believed boys were smarter than girls. While applying for college, many universities openly excluded girls from majors such as marine engineering and geological exploration, and lowered admissions standards for boys who chose to study foreign languages and broadcast journalism, which historically attract girls. I constantly saw want ads that either excluded women or specified that women applicants needed to be tall and attractive. . . . In China today, women face widespread discrimination at work; many companies refuse to even hire women. Sexual harassment is commonplace. Domestic violence is pervasive. According to a 2013 multi-country study conducted by the United Nations, more than 50 percent of Chinese men have physically or sexually abused their partners.[16]

These conditions within which women live have dramatically upended the "party line" that Chinese women have achieved full equality with men or that they have equal access to rights, income, and social protections.

As a logical extension of this growing inequality, Chinese feminism has emerged as an increasingly important social movement dedicated to exposing the violence, intimidation, and threats women experience just for speaking out about gendered inequalities. Further, the need for a robust and organized feminist movement has been articulated by a growing number of Chinese feminists. Xiao writes about the necessity of engaging in feminist activism in such a cultural context: "Many women before us have taken the accommodationist route, but little has changed. Strong public pressure is necessary. We cannot afford to go about our campaign quietly.

Since public protests and demonstrations are banned, we rely on a unique platform—performance art—to challenge social conditions. We've taken our message to the streets and subways and fought for a safe public space for women."[17]

Because of prohibitions about public gatherings and the repression of the feminist movement in general, many Chinese feminists have resorted to street-based actions that inject unexpected and performance-style activism in public spaces.[18] By 2012, around one hundred university-educated feminists regularly participated in performance art and activism across China, targeting a number of subjects ranging from violence and harassment to employment and university admissions.[19] These younger women, notably outside of the control of the Communist Party, have cultivated a public and confrontational style of feminist resistance. Xiao has joined her fellow activists for a variety of public performance stunts, including an anti–domestic violence event on a crowded Beijing street where they wore bridal gowns splattered with fake blood, carrying signs that read, "Love is not an excuse for violence."[20] (While wearing these bloody bridal gowns, they also performatively hugged Kim Lee, an American citizen living in China, in the courtroom following her domestic violence court proceedings; Lee publicly posted pictures of her battered and bruised body on social media, took her husband to court, and was awarded USD $8,000 in damages, the highest amount ever offered in a divorce case related to abuse.)[21]

This action occurred in tandem with a 2013 United Nations report that found that *half* of Chinese men surveyed admitted to committing some type of violence toward women and nearly a quarter of them admitted to having raped a woman, signaling the extent and gravity of the problem they sought to combat.[22] (Recently, these numbers have skyrocketed, as domestic violence complaints rose threefold during the COVID-19 pandemic in February 2020, prompting one feminist activist, Guo Jing, to design an intervention called the Anti–Domestic Violence Little Vaccine to recruit domestic violence volunteers and activists.)[23] Many of the activists involved in the anti–domestic violence activism had themselves been victims of violence during their childhood, with Li Maizi noting, "In China, rape culture is so strong that almost no one dares to admit they've been sexually assaulted because they're terrified of being blamed for it."[24]

FIGURE 5.1. Li Maizi, Xiao Maili, and Wei Tingting (left to right) take part in a 2012 protest against domestic violence in Beijing. Photo courtesy of Lu Pin.

Indeed, the Chinese Health and Family Life Survey found that 32 percent of married urban Chinese women had been raped by their husbands, and the tendency for Chinese citizens to blame women for rape is much higher than it is for people who live in other industrialized nations.[25] Reacting to these conditions, feminist activists issued a public petition immediately after their bridal gown stunt, saying, "We don't want a hollow, empty and only symbolic domestic violence law. We want a law with actual power. . . . We hope to be informed of, take part in, and monitor the lawmaking process."[26] The petition received twelve thousand signatures, the largest women's rights action to date at that time.[27]

Their public and performance-based activism did not stop there. Xiao and her colleagues also organized an "Occupy Men's Toilet" campaign to protest the unfair ratio of male to female public toilets in Beijing. Xiao also wrote a scathing open letter—frequently taken down from major social media sites—to her university protesting their handling of sexual harassment on campus.[28] Subsequently, she and many other women shaved their heads to protest college admissions discrimination against women, and they have raised awareness about the high rates of child sexual abuse in China's schools.[29] They have also circulated online petitions criticizing misogynist comedy sketches during major television events and, following the #MeToo movement's start in 2017, they filed a #MeToo petition at Xiao's university.[30] She writes of these actions, "The government, rather than fixing the system and punishing the perpetrators, simply blames the victims."[31] Many of these actions have resulted in some policy changes throughout China, as some universities have abolished their discriminatory admissions policies, the city of Beijing has built new women's toilets, and a landmark 2016 domestic violence law has had a remarkable impact on changing public opinion and, until the pandemic, lessening the occurrence of domestic violence throughout China.[32] As feminist activist Lu Pin writes of these changes, "Mass media was playing an important role in turning the tide on domestic violence, but it was only made possible because of the persistent lobbying and campaigning conducted by dedicated activists and determined women's rights groups."[33]

As part of the backlash for these activist efforts, young feminists in China have become targets for governmental oppression, particularly as they push back against the Communist Party's vision of women as, in Fincher's words, "reproductive tools to sculpt the nation's destiny." She adds, "Chinese leaders believe that the very survival of the Communist Party depends on the subordination of women for social stability and to produce future generations of highly skilled workers."[34] Some legal scholars have suggested that the repression of grassroots movements in contemporary China is often sporadic and symbolic but that feminist activism has consistently been hit with some of the most aggressive crackdowns on political dissent on record.[35] Despite this, in China's middle class, women have started to revolt against marriage and childbearing and have begun to reject patriarchal values of control over women's bodies and freedoms. Armed with the internet, Chinese women have exerted remarkable pressure on the Chinese government to retract misogynistic propaganda.[36]

That said, the Chinese government has gone to remarkable lengths to suppress feminist activism, including banning social media accounts, arresting activists, blocking public gatherings, tightening ideological controls on gender and women's studies programs in universities, and shaming and humiliating women who resist governmental propaganda.[37] They have also begun, recently, to collect biomedical data on those considered "threatening" to the Communist Party, including activists, migrant workers, and Uyghur Muslims, and to subject them to increased surveillance monitoring.[38] In February 2016, the Chinese government shut down the country's most influential women's rights organization—the Beijing Zhongze Women's Legal Counseling and Service Center—in an effort to curb any defense provided for women to engage in rabble-rousing, troublemaking, and public agitation.[39]

THE ARREST OF THE FEMINIST FIVE

On March 6, 2015, just before International Women's Day, the Chinese government arrested five well-known Chinese feminist activists in Beijing—Wei Tingting, Li Tingting (Li Maizi), Wu Rongrong, Wang Man, and Zheng Churan (Datu). Though the five women had started a campaign against sexual harassment on public transportation that was fairly small and contained—they were handing out stickers about sexual harassment—the arrests ended up building a support network for their movement from all over the world. They were (absurdly) initially arrested for the offense of "picking quarrels." One reporter noted, "In cracking down on these largely anonymous young women, the Chinese government itself provided the spark for the creation of a powerful new symbol of feminist dissent against a patriarchal, authoritarian state."[40] They were lauded as heroic, and their efforts and actions were publicized widely and held in high regard by women across China.

Due to this notoriety, they would later become known as the Feminist Five or the Five Feminist Sisters by some media outlets. The police detained the women in a small, unheated room of a Beijing police station with the temperature falling to below freezing. As *Dissent* writer Leta Hong Fincher says of Li Maizi, "The interrogations began immediately: Why was she organizing subversive activities about sexual harassment? Who was she working with? Who funded her organization, Yirenping? Li was freezing, hungry, and angry. She refused to cooperate with the men interrogating her."[41]

Li had never imagined that the governmental repression of women's rights activism would be this strong, noting that she had only intended to hand out stickers about sexual harassment and that she and her fellow activists had done nothing to oppose the government.[42] In an attempt to get these activists to talk, one security agent took Li outside the room to show a group of women waiting near the entrance, noting that they had arrested such a huge number of feminists that night that they had run out of interrogation rooms. Li described being led through an underground passage surrounded by guards: "At that moment, I knew there was no way they were letting me go home," Li said of this experience. "Those men acted like they had just won some glorious battle."[43]

The conditions of the detention were astonishingly bad. Li described being interrogated at least once per day and refusing to speak in the face of humiliations, attacks, assaults, and name-calling. Police attacked Li for being *lala*—a lesbian—and called her a whore; they forced her to scrub floors at night and do other menial labor in the detention center, shined bright lights in her eyes, and accused her of spying for foreign governments. Even her parents received threats. She relied on the mantra "Perseverance, Bravery, Endurance" to get through the interrogations.[44] Another one of the Five, Wu Rongrong, had been scolded and threatened by the police during her detainment, and one police officer told her he would throw her in the men's prison to be gang-raped. Wei Tingting had her glasses taken, her laptop hacked into, and her warm clothes removed so that she would freeze in her cell. Her colleague, Zheng Churan (nicknamed Giant Rabbit), described the repeated interrogations as so stressful that clumps of her hair fell out.[45]

Eventually, after thirty-seven days in prison, authorities released all five women, though they remained "criminal suspects" a year after their release and were still under investigation for the charge of "gathering a crowd to disturb public order."[46] Many of the five women reported having posttraumatic stress disorder following their release. Zheng Churan described how state security continued to call on her at home: "Anytime I heard a knocking sound, I was terrified and my heart would start beating really fast. I would remember the dark, hazy images from my detention, because they had confiscated my glasses and I couldn't see properly. After my release, I think I suffered from a kind of Stockholm Syndrome, where

I tried to cater to some of the requests of the state security."[47] Four or five months later, she regained a sense of optimism about China's feminist movement, mostly due to the overwhelming outpouring of support the Feminist Five had received. She focused her efforts on building alliances between middle-class and working-class women, in a kind of direct threat to the Community Party (which largely relied on elite intellectuals joining forces with millions of peasants and workers).[48]

In building solidarity with other Chinese women, the Feminist Five have joined arms with other Chinese feminists throughout the country who wanted to have a more public platform for their anger while working against the "toxic vitality of sexism in China today."[49] When they were detained by the Chinese government police based on charges of "picking quarrels and provoking trouble," this galvanized young Chinese women and sparked outrage among women throughout the world. In response to these unjust arrests—and the conditions they faced during detainment—a number of prominent politicians throughout the world spoke out in support of their cause.[50] Protests of solidarity sprang up in the United States, United Kingdom, Hong Kong, South Korea, India, Poland, and Australia.[51] These arrests seemed to represent a turning point for many people interested in global human rights, particularly as they witnessed the poor treatment and detention of women who were engaging in relatively low-stakes activist work.

Many feminist scholars, writers, and activists throughout the world found the arrest and detainment of the Feminist Five to be a chilling example of how governments set precedents that threaten and intimidate those fighting for equal rights. Xiao wrote critically of these arrests, saying, "The government has become scared of a group of young women because of our ability to mobilize a large network of supporters. . . . The police punished my friends to intimidate other social and political activists."[52] Scholars around the world have expressed alarm, and one scholar, Teng Biao, has recently called these arrests the "worst crackdown on lawyers, activists and scholars in decades."[53] Feminist scholar Wang Zheng said of the arrests, "I'm happy they are released but they should not have been arrested in the first place. If women are already being arrested when they are only raising awareness for a cause such as this, then what can we expect in the future? Worst of all, they were treated as criminals by the police."[54]

These arrests sparked a number of reactions throughout the mainstream media and on social media. After the arrests and detention of the Feminist Five, feminists began wearing masks and photos of the women in a show of solidarity. Stickers calling for their release were posted in men's toilets, and a public count of how long they had been detained began circulating online.[55] The hashtag campaign #FreeThe-Five went viral on Twitter, Instagram, and Facebook. Further, because the arrests coincided with preparations for Chinese president Xi Jinping to cohost a United Nations summit on women's rights in New York to mark the twentieth anniversary of the 1995 Beijing World Conference on Women, the arrests of the Feminist Five created an even more widespread international outcry from human rights organizations and world leaders. Then US vice president Joe Biden tweeted that "rights of women and girls should never be suppressed."[56] Hillary Clinton tweeted about the arrests, "Xi hosting a meeting on women's rights at the UN while persecuting feminists? Shameless."[57]

Many believe that the arrests also ignited a series of important conversations about the status of feminism in China and the importance of feminist activism throughout the world. As one reporter wrote, "Although the five women were released on April 13, their arrest and the position of women at large remain well-discussed topics on China's social media platforms, with some claiming that China has no feminism."[58] Xiao herself disputes this idea of an absence of Chinese feminism, saying, "Feminism was never a taboo topic in China because our messages were consistent with those of the government, which calls itself an advocate of women's rights. But all that changed with the arrest of what the media dubbed the 'Feminist Five.' In an unexpected way, the police helped create more public interest in feminism in China."[59]

By some accounts, feminism is in ascendancy in China, with digital feminisms booming, awareness of the need for women's economic independence on the rise, and renewed interest in critiquing the mystique of housewife identities and quiet motherhood. The arrests of the Feminist Five tried to suppress feminist activism but ironically seem more to have sparked an interest in the possibilities of feminist visibility in a political landscape often hostile to women in positions of power. Still, after the arrests, the Feminist Five said that they had to think creatively about how to engage in feminist activism. Li Maizi told *Dissent*, "The political environment is very difficult now. We have to think very carefully about new methods to push forward China's feminist movement."[60]

CHINA'S ARMPIT HAIR CONTEST

While interest throughout China in women's body norms has increased in recent years—with more conversation and attention critiquing the narrow standards of beauty within which Chinese women struggle—body hair has only recently entered the public sphere as a distinctly feminist issue. In 2014, interest in the politics of visible body hair began after a flood of social media attention triggered conversations about women shaving, or not shaving, their body hair. A small contest (with no prize) called "Girls not plucking armpit hair" drew widespread attention on Weibo.[61] Over twenty-eight million people viewed the thousands of pictures uploaded to Weibo in August 2014, with many images showing women proudly displaying their underarm hair.[62] Tensions emerged from this "contest" when nearly seven thousand people debated online whether women should shave or keep their body hair.[63] (This competition also brought plenty of media attention to my body hair assignment—see chapters 1–2—with some Chinese reporters directly assigning responsibility to me for "ruining China" and inspiring this 2014 contest.)[64]

The year 2014 saw the emergence of Tumblr's Hairy Legs Club (where women posted photos of their leg hair and commented about social expectations of beauty), Miley Cyrus posting photos on social media of her dyeing her armpit hair, along with widespread international media attention for my body hair assignment.[65] Two years prior, feminists in the United Kingdom had organized the Armpits4August campaign, urging women to grow their armpit hair for a month for the charity organization Verity, which emphasizes research on polycystic ovary syndrome (PCOS). More recently, the Januhairy campaign for women to grow body hair in support of body positivity was launched.[66] These campaigns have garnered plenty of social media attention.[67] Beauty editor Maria Del Russo noted that social media is an intuitive conduit for thinking critically about body hair: "I think the reason more and more women are using social media to show off their body hair choices is connectedness. Since the idea of women having body hair is not considered the 'norm,' women who feel that it is their norm are likely attempting to make connections with other women who feel the same way."[68]

Hair has also recently played a role in political protest in China. In July 2015, following the event known colloquially as the "709 crackdown," where hundreds of human rights lawyers and activists were detained, arrested, and jailed, four wives of lawyers gathered in the central court-yard of a sleepy Beijing apartment complex and cut off their hair in front of their neighbors and a small group of invited foreign journalists. *Reuters* reported on the event, saying, "The women took turns shaving each oth-er's heads placing the hair in see-through plastic boxes alongside pictures of them with their husbands, before heading to China's Supreme People's Court to petition over their husbands' treatment."[69] One of these women, Li Wenzu, who had not seen her husband since his detention, told report-ers that shaving her head was her protest against the way the government had delayed proceedings on her husband's case and prevented her from appointing her chosen lawyer. She pronounced during her head shaving, "We can go hairless, but you cannot be lawless" (the phrase is a pun given that the words for "hair" and "law" sound similar in Chinese).[70]

The jockeying between serious and playful, heavy and light, weighty and frivolous allows hair to move between registers of political activism

FIGURE 5.2. Li Wenzu, the wife of prominent Chinese rights lawyer Wang Quanzhang, gets her head shaved in protest over the government's treat-ment of her husband in Beijing, China, December 17, 2018.

and personal grooming. As such, it offers a unique inroad for a flagrantly public intervention about cultural attitudes toward women. Given that Xiao Meili had successfully helped to organize numerous public performance stunts in the past, often with much success in impacting public policies and social attitudes, she decided to launch a full-fledged hairy armpit contest in late spring 2015. Two months after the arrests of the Feminist Five, in May 2015, Xiao created the armpit hair contest, this time reaching out to a wide swath of Chinese women from a variety of class backgrounds and across China. She launched the event on the wildly popular Chinese social media microblogging website Sina Weibo.[71] Xiao asked women who wanted to participate to take a selfie of their armpit hair and to post the photo showing off their hairy underarms. In total, forty-six women participated in the contest and posted photos under the hashtag "women's underarm hair contest" (#女子腋毛大赛#).[72] She and a few of her friends planned to judge the contest, and winners were based on the number of reposts and "likes" an entry attracted.[73] They specifically wanted to find the most "characteristic, beautiful, and confident" displays of armpit hair.[74]

When interviewed about the intent behind the contest, Xiao told the *New York Times*, "Men have more freedom in terms of what to do with their bodies. I'm not calling on everybody to grow underarm hair. I'm just saying if some people don't want to shave, the rest of us should not think their underarm hair is disgusting, unhygienic, uncivil or not feminine enough."[75] She also admitted that even some of her friends did not understand the intent of the contest, though Xiao stood by it as an important social intervention.

The contest, which ran for about a month, was viewed nearly two million times and had over a thousand comments, including many from feminists and scholars.[76] Six "winners" were selected based on the number of reposts and "likes" online. (Prizes included one hundred condoms for first prize, a vibrator for second prize, and ten female urination devices for third prize, all donated from a fundraising activism walk Xiao undertook from Beijing to Guangzhou the previous year to raise awareness of child sexual abuse in China.)[77] Participants ranged from those in their early twenties to those in their forties. The winner, Zhu Xixi, told reporters that she enjoyed posting a picture of herself with hairy armpits and admonished her ex-boyfriend for the double standards women experience with their body hair: "When I was still heterosexual, my boyfriend at the time just took it for granted that I shaved my armpits for the sake of wearing sleeveless T-shirts—until I shaved all of his underarm hair and let him experience what girls go through."[78]

Many other women had strong reactions to the contest, and most posted positive reactions about trying to grow their body hair. Xiao Meili wrote of the empowering qualities of the contest: "Women's armpit hair is considered to be offensive, rude and ungraceful—how come it makes people so uncomfortable? Women's underarm hair can be adorable, interesting, humorous, sexy, serious, connotative and ever-changing."[79] The second-place winner, "Chacha," wrote of the contest: "I love my underarm hair. It's part of my body. I hope girls can reveal it without fear."[80] Another participant cited the medical reasons for growing out armpit hair: "Pulling or shaving armpits might lead to skin infection, as there are many lymph nodes in the armpits. It's not good for your health. Nobody cares if you shave your armpits as long as you keep it clean."[81] Still others talked about how they looked just fine, refused to feel ashamed about their armpit hair, and maintained that armpit hair looked beautiful on women.[82]

For some women, participating in the contest meant challenging family norms about gender and the body. One participant, Liu, decided to participate after she had taken a gender studies course. She had begun to change her attitude about body hair and decided to have a fellow photographer classmate take a photo of her for the contest. Her mother, who resided in a small city in Jiangxi Province, called soon after to ask if she had been kidnapped and forced to take the photo. "She didn't even notice the armpit hair. She just thought a photo [of nudity] was crossing the line."[83] Still, Liu found value in participating, particularly as her friends called the photo a "good deed" and her male friends were quietly "freaking out."[84]

Not surprisingly, the armpit hair contest also drew some pointedly hostile and negative attention, with some viewers calling armpit hair ugly, smelly, and irrelevant to feminism. One person commented that women who grow armpit hair are "lazy." Another viewer wrote, "Why is it relevant to women's rights? Whether it's men or women, revealing hairy armpits when wearing sleeveless tops is inelegant. We can smell it on the bus and subway."[85] One critic on Weibo wrote, "Shaving or not is a personal choice. Why flash it? Armpits are quite private after all. I just hate being this high profile." Another critic of the contest wrote on Weibo, "This is not a question of pleasing anybody. According to our universal aesthetics, it's just not elegant."[86]

CHANGING BODY HAIR NORMS IN CHINA

Xiao responded to these negative critiques by posting a brief history of women's body hair removal, along with a reminder of the purpose of the contest, which was to challenge narrow definitions of feminine beauty and highlight that hair removal should be a choice, not a compulsory part of women's grooming routines. She reminded participants and viewers that shaving underarms was, for women in China, a relatively recent practice, and that it became a widespread custom only in the 1990s. She told the *New York Times*, "For my mother's generation, a woman not shaving her armpits is totally natural."[87] She went on to say, "Women's underarm shaving in China only has about 20 years of history and that is because of advertising, which has changed people's minds."[88] One of the contest participants backed up Xiao in her efforts to educate the participants, writing, "The goal of this contest is not to suggest that women should have hairy armpits, but to make women realise that they have the ownership to their own body—women shouldn't be forced to shave armpits under the pressure of stereotypes or the mainstream aesthetic."[89]

Chinese women's feelings about body hair have shown a strong generational divide, with older women traditionally not shaving, while younger women do shave. Historically, Chinese people have long considered a woman with no pubic hair as a symbol of misfortune, such that it was commonly held for many generations that a woman without pubic hair could cause her husband failure in his business pursuits.[90] As one reporter commented, "Traditionally, Chinese people do value women's skin to be smooth and clean, but are not especially sensitive about body hair. Chinese girls did not learn about body hair grooming from their mothers, but from commercials and their peers."[91] Most women in China have, until recently, allowed body hair to grow, and some attribute changing attitudes toward body hair to a female population that is more fashion conscious and prone to expose more skin.[92] One twenty-nine-year-old legal secretary told the Telegraph, "Shaving underarms is absolutely obligatory," while another woman who worked as a sales representative said, "I used to think the hair on my arms were kind of cute, but my friends pointed them out a couple of times and I decided it was best just to get rid of it."[93] A twenty-six-year-old teacher noted that she shaved her armpits "so as not to embarrass foreign students."[94]

Tensions between valuing hairiness and prizing hairlessness have historical roots in the rapidly changing culture of body norms for Chinese women. Studies of Chinese body norms have shown that these norms have significant flexibility in response to changing cultural and social values, both currently and historically. For example, Chinese women have recently moved away from valuing round, full faces, instead preferring slim bodies and small faces.[95] Further, historian Dorothy Ko has argued that, starting in the sixteenth century, Chinese cultural norms shifted such that bodily modifications like foot binding came to be seen as a form of bodily adornment much like clothing, thus signaling a shift away from bodily subjectivity and toward women's bodies becoming "objects" with cultural and political implications. Ko writes, "In the late sixteenth and early seventeenth centuries, footbinding was considered part of female attire, an adornment to be exact, not a form of bodily mutilation. It was supposed to embellish, adding something to the female body, not breaking and hollowing it by taking something away."[96] More specifically, foot binding became linked to women's hairdos and clothing, thus collapsing "coverings exterior to the body (clothes), an auxiliary part of the body that can regenerate and be clipped (hair), and the body itself (limbs)." In short, "all were 'attire' that could be manipulated and altered at will by the person displaying his or her political allegiance and cultural identity," paving the way for Chinese women's bodies to be seen as emblems of cultural values.[97] Related to this, deep reservations about emulating versus resisting Western norms of femininity and beauty pervade the histories of Chinese women's body norms and extend into contemporary debates about hairlessness as a cultural, political, and social value.[98]

Fast-forward to 2005, when the Reckitt Benckiser Group attempted to introduce Veet, a hair removal cream, to Chinese women, encouraging them to remove their body hair and emulate Western women's hairless practices. Notably, sales were sluggish, and most Chinese women did not have enough body hair to worry about hair removal products. In response, Reckitt Benckiser introduced advertisements equating hairlessness for women with health, confidence, and "shining glory."[99] Veet targeted subways and restrooms, introduced TikTok videos about Veet, and developed a mobile video game where users "shaved" hairy legs and armpits by shaking their phones (and more than sixty thousand Chinese people played this game).[100] Veet also flooded university campuses with free samples and enlisted actress Yang Mi as a spokesperson in order to target urban Chinese women. As a result of this aggressive advertising, Chinese women seem to have had a notable spike in self-consciousness about their body hair, much to the delight of the company. Sales started to rise 20 percent annually. Their Chinese company spokesperson, Aditya Sehgal, gleefully told reporters, "It's not how much hair you have, it's how much you think you have. If your concern level is high enough, even one hair is too much."[101] Building on this, Benjamin Voyer, a social psychologist and assistant professor of marketing at ESCP Europe Business School, said of Veet's innovative tactics, "It creates an awareness, which subsequently creates a feeling of shame and need."[102]

This sinister and wholly intentional body shaming of Chinese women orchestrated by these marketing executives is exactly what Chinese feminist activists have worked to fight against. Xiao Meili noted that the concept of underarm hair being "uncivilized" or dirty comes from the West and has been spreading quickly, leaving a negative impression on young women newly negotiating norms of the body.[103] She reiterated that the goal of the armpit hair contest was not to set a new norm of women adopting hairiness, but to create space for looking critically at the social norm of armpit hair: "We are not trying to force people to not shave, but we are against the social norm that armpit hair is unacceptable and disgusting."[104] The contest sought to undermine capitalistic and Westernized notions of hairlessness as ideal and compulsory.

BODY HAIR AS POLITICAL ACTIVISM

While the body hair contest may have drawn some attention regardless of the fame of its participants, as images of hairy women often travel quickly on social media platforms, the 2015 armpit hair contest garnered more major news coverage because of its well-known contenders. Three of the participants—Wei Tingting, Li Maizi (also known as Li Tingting), and Zheng Churan—were well-known Chinese feminists, members of the Feminist Five, who were arrested and detained only two months earlier for their campaign for gender equality.[105] When the news media heard that prominent Chinese feminist activists had participated in the contest, the rhetoric in the media shifted toward a more panicky and anxious reaction to the contest.

These three activists had much to say about the armpit hair contest as a form of feminist political activism. Wei Tingting wrote on Weibo, "The pictures have proved that women can celebrate their bodies, desire and love, whether homosexual or heterosexual, whether their underarm hair is long or short and in spite of raised eyebrows from passers-by."[106] Li Maizi, another one of the Feminist Five, wrote of her experience with the armpit hair contest, "Lots of people gathered around to watch and looked at us funny. The armpit hair contest challenged the public's understanding of women's bodies. It also challenged me to see my own true body and thus made me braver."[107] After posting a photo of her hairy armpits with the words "Punish Domestic Violence and Love Armpit Hair" over her body, she reflected on the meaning of armpit hair as a political statement: "I think this competition is very meaningful. Consumerism is gender-based. The market is filled with all kinds of shaving products for women. We need some space to think about why women are obliged to shave ourselves."

Other Chinese feminist activists have observed these actions with awe, solidarity, and a renewed commitment to continue the activist struggle toward justice and freedom. Activist Lu Pin, speaking from New York, talked about the value of forming alliances across national boundaries and continuing to do the provocative work of feminism. She told *Dissent*, "As a woman, I have no country. . . . The position of our core activists is extremely fragile and we don't know when the police will come and arrest someone again—it could be today or tomorrow."[108] Still, feminist activists in China remain undeterred, looking to build new solidarities and open up new possibilities for women, their bodies, and feminist activism.

Continuing efforts to protest sexual violence, domestic violence, and women's exploitation, feminist activists have renewed their efforts to engage in consciousness-raising, performance art activism, and on-the-ground work to raise awareness about violence against women, even after the arrests of the Five. Xiao's girlfriend, Zhang Leilei, who has continued the activist work with Xiao for several years, wrote on WeChat, "No matter how much they try to shrink our space, nothing can stop feminists from sprouting up everywhere. At any moment, we have the power to burst forth in all our magnificence."[109] Despite the harsh government crackdown and efforts to separate women from each other, degrade their activist work, and intimidate them from speaking out, the struggle continues. As Li Maizi said when reflecting on the body hair contest and the meaning of women's rights more broadly, "For women, we need to free our minds and our bodies. For me, my body is a battlefield."[110] Xiao herself offered some advice to feminists both in China and throughout the world: "Whether it's violence by public authorities or domestic violence, the patterns are the same. The more you accommodate, the more you get harassed. If you don't resist, the cycle of violence will worsen. So fight for your rights, never compromise."[111]

PART 3 |

BODY HAIR REBELS

6 |

Growing a Thicker Skin

The Emotional Politics of Body Hair

> This projection of "emotion" onto the bodies of others not only
> works to exclude others from the realms of thought and rationality,
> but also works to conceal the emotional and embodied aspects of
> thought and reason. . . . The "truths" of this world are dependent on
> emotions, on how they move subjects, and stick them together.

—SARA AHMED, *The Cultural Politics of Emotion*

FROM TEMPORARY FORAYS INTO BODY HAIR REVOLTS TO ACTIV-
ist and artistic work with body hair, this book has thus far looked at the
ways that women's body hair can resituate and recast gender norms and
beauty ideals while undermining political systems of misogyny. We now
turn to three chapters that feature the voices of longtime body hair rebels
from the United States, featuring those who have consciously chosen to
grow out their body hair as a mode of resistance against the so-called
ideals of hairlessness for women. These narratives, collected through
semistructured interviews in June 2020 at the height of the first wave of
COVID-19 quarantines and the George Floyd/Black Lives Matter protests,
speak to the complexities of what it means to purposefully resist gendered norms of the body in a culture that derides women's hairy bodies
as "gross," "disgusting," and "dirty."

This chapter draws from interviews with twenty-two people—nineteen
cis women, one trans woman, and two nonbinary people—from diverse
backgrounds in terms of race, class, sexual orientation, age, parental and

relationship statuses, and geographical locations across the United States. All of these people have intentionally grown out their body hair for a long period of time. I use the narratives generated in these qualitative interviews to expand the conversation on body hair to a variety of topics that highlight the emotional qualities of women's body hair, both in terms of how women themselves feel about their body hair and in terms of how others react to women's body hair.[1] First, I look at the key reasons women choose to grow their body hair, highlighting the diverse range of motives for why women reject the social norm of women's hairlessness. I then consider the emotional experiences of hair, particularly the joy and ambivalence women feel about their body hair, followed by a consideration of the different meanings women assign to different regions of their body hair, including armpit hair, leg hair, pubic hair, facial hair, and "rogue" body hairs. I conclude by examining why women feel emotional about their hair and what these emotions reveal about gender and power. Ultimately, this chapter is a meditation on the interplay among bodies, gender, affect, and power, and how both social regulation and personal freedom can be experienced through the layering of emotions onto the body.

A BRIEF HISTORY OF AFFECT STUDIES

In her meditation on the cultural politics of emotions, feminist scholar Sara Ahmed writes that emotions themselves have become associated with women, "who are represented as 'closer' to nature, ruled by appetite, and less able to transcend the body through thought, will and judgment . . . emotions get narrated as a sign of 'our' prehistory, as a sign of how the primitive persists in the present."[2] This divide—between emotion and reason—led to a hierarchy between emotions, as some emotions became indicative of cultivation and refinement, while others signaled weakness and lack of control. This has led to emotions informing the nature of social hierarchy itself, as "emotions become attributes of bodies as a way of transforming what is 'lower' or 'higher' into bodily traits. So emotionality as a claim *about* a subject or a collective is clearly dependent on relations of power, which endow 'others' with meaning and value."[3]

Ahmed also argues that emotions do not merely reside as an interior, individual experience but, rather, move between people (as "stickiness" or adherence) as a social phenomenon. One person's feelings become another's experience, through sympathy, empathy, "fellow-feeling," and, in some cases, rejection or alienation. This contagious nature of emotions, and how emotions transfer from one person to another in a collective sentiment, has a long history, particularly in relation to causing fear and panic among the elite. (If, for example, people could "catch" feelings from other people or from written texts, they would then be capable of generating and spreading revolutionary sentiment as a collective body.)[4] Emotions also become projected onto bodies themselves, as bodies serve as the containers or repositories of emotional baggage carried through and within a culture. As Ahmed writes, "Feminist and queer scholars have shown us that emotions 'matter' for politics; emotions show us how power shapes the very surface of bodies as well as worlds. So in a way, we do 'feel our way.'"[5]

The field of affect studies, or affect theory, offers a blueprint for how to begin to understand the immensely complex nature of emotions and how emotions infuse and inform individual and collective bodies. Building on the sociology of the body, affect theory was largely pioneered by Mike Featherstone, Bryan Turner, and Chris Shilling in the late 1990s and early 2000s and subsequently taken up by feminist sociologists, feminist psychologists, and critical humanities scholars such as Sara Ahmed, Patricia Clough, Lauren Berlant, and Elspeth Probyn.[6] An emerging field, affect studies argues that emotions and affect can become a defining force of social relationships, codifying and sorting bodies, merging and separating people from each other, and defining the relationships among humans, animals, the earth, and even inanimate objects.[7] Emotions become cultural artifacts rather than states of individual psychology, mapped onto the social landscape in ways that mitigate how people relate to each other and their world.

To study affect, then, is to imagine it as operating beyond the cognitive, as changing the fundamental nature of relatedness and relationships, and as an entity that can absorb and mitigate the transmission of power. As media scholar Lisa Blackman argues, "Affect refers to those registers of experience which cannot be easily seen and which might variously be described as non-cognitive, trans-subjective, non-conscious, non-representational, incorporeal and immaterial."[8] She goes on to write,

"Affect is not a thing but rather refers to processes of life and vitality which circulate and pass between bodies and which are difficult to capture or study in any conventional methodological sense."[9] Affect theorists have grappled with the fundamental unruliness of emotions, how they resist easy categorization, bleed into one another, disrupt and upend hierarchies, and operate both as mechanisms of social control and as markers of freedom and liberty.

Emotions exist in a permanently *liminal* state, lingering between things and mediating relationships between things. In their introduction to affect theory, Gregory Seigworth and Melissa Gregg write, "Affect arises in the midst of *in-between-ness*: in the capacities to act and be acted upon. . . . Affect is found in those intensities that pass body to body (human, non-human, part-body, and otherwise), in those resonances that circulate about, between, and sometimes stick to bodies and worlds, *and* in the very passages or variations between these intensities and resonances themselves."[10] They argue, most basically, that affect can accumulate across modes of relations and relatedness and that bodies acquire a capacity to affect and be affected, particularly when they work collectively. With emotions, people constantly become something else. Further, because emotions are experienced so deeply within the body, it makes sense that people experience emotions as bodily just as they feel emotions *about* their bodies. We do not merely think about our bodies but feel our bodies and feel through our bodies.

Seigworth and Gregg have argued that distinctions among the body, affect, and the outside world are impossible to tease apart, that affect is "integral to a body's perceptual *becoming* (always becoming otherwise, however subtly, than what it already is), pulled beyond its seeming surface-boundedness by way of its relation to, indeed its composition through, the forces of encounter. With affect, a body is as much outside itself as in itself—webbed in its relations—until ultimately such firm distinctions cease to matter."[11] In other words, bodies and emotions, or even bodies and their social contexts, are impossible to disentangle, which then obscures the central role emotions play in shaping and contouring people's understandings of their bodies. The invisibility of emotions allows them to more efficiently dictate the social fabric of bodies and relationships. In the case of body hair, for example, people often fail to recognize the deep emotions they have about their own and others' body hair, which then allows those emotions to dictate their choices and practices even more efficiently and directly. If one fails to recognize that they pluck their eyebrows or shave their underarm hair in order to avoid others' disgust or to dodge their own feelings of shame, such choices can feel relatively benign and operate instead as "just how things are done."

Affect theory thus has important implications for the body and the choices people make about their bodies, particularly how people experience their physical, embodied, and aesthetic lives. For example, not fitting into clothing or finding clothing that one likes can cause considerable stress to people, suggesting that clothing choices are not merely aesthetic but also quite emotional.[12] Sociologist Lucia Ruggerone finds that sociologists and cultural studies scholars have focused extensively on fashion and identity, for example, but have largely ignored the feelings people experienced about and in their clothes (what she calls the "feeling of being dressed"). She also argues that the selection of clothing is not an intellectual decision but an affective one, where people compose and design their bodies around how they feel.[13] She writes of this phenomenon, "In our culture feeling good has been surreptitiously assimilated with looking good."[14] This raises numerous questions about how women could relate to their clothing differently, through affect: "What new social scenarios would open up if a large number of women started overlooking their appearance and prioritizing instead an affective bonding with clothes?"[15]

People also have complicated emotional relationships with their tattoos, particularly as some interpret their tattoos to represent internal states of feeling, while others see them as public expressions, markers of social identities, or declarations of symbols of the self.[16] Tattoos can symbolize the relationship between the body, self-identity, and society, and the process of getting a tattoo often involves a variety of emotional relationships and reactions, from trust in the tattoo artist to regret about the tattoo turning out poorly to a mismatch between desired expression and how others interpret the tattoo.[17] Getting a tattoo, then, is not merely a personal aesthetic choice but one governed by emotional and affective resonances.

Similarly, people's feelings about their hair often connect deeply to their emotional states, particularly avoidance of shame and disgust.

Women who grow visible facial hair often have strongly negative feelings about it, with two-thirds continually checking in mirrors to monitor for it and 40 percent of women reporting discomfort with their facial hair in social situations.[18] Black women, and white women with red hair, often reported feeling that their natural hair was not beautiful and expressed discomfort and shame about their hair.[19] Blond women also reported emotional conflicts about their hair, as blond hair got associated by others with innocence, sexiness, sexual promiscuity, and stupidity; consequently, blond women reacted emotionally to these labels by joking about it, confirming these stereotypes, overcompensating, fighting back, and passing.[20] LGBTQ+ people also struggled with their hair, as one study of queer people in job interviews found that "appearance labor" about their hair and clothing burdened them during the job interviewing process.[21] These examples reveal that affect and emotion drive how people view their hair and how they manage possible negative stigma associated with certain kinds of "wrong" or "bad" hair.

METHOD

To give some context about the interviews used in chapters 6, 7, and 8, I introduce the women featured here and explain how I found them and what sorts of questions I asked them. Not only do these interviews illuminate certain aspects of body hair experiences otherwise left out of the current scholarly analyses but they also serve as a way to think more deeply about the relationship women have to the social and cultural contexts that often regulate and control bodies. Such regulation often denies bodily autonomy and diversity of experiences, drawing on emotional mechanisms for control (e.g., "I want to avoid looking bad"; "I don't want to feel ashamed") in order to diminish women's satisfaction with their bodies. While these stories complicate the notion that body hair rebels always enthusiastically grow out their body hair joyfully and freely—in fact, many women in this group felt hindered by their negative emotional states about their body hair—these stories add texture and nuance to women's marginalized bodily experiences. How people talk about body hair presents a fascinating mix of the individual and the social, the interior and exterior, the self and the other. These stories also speak to the unevenness of women's body hair experiences, clearly highlighting the unruly edges of the body that too often get "shaved away." I left these interviews with more questions than answers, more complicated understandings of body hair and gender, and a range of emotions in myself that spanned all the way from infuriated and confused to hopeful and elated.

In all, I interviewed twenty-two people (nineteen cis women, two nonbinary people, one trans woman) over the course of three weeks in June 2020. Due to the COVID-19 outbreak and mandatory quarantine and lockdown still happening in many states, all interviews were conducted remotely via Zoom.[22] Because I wanted to speak to women from many different social backgrounds and statuses, I used a purposive sampling technique to select women and nonbinary people from a variety of racial/ethnic backgrounds, sexual identities, and ages. Participants were recruited from the "volunteers" and "et cetera" sections of Craigslist in numerous US cities and towns, ranging from big metropolitan areas like New York City and San Francisco to smaller/midsize cities like Santa Fe, New Mexico, and Asheville, North Carolina.[23] The advertisement noted that women over age thirty-five, trans and nonbinary people, lesbian and bisexual women, and people of color were particularly encouraged to apply. Participants were paid $20 for doing the study, which received approval from my university's research ethics board. Interest in the study was sizable and enthusiastic, making it quite easy to recruit participants from diverse backgrounds. Identifying data was removed, and each participant received a pseudonym to ensure anonymity.

The people in the sample came from a wide range of identities and demographic backgrounds, including substantial racial diversity: eleven (50 percent) white and eleven (50 percent) people of color: six Asian Americans, two Mexican Americans, one African American, and two biracial women—one with half–Native American ancestry and one with half-Moroccan ancestry. The sample also spanned a range of sexual orientations: nine people (41 percent) identified as heterosexual, seven (32 percent) identified as bisexual, four (18 percent) identified as lesbian, and two (9 percent) identified as queer. The age range spanned twenty-one to sixty-three, with twelve people (55 percent) twenty-one to thirty-four years old and ten (45 percent) thirty-five to sixty-three years old (mean age = 34.05; standard deviation = 13.11). Geographical location also varied, with seven participants from the San Francisco Bay Area; four from New York City; one from Los Angeles, California; one from Portland, Oregon; five from small towns in Pennsylvania, Mississippi, Texas, and North Carolina; two from suburban cities Colorado and Illinois; one from a large college town in Wisconsin; and one from Santa Fe, New Mexico. Class diversity was also well represented, as were parental and relationship statuses and, surprisingly, political identification, which ranged from mostly conservative to very progressive/liberal (though the sample skewed toward more liberal perspectives).

All of the participants agreed to speak to me for a sixty-to-seventy-minute audio-recorded Zoom interview, where I asked them a range of questions about their body hair behavior, practices, experiences, and feelings, alongside questions about their political activism and ideologies and the broader picture of their body experiences (e.g., menstruation, abortion, other forms of body resistance). I asked participants questions like, "How have you talked about body hair with your partners, friends, family, and coworkers?" and, "How do choices about body hair differ between white women and women of color, or between wealthier women and poorer women?" Questions were open-ended and served as a springboard for larger conversations that emerged from the initial questions, leading to several probing questions and free-flowing conversations about body hair. Interviews were transcribed verbatim, though I removed verbal pauses and utterances like "Um" and "Uh" in these narratives for readability.

WHY DO WOMEN REFUSE TO REMOVE THEIR BODY HAIR?

In these narratives of growing out their body hair, women often described their decisions to stop shaving in highly emotional terms. Women had a huge diversity of reasons and motivations for not removing their body hair, including practical and medical reasons, personal comfort and ease of not shaving, partner preference and/or partner acceptance, environmental reasons, and explicit rebellion against oppressive gender norms. Each of these fell on the spectrum between the seemingly apolitical frameworks for women growing out body hair and the explicitly political/feminist reasons that women rebelled against the hairlessness norm for women.

Further, the underlying emotional dimensions for these choices—particularly around partners' feelings and their own passions for environmental justice or personal freedoms—showed how emotions both regulated their decisions and pushed them toward more openness and comfort with body hair.

Practical and Medical Reasons

Five women cited practical reasons for not shaving, divorcing their body hair choices from a political or politicized context. For example, growing out body hair for medical reasons appeared in two women's narratives. Ruby (fifty-eight/white/heterosexual) described growing out her body hair after a stay in the hospital, being put on blood thinners, and deciding for health reasons to keep growing her body hair: "My legs are blondish, so you don't really see it if it's long and don't really know it's there anyway. I stopped shaving mainly for medical reasons, but now that I'm not shaving, it seems natural." Ainsley (twenty-three/white/heterosexual) decided to grow out her body hair after repeated skin infections from shaving her underarms:

> When I was a teenager, I was also super self-conscious, and I would shave and shave and shave almost every day because you think everyone is looking at you, and it got to the fact that I actually had MRSA twice, so I kept getting these skin infections, and the doctors would say, "Hey, try not to shave." I would just be on so many medications, and my skin would blow up, and I was like, "You know what? This isn't worth it. Honestly, who's going to look at it?" In my armpits I would get ingrown hairs, and then those would get super big, super irritated. I was like, "I just got to stop this."

Ainsley went on to explicitly remind me that her growing body hair was not a feminist statement, saying, "It was my body's reaction more than anything. It wasn't anything like, 'Oh, girl power!' If my skin was more tolerable, then I would definitely still be shaving on a regular basis."

Women also cited the practical, time-saving reasons for growing out body hair by emphasizing that shaving was unnecessary and that no one cared if they grew body hair. Lin (thirty-four/Vietnamese American/ heterosexual) said she grew her body hair in order to stay warm and avoid having to shower: "I thought, well, it's very cold right now, and I don't really feel like shaving because I was kind of on the cheap side and there was no heating or air conditioning, so I would always wear layers of jackets because it was so cold. I didn't want to get up early to shave in the dark and feel cold. If I were to take a shower in the morning, it's like dumping a bucket of ice on my body." She also said that her coworkers did not care and that she lived alone: "I was the only woman on my team, so I felt like the guys could care less, and a lot of them are married with kids, so I didn't really have anybody to impress. I was just like, 'I don't have to impress anybody, so why do I have to do this? I could just save time and roll out of bed and go to work.'" Natasha (twenty-eight/white/bisexual), a recent Russian immigrant, talked about how shaving added yet another demand to her busy schedule taking care of her children at home: "I got married, and I have two kids. I don't have time for doing depilation at different salons, because you have to do it on a regular basis." Natasha's words serve as a reminder that, while time-saving techniques could be read as nongendered and apolitical, women often have less time because they juggle the endless obligations of working full-time and engaging in domestic and family labor.

At times, women grew out their body hair because of the physical hazards of shaving and the sense that shaving was unnecessary for health reasons. Bijou (twenty-two/African American/heterosexual) described getting ingrown hairs alongside her growing realization that no one noticed women's body hair:

> I developed ingrown hairs or folliculitis, and it kind of scared me because I thought it was something else. I went to the doctor, and he suggested I stop shaving for a bit. I just decided to stop shaving after that so I wouldn't have to deal with that anymore. Also, I don't wear a lot of sleeveless tops or tank tops, and I just don't think people really care. People don't really notice it or have never told me, like, "Ew, why don't you shave under your arms?" I never felt that I had to. It just feels more natural and better.

These narratives suggest that, for some women, growing body hair was purely a way to avoid negative physical symptoms and discomfort from shaving, comply with medical recommendations from their doctors, or align themselves with their desires to be practical.

Personal Comfort and Ease of Not Shaving

As a second reason for why women grew out their body hair, a third of the women cited the personal comfort and ease of not shaving, noting that it saved time and money and felt comfortable to them. Francis (forty-seven/Mexican American/lesbian) cited the convenience of not shaving: "Why would you do something that is expensive, time-consuming, and annoying? No thanks!" Olive (sixty-three/white/heterosexual), the oldest woman I spoke with, described visiting the Netherlands in 1975 and noticing that women her age did not remove their body hair at all: "I was a stranger in a strange land, and I was trying to learn the language and the customs and everything. I just realized that nobody else was shaving their legs so I don't need to do that. It wasn't a big decision. It was just like, 'Okay, I'll hold my fork this way, and I'll drink this for breakfast.' I was just trying to be like everybody else there." She described her return to the United States as a moment of realizing she wanted to continue not removing her body hair for the rest of her life: "When I came back to the US, I just didn't shave anymore. I thought, 'What a waste of time! Why would I keep doing that?' I didn't even think of it as a decision. That's how we're made, and there's nothing wrong with how we're made."

Similarly, other women decided to grow out body hair because of the ease of it. Kalani (twenty-one/Sri Lankan American/heterosexual) described shaving as irritating and bothersome: "It just became too much of a nuisance because it had to be done every couple of days because otherwise it gets prickly. It was just more a nuisance and more of an annoying thing to do all the time. I see it as natural. There are plenty of women who don't shave, who have just as much body hair as me." Vera (thirty/Chinese American/heterosexual) described the comfort of not shaving during the COVID-19 quarantine, citing the lack of social judgment as a key reason for growing body hair: "I don't really need to go out and see anyone, and my boyfriend and I are in a long-distance relationship, so I don't see him and I don't really care too much. I also transitioned from working in the office to working at home, so if I'm not being judged by other people, I would rather let it grow out."

Growing body hair also aligned with some women's gender identity, particularly for women who had more masculine presentation, aesthetics, and clothing choices. Heather (forty/white/bisexual) said that body hair fit with her desired gender presentation: "I just wanted to be more natural and not as feminine. I don't dress very feminine, so it kind of fit for me. I see myself as tomboyish. Also, just taking less time in the shower!" Collectively, these narratives did not explicitly link body hair choices to political contexts or outright rebellion against gender norms, though Heather's narrative came the closest to doing so. Still, these stories suggest that women imagined body hair as natural and easy and that it made them feel comfortable in their bodies.

Partner Preference and/or Partner Acceptance

While many women described their partners' feelings as a key factor in deciding whether to grow their body hair, three women said that they had had partners who explicitly preferred women with body hair. For some women, their partners' attitudes encouraged them to grow body hair when they otherwise would not have, while for other women, it affirmed their desires to grow body hair and served as a source of encouragement and support. Martina (fifty/Mexican American/bisexual) said that she grew out her body hair in response to a female partner who requested that she grow it: "My partner preferred it at the time, and I just got really tired of the whole routine of hair removal, you know? It was unnecessary. Why are we born with body hair if we're not supposed to have it? My partner wanted me to have body hair because it had to do with sex. It almost made her feel like I was a child if I didn't have hair, because only children don't have body hair, just kind of weird, or like a doll or something." She went on to describe her previous elaborate body hair removal routines: "I've been doing it my whole life, spending lots of money on it, lots of time. I've used depilatories before, and they're toxic. I've used them on my face even. A lot of women use electrolysis, and that's expensive and time-consuming, and it comes back. It's just sort of easier to not remove it. . . . I mean, who really cares? And if my partner prefers it, then who's to say what I cannot do?"

Even for women whose partners may not have explicitly *requested* body hair, their partner's acceptance or tolerance of their hair mattered a great deal in their decision-making about body hair growth. Eve (thirty-eight/white/lesbian) said that her partner liking body hair greatly impacted her decision to grow her body hair: "I felt like I was more of myself and more comfortable. My partner liked it and didn't mind, so I just kind of stuck with it. The longer I had it, I'm like, 'Oh, this is better!'" Ula (twenty-two/Chinese American/bisexual) also cited her partners' acceptance or judgment about hair as influencing her body hair decisions to shave or grow hair:

> I was lazy at first and started dating this person who would often comment, "Oh, you have so little body hair. I don't really notice it." I think that just made me feel a little more comfortable with not shaving. I stopped shaving because I got affirmations from people that they didn't mind. When I was with a different partner, I got a lot of comments that I should shave my pubic area. That made me want to shave more. I think just the reluctance to have sex when I didn't shave made me feel that way. It really hurt, so I think that contributed to it.

This clear influence of partners in encouraging body hair, accepting body hair, or discouraging body hair showed the importance of the role of romantic and sexual partners in women's ideas about their bodies and the freedoms they perceive with their bodies. Still, the notion that women grew body hair to please a partner suggests that women may simply reframe body hair growth as yet another mechanism to please partners rather than themselves.

Environmental Reasons

Moving toward a more political perspective on body hair growth, four women cited environmental reasons for growing their body hair, particularly around issues of water usage, sustainability, and wanting to avoid adding razors to the landfills. Casey (twenty-six/white/lesbian) described growing body hair as a way to think more consciously about water usage: "I've always been water conscious because I'm from the desert. It's always been on my mind, how to conserve water, so it's one of those things, 'Why do I have to take a thirty-minute shower when I could take a five-minute shower and not worry about shaving?' Additionally, I have very thick hair, and if I shave my legs on one day, they're going to be prickly the next day, and you have to shave again." Similarly, Sequoia (twenty-three/white/bisexual) cited her local cultural context around environmentalism and left-wing politics as a key influence for not removing body hair: "I live in Asheville [North Carolina] and it's kind of a hippie little town. Nobody cares. I just don't care as much. It's a hassle to shower. I've just read things about how showering too much is bad for your pH levels anyway." She went on to describe her desire to avoid razors and pollution: "It's just freeing. That's how it's supposed to grow. We wouldn't have razors if we all lived in the jungle. I like just not going out and buying those and not even having to deal with them. I don't want to buy miscellaneous things I don't need." This environmental consciousness argument speaks to the ways that people's choices about their bodies connect to larger narratives about gender, power, and social norms. These findings also map onto studies that found that women and feminists more often cared about pollution and environmental degradation than did men and nonfeminist women.[24]

Rebellion against Oppressive Gender Norms

As the most common explanation for growing out body hair, nine women described growing body hair as a political act, a rebellion against oppressive gender norms, and a signal of their desire for more gendered freedom. For example, Gloria (fifty-six/white/heterosexual) said that not shaving felt like a conscious and overt form of rebellion, and she related this to her lifetime of traveling across cultures: "Fuck social norms. I travel all over the world, and I have for years. I've been exposed to so many cultures and so many societies where most people don't shave. It's normal and natural." Along these lines, Indigo (thirty-five/White/Bisexual) felt betrayed by shaving, particularly as it cut her off from certain spiritual practices: "I'm definitely responding to pressures sometimes, and sometimes rebelling against those pressures as well. I started growing out body hair when a boyfriend told me about the Sanskrit concept of 'Prana Antenna,' or energy centers, back in my hippie days. I just saw how conditioned I was. I thought I was such a freethinker, and I was like, 'Oh wow, I've been completely shearing myself all this time to be accepted as beautiful or to be on the market dateability-wise.'" She went on to add, "It just feels better to not shave. It's just so much nicer to strip away all of those pressures to shave. Like if I were on a deserted island by myself, would I choose to shave? No. Not at all. It just my natural body, and it just feels good."

Growing body hair also served as a way of rebelling against gendered expectations for women. For example, Zara (twenty-two/white and Moroccan/queer) started growing her body hair in response to feeling insulted by a sexist remark she saw online: "It kind of started, in a way, out of spite. I remember I was in high school and there was a video that came out where this kid wanted his girlfriend to shave her arm hair, saying that she was unattractive or whatever. I just thought it was so stupid, and I was like, 'Oh, well, I never want to date anyone who's like that, so I'll grow my arm hair so that kind of person wouldn't be attracted to me in the first place.' It was kind of a strange way of thinking about it." Tori (twenty-six/Asian American/bisexual) also associated not shaving with refusing to conform to restrictive gender norms: "I just feel it's not something I need to do hygiene-wise or just to fit into society for whatever. I don't feel I need to conform like that. . . . I just got to the point where I was like, 'You know what? I don't need to do this for me. I don't need to do this for anybody else.' I was more okay with it, and I felt good." Quinn (twenty-one/white and Native American/lesbian) also described growing her body hair as an intentional revolt against gender norms: "It started out as a bet between me and this other gal to see how long we could go without shaving our legs. I also wasn't very good at shaving. I would cheese grater my legs, so it was never something I was particularly endeared to. But after we started that bet, it gave me the permission I needed to kind of say 'Fuck it' to the whole routine." Speaking about her ideology connected to body hair, Quinn said, "I do see it as a very natural thing. I'm in environmental studies, and so I get to handle a lot of other mammals. When I was younger it was something I didn't even conceptualize as something to be removed, and then I went through a brief period where I was told it was kind of gross, and then I guess I kind of gradually evolved into me not caring if other people thought it was gross."

Having body hair also coincided with ideas about identity and a desire to deconstruct or play with gender norms. This sense of fluctuation—between hairlessness and hairiness—and interviewees' reflections about how this spoke to ideas about gender and gender fluidity highlighted the dynamic relationship between gender and body hair. Jasmine (twenty-eight, Taiwanese American/heterosexual), who identified as a trans woman, shifted from shaving her body hair to letting it grow: "I let it grow after I started transitioning more, because in the beginning of my transition I actually wanted all of it to be gone. I guess when you are raised as a guy, you are raised thinking girls don't have any body hair, but then after I started transitioning, that's obviously not the case, so I also just stopped caring about it. Hair is natural." Dana (thirty-six/white/queer), who identified as nonbinary, described a fluid relationship with their body hair: "I really don't care. I'm queer anyway, so I don't really think that the partners I would choose would even care about that. I like to think of body hair as a ritual. It'll be on solstice, I'll reset, like start over just to see how it grows out. It's more of like that kind of experience. I don't really like shaving anyway. It's better not to." They went on to outline their broader views on body hair, again highlighting feelings of naturalness and fluidity: "I do see it as natural. Whether you're male or female—it's not even a gender thing, really. Everybody has hair. We're humans. I almost don't even understand why so many females feel pressured to shave because I don't necessarily see it as unattractive when a woman has body hair. Maybe it's just a media thing or something."

These diverse narratives about why women grew out body hair suggest that women arrived at that decision for numerous reasons, both practical and ideological. For some women, growing body hair caused ambivalence and even disappointment, and for others it felt like a way of honoring their comfort about their natural bodies. Still others grew body hair for ideological, feminist, moral, and ethical reasons, including environmental responsibility and a rejection of constricting, sexist, and misogynistic norms about bodies. Body hair can hold many tensions in place, between playful and serious, intention and accident, trivial and profound, practical and spiritual, and feminine and masculine.

EMOTIONAL EXPERIENCES OF BODY HAIR:
THE JOY OF BODY HAIR

Building on the reasons women grew out their body hair, I also asked women what they liked about not shaving their body hair. The question yielded a wide array of responses, again highlighting tensions between practical and resource-based answers (e.g., saving time, money, energy) and more ideological answers (e.g., being proud of rejecting norms). The most common response women gave highlighted their desire to conserve resources, particularly as they saved time by not shaving. Natasha (twenty-eight/white/bisexual) enthusiastically discussed the time she saved as a mother of young children: "I like that I spend less time in the bathroom, because to shave underarms, it is very fast, but to shave your legs, it takes longer. When I have kids, I don't have too much time to spend in the bathroom." Kalani (twenty-one/Sri Lankan American/heterosexual) liked not wasting time on hair removal: "That's fifteen minutes I could be doing nothing or relaxing. It frees up time with my legs, and I'm not worried about getting cuts." Olive (sixty-three/white/heterosexual) felt similarly about the benefits of extra time, saying, "I like that I have extra time and that I don't get nicks and cuts. I'm comfortable with who I am."

Women also appreciated saving money by not shaving, noting that razors, waxing treatments, and shaving paraphernalia were all quite expensive. Ainsley (twenty-three/white/heterosexual) talked about the twin joys of saving money and avoiding razor burn: "I save *so much* money on razors. You don't realize how much it adds up, because I would get like super nice ones, and I kept getting infections. Also, my skin would get infection after infection and get hives and razor burn and there would be pimples on my legs. It'd be horrible and hurt so bad." Bijou (twenty-two/African American/heterosexual) acknowledged the money saving and lack of ingrown hairs as joyful: "I like that it's inexpensive and you don't have to go and get waxed or buy shaving tools. It's comfortable. There's no pain. You don't develop ingrown hairs. You don't spend time removing your body hair." Ruby (fifty-eight/white/heterosexual) likened not shaving to breastfeeding in its affordability: "People spend good money on waxing. Not waxing is cost-effective. It's kind of like breastfeeding. It's there, and you use it, and it's free. It doesn't cost anything. It's cheaper."

Jasmine (twenty-eight/Taiwanese American/heterosexual) added that she also appreciated saving water: "It saves water, 'cause I usually shaved in the shower. It saves some time as well. It saves resources to not shave. I don't really do it for a statement."

Highlighting the emotional relationship women had to their hair, several women talked about the relief and lack of worry that growing body hair created for them, noting that freedom from worrying about their body hair helped them to feel calmer and more peaceful. Indigo (thirty-five/white/bisexual) exclaimed that she loved the lack of worry that came with growing body hair: "I just like not thinking about it at all, like it was always just something that took so much time and worry. This letting go of caring about it is just liberating. That's the best part. It just feels like any other day, kind of like how men must feel!" Tori (twenty-six/Asian American/bisexual) also noticed the lack of worry and feeling free to be herself as key reasons for growing her body hair: "It's really nice just to not worry about it, just to have one less thing to do. It just makes me happy to not conform to standards of beauty or whatever. I can just kind of be who I am naturally."

Women also avoided negative physical sensations of shaving, which many found enriching to their lives. Eve (thirty-eight/white/lesbian) noted that her sensitive skin made shaving hazardous: "I have pretty sensitive skin, and so, when I would shave, I would get razor bumps and stuff like that. I love that my skin feels softer and more natural when I don't shave. I don't have to worry about reaching and finding every hair. It's just something I don't have to think about anymore, and that's nice." Zara (twenty-two/white and Moroccan/queer) also described positive physical consequences of not shaving alongside curiosity about her own body: "I like to just see how long it can grow. That's kind of an interesting thing to see. The first time I grew it out, it was a lot darker than I expected, but it was also softer than I expected. I also like that I don't have my skin rubbing against each other. I don't nick myself anymore either. It's also nice not to feel the pain of waxing and not to get ingrowns." Ula (twenty-two/Chinese American/bisexual) also mentioned the combination of the lack of physical discomfort and feelings of freedom: "It's nice to not have to answer to anyone. Also, after I shave, when it grows back, it kind of has these ingrown hairs, so that's never fun. So I don't get those anymore, and that's nice."

People also felt more comfortable with their bodies when growing their body hair, citing this comfort as a freedom from the constraints of gendered beauty norms. Dana (thirty-six/white/queer) described body hair as feeling natural to them: "I just like that I get to be myself. I don't have to hide or prepare to look a certain way. I like to groom and take showers and feel good about myself, but I don't think shaving has to do with that." Heather (forty/white/bisexual) equated body hair growth to independence from hassles, saying, "It kind of feels like freedom. It's not grooming all the time, taking extra showers because I have to groom. It just feels like freedom." Casey (twenty-six/white/lesbian) described body hair as liberating: "I love the lack of hassle of not shaving. I love my freedom. I love being myself. I feel good, and I feel comfortable." Sequoia (twenty-three/white/bisexual) felt that her body was more natural when hairy: "I just like that this is how I would look if we did not all have razors and things like that, if we would just be living in a community. That's what I want to do, just live in the woods."

Building on this, a few women talked about body hair as a symbolic form of rebellion that made them proud of their bodies and excited about the potentially politicized aspects of growing body hair. Gloria (fifty-six/white/heterosexual) felt proud of her body hair, noting its rebellious qualities when she openly showed it to others: "The positive part is I feel proud when myself or other people can pull it off or choose to pull it off in a society that is often saying, 'No, don't do that.' You can hide your armpit hairs quite easily, but you can't hide your skin tone, your race. . . . So if I show it, I'm a little bit proud, like a fat old white lady, I'm not judged like a lot of other people are every single day in America." Quinn (twenty-one/white and Native American/lesbian) also felt that growing body hair was an antidote to the all-too-common shaming of women's bodies: "I like the freedom of it. I also feel like it's a rebellion, like you're kind of honoring something that you were told to get rid of or that you were told was shameful, and it's like, 'Ha! I'm just gonna let my body grow as it pleases.' It's just a normal thing about being a mammal." She added that she has sometimes felt solidarity with other hairy women, saying,

"Sometimes I find with friends or people I'm just meeting, if they have unshaved legs, sometimes you can kind of befriend them on that note." These stories reflect a keen awareness that body hair on women can be threatening to the status quo or present a challenge to how women's bodies are narrowly constructed, just as it can free up time, resources, and energy for other activities and interests.

DIFFERENT EMOTIONS ABOUT DIFFERENT REGIONS OF BODY HAIR

Women also experienced the emotional weight of body hair differently for different regions of the body, as leg hair, armpit hair, pubic hair, facial hair, and nipple hair all had different emotional resonances for women. Further, women felt quite emotional about their body hair in general. These reflections highlight not only the emotional relationship between individuals and their bodies but also the emotional impact of women interacting with the social world.

In particular, over half of the participants mentioned that the social aspects of hair greatly impacted the emotional experience of body hair, in that who saw the hair contributed to how they perceived and experienced it. Tori (twenty-six/Asian American/bisexual) described the different regions of hair as connected to the social feedback she received: "I'm more self-conscious about my pubic hair just because it is in such a private area. Armpit hair is more of a public area. With leg hair, a lot of times people are wearing jeans or something like long pants, or they're sitting at a table, so you can't see it. But with armpit hair, it's just right there, on the upper body, so when someone reaches for something you can see it." Bijou (twenty-two/African American/heterosexual) gauged her own feelings about body hair based on how much others might take offense at it: "I feel the least self-conscious in public about my leg hair, mostly because it's not very noticeable—I don't have very hairy legs, and I don't think people pay attention—and then the second least self-conscious about my underarm hair, and then I feel the most self-conscious about my pubic hair if I'm wearing a bikini, so I guess because I think that people find pubic hair on a woman the most offensive." Dana (thirty-six/white/queer) outlined their reasons for feeling differently about different body hair regions, citing the visibility and symbolic meaning of hair: "With leg hair, that's natural. Everyone has leg hair. With armpits? Yeah, I wonder. Maybe because it's more visible, and if you're wearing a T-shirt, you'll see that. But leg hair, maybe you wouldn't notice so much. I don't know. And pubic hair, I guess that's like a sexual thing. Do people still shave all that? That's hard to believe. Do they want to look like a child?"

Worry about how others judged or evaluated women with body hair also led to women attaching different emotions to different body hair regions. Martina (fifty/Mexican American/bisexual) worried about others questioning her gender and sexual identity because she grew her body hair: "Usually when men see a woman with armpit hair, they do a kind of double take, like, 'Oh are you a man?' or whatever. They start thinking in terms of, like, sexual preference or whatever. It's nobody's business but me and the other person." Eve (thirty-eight/white/lesbian), who worked as a yoga instructor, struggled with feeling like having body hair challenged other people's perceptions of her femininity and her fitness as a yoga teacher: "In yoga I'm always putting my hands up, so it's very obvious, whereas leg hair, it's not as thick, so you can't really see it that well. I think people don't expect armpit hair, so it's like, 'Whoa.' You have a certain image about yourself, or people look at you in one way, and then if they see it, it's just more of a shock. It's not something people expect, almost like when a guy lifts their arms, they don't expect it to be shaved."

As another contextual factor in women's emotional experiences of their hair, some participants mentioned that changes in the weather mattered in how they felt about their body hair. Casey (twenty-six/white/lesbian) mentioned that they felt a variety of different feelings about hair, largely dependent on weather: "With leg hair I feel like it's what grounds you. It's strong, and it's like bark on a tree. I feel like if you're comfortable with your legs then you're going to be fine no matter what. With underarms, because some people might say if it's too long, especially during the summer, that's how I feel, and I think it can be kind of gross. With pubic hair, in the winter months I don't care, but in the summer, when it's hot, I do care." Heather (forty/white/bisexual) also attached seasonal patterns to her feelings about her armpit hair: "For the underarms, it's a little hard to tolerate in the hot weather, so I will occasionally shave it just so I don't smell or have odor."

Related to this, and in line with much previous research on how lower-status people worry about, and are accused of, smelling bad,[25] some women felt concerned about their body odor. Vera (thirty/Chinese American/heterosexual) worried about how she smelled with armpit hair, which made her feel more negatively toward her armpit hair compared to other regions of body hair: "I can smell myself if I get really sweaty and have armpit hair. It just traps the sweat versus pubic hair and leg hair." Jasmine (twenty-eight/Taiwanese American/heterosexual) also felt that armpit hair had a different connotation because of its potential to smell bad, especially when compared to pubic hair: "Armpit hair doesn't really have any negative feeling for me as long as it doesn't smell because of the hair. And pubic hair doesn't really matter to me at all, like I don't know why it would matter to the people you're having sex with."

Women tended to feel most negatively not toward their leg, underarm, or pubic hair, but toward their facial hair. In particular, women described facial hair in highly negative terms, even if they enjoyed having body hair in other regions of their body. Perhaps because of the difficulty of concealment, many women found it cumbersome and painful to cope with and manage their facial hair.[26] Ula (twenty-two/Chinese American/bisexual) felt horror when thinking about her mustache hair, even to the point of judging other women's mustache hair: "My mustache area, I remember when I was a kid and it kind of grew a little bit here. People would make fun of me and say, 'Oh you have a mustache! You're a dyke!' People would say that! So I think that's definitely impacted how I see things. If I do see a woman who has a quite visible mustache, it would make me feel kind of uncomfortable." Indigo (thirty-five/white/bisexual) also expressed sadness and shame when talking about her facial hair, particularly her mustache and unibrow: "I care about my facial hair, my mustache and my unibrow. I feel like it's unacceptable to society to have hair on my face. Maybe it's aging or being thirty-five now, but it's an uphill battle within my own mind about my appearance. My eyebrows have become such a symbol lately too, of me not taking care of myself, like it's *totally* unacceptable." Zara (twenty-two/white and Moroccan/queer) described her facial hair as problematic because of its association with masculinity: "Facial hair in general is so visible and is so associated with masculinity.

If you want to be a typical soft woman who fits the ideal, then you can't have that. It's just too much similarity to masculinity."

In addition to voicing these feelings about facial hair, women also expressed distress and disgust about having stomach and nipple hair. As these "rogue hairs" on other parts of their body were not often discussed among friends or between family members, many women felt more alone or embarrassed by having these miscellaneous body hairs. Ainsley (twenty-three/white/heterosexual) strongly disliked the hair on her lower stomach (known colloquially as the "happy trail"): "This seems silly, but the only place I really don't like hair is right below the belly button. Sometimes I get a tweezer and I pluck that occasionally. I don't know why, but it's harder than having pubic hair for me. It's an area that typically guys have but not all girls have so I feel like I have to get rid of that area. No girl says, 'Oh yeah, I shave my happy trail.' I try to pretend that I'm OK growing it out, but I'll pluck it." For Kalani (twenty-one/Sri Lankan American/heterosexual), her dark stomach hair bothered her the most, as she felt she compared negatively to white women with lighter hair: "I also shave my stomach a lot, because societally I feel like I would get more judged for not shaving my stomach. I don't know if that's a common thing that women who are white or just have less body hair shave, but I assume others shave that less. If I had to choose between not shaving my armpits or my legs or my stomach hair, I would get rid of my stomach hair first. It feels like a 'hard no' because it's more of a taboo to have a hairy stomach as a female than anything else." Kalani also described feeling upset about having wiry nipple hair, saying, "I'm super aware of my nipple hair. It's quite coarse. As a Southeast Asian woman, I have a lot of wiry nipple hair, and I pluck it with a tweezer. That's not really good because that area is prone to scarring."

In contrast to these more negative portrayals of women's body hair, some women also felt many positive emotions about their body hair, from comfort and ease to joy and acceptance. Sequoia (twenty-three/white/bisexual) described her armpit hair with positive emotions and affect: "I feel like I really like my armpit hair more than anything. I don't know why. It doesn't really look good, but I just really like it, and it feels good under there. It's natural." Olive (sixty-three/white/heterosexual), who had grown her body hair out for the longest period of time compared to any other women I spoke with, also described affectionate feelings toward her body hair: "I've never really given much thought to my pubic hair, but I kind of like my leg hair." Quinn (twenty-one/white and Native American/lesbian) emphatically embraced her body hair while also talking about the emotionality of hair in general: "As people, we have really emotional reactions to most of our body parts. They're part of us, and I think that, with regard to hair, you can't really untangle that from what we've been told about how we need to maintain it and from what we've seen in the world around us. Like I never really saw hairy ladies when I was growing up, and I didn't ever think I would be one, but I guess I physically am." She went to reflect on the importance of not feeling shame about body hair: "For a lot of people, there's a lot of shame embroiled into it, and you don't want to be seen as an outcast for that reason, so you might as well take off all your body hair just to lessen that as a reason that people would reject you."

WHY IS HAIR EMOTIONAL?

Though different regions of hair inspired different kinds of feelings and emotions, women also explored the general sense that hair felt emotional, both to them and to others. When I asked them why they thought hair was emotional, they had an array of responses that highlighted the complicated interplay between the body, their emotional lives, and the broader cultural contexts that denigrate women's body hair.

For some participants, hair had a deeply personal quality, which gave it an emotional tenor. Casey (twenty-six/white/lesbian) reflected on how different people in their lives have gotten emotional when having to cut their hair: "I've asked women, 'Why don't you shave your hair?' and they're like, 'Nooooo,' and they got really upset. My heart goes out to people who actually have to shave their hair for certain reasons. It makes me really sad. I know my aunt wasn't allowed to have long hair. She had really long, beautiful black hair, and then she got cancer, so her friend shaved her hair. . . . For me, I can go without shaving my legs, but if someone touched them, I'd be like, 'No, back off.' I'd be emotional too."

Sequoia (twenty-three/white/bisexual) described a highly emotional relationship to her body hair, though she felt confused about why she felt this way: "There is really an emotional attachment to my hair or body hair in general, and it is weird. I'm not exactly sure why. Men are more like, 'It will grow back,' or whatever."

Some women attached the emotionality around body hair to capitalism and critiques of the social conditions of women's lives. Gloria (fifty-six/white/heterosexual) linked the emotions of hair to the pressures for women to buy products: "Maybe it's driven by the norms of what's beautiful. Maybe it's also driven by capitalism and products. I remember when I was younger, you could get a razor, and it was a men's razor with one blade. Now you can get up to five blades. It's got lotion, not lotion, in the shower, out of the shower. It just seems like there are so many freaking products! Maybe that's part of the messaging. You can get whatever you need for whatever it is, whenever you want it." Quinn (twenty-one/white and Native American/lesbian) saw the emotions about body hair as connected to cultural stories about deviance and the regulation of women's bodies: "I guess in the past two hundred years, body hair removal has been so intrinsically linked to women's bodies and body routines. I think people kind of have a visceral reaction, like they're seeing deviance or something. I can't really think of any other body modification or lack thereof that would make people that grossed out. People seem *personally* offended sometimes when you don't shave!" She added, "We're not a collective body. We're a bunch of individuals walking around with different degrees of hair. People seem to imagine a social contract of shaving."

Kalani (twenty-one/Sri Lankan American/heterosexual) attached the emotionality of body hair to the personal experiences of social control that women went through in other parts of their lives:

Hair can be a really emotional thing, like when I get my head hair cut too short. I lose my mind, and I start crying when I get home and see how short it is. It can be very, very emotional personally for people, but I think the societal push to get women to be shaved and waxed and trimmed and clean and prim and proper is just a micromanaging of women that exists all the time.

Whether that's your uterus or whether you can get an abortion or not, whether women have safe availability of IUDs or the ability to buy tampons and not be embarrassed about it, it's the same thing with hair.

Zara (twenty-two/white and Moroccan/queer) also felt that body hair was emotional because of the way women's bodies were controlled and monitored: "I think it's a way of control. It's just another way to get us to maintain a beauty standard. It's kind of similar to saying someone is the wrong weight or the wrong size or something. It's another constraint, another thing you have to put your time and energy and money into. It's so much money to get waxed. I must have spent hundreds of dollars in high school, and if I had saved that money, what would I be doing with it now?" Jasmine (twenty-eight/Taiwanese American/heterosexual) echoed these claims, saying that women's hair symbolizes their freedom and autonomy: "I think it's because people don't want women to have their own views on things or to do things in their own way."

Several women commented on the double standards directed toward men versus women, where men have freedom to do what they want with their hair, while women do not. Tori (twenty-six/Asian American/bisexual) noted that women's bodies faced far more constraints than men's bodies: "There are definitely harsher standards for women than men. I don't know any guys who have ever shaved or trimmed their body hair, but literally all of my female friends growing up, including me, we'd all do something to remove our body hair, and that's not really fair. Women are trained that their bodies are something to look at, whereas men's bodies are a tool, like a utility. I think that's just totally unfair that women have to go through all of this primping and pampering and whatnot, but men don't. It's ridiculous!" Eve (thirty-eight/white/lesbian) also noted this double standard and how it produces emotions about women's body hair: "I think it's just because women's body hair doesn't look as pretty, and they expect females to be more groomed and taking care of themselves, like a certain image, whereas men, it's fine and expected and hair is just there." Similarly, Bijou (twenty-two/African American/heterosexual) felt that the double standards between men and women stemmed from men wanting women to alter their bodies: "Women are supposed to have very smooth and soft skin and look flawless, and hair doesn't give the appearance of being flawless and smooth because sometimes body hair is very coarse. That's where the emotional reactions come from when it comes to women. With men, it's different because the male hormone, testosterone, helps men grow hair on their face, so hair is seen as manly."

Women also commented that culture lacks imagination about what women's natural, unadulterated bodies look like and what women's bodies are for. Ainsley (twenty-three/white/heterosexual) felt that hairy women were labeled as "freaks" and were largely rejected and ignored: "Women with body hair are seen as more masculine, like 'You're a dude' or 'You're unclean!' Like you don't have enough money to care to shave. You want to look gross. It's negative, like the bearded lady. You're a freak if you have hair in these places, even though it's natural. It's natural to have hair on your nipples, or hair on your chin, or hair on your lip. The media portrays women with hair as abnormal weirdness." Going a step further, Dana (thirty-six/white/queer) worried that women were not even treated fully as people: "Sometimes I think that women's bodies are just seen as sexual objects for men. They're almost not even seen as a separate human that grows hair. It's just this clean object that's smooth. I know that sounds crass." Together, these narratives reveal that hair elicits a variety of emotional reactions in women, and that women directly connect the emotionality of hair with the social control of women and their bodies.

REFLECTIONS ON AFFECT AND BODY HAIR

The narratives in this chapter highlight the ways that body hair becomes attached to emotions, both for individuals who negotiate their body hair and for people in a culture that largely denigrates and makes invisible women's body hair. The notable tension between the ways that women internalized social and cultural norms that portrayed women's body hair as "gross" and some women's clear framing of body hair as connected to political ideologies highlights the huge range of emotional experiences that women had with their body hair. Some women consistently denounced double standards of beauty between men and women and envisioned a world where women had more freedoms with their bodies, while others felt uncertain and confused about how to resist pressures to dislike their body hair. Even the narratives about joy and what women *liked* about body hair remained fraught with ambivalence, tension, and hesitation.

That said, the emotionality of body hair infuses it with unique potential as a tool of political and social rebellion. Many women understood that the treatment of women's body hair—particularly reactions of disgust and rejection—symbolized the broader cultural tendencies of treating women as objects or reducing their worth to their physical compliance with beauty norms. Women felt uneasy about capitulating to mandates to erase their facial hair, pluck their nipple hair, and shave their stomachs. They felt angry about having to modify their bodies to fit in or earn approval from others, and they saw body hair as a litmus test for how much freedom and autonomy women really had about their bodies. Still more, some women were acutely attuned to the capitalistic frameworks around women's body hair, and how capitalism tapped into women's emotions (e.g., fear, vulnerability) about "fitting in" in order to sell them products they did not want or need. Their emotional pleas to make room for feeling affection for their body hair, or embracing it as an expression of resistance, reveal the ways that affect informed and infused how women saw themselves and their social worlds.

This rich and textured picture—of women feeling their own emotions about their body hair and also seeing the ways that body hair inspires emotions in others—illuminates how emotions can become tools of social control and markers of newfound freedoms. As Sara Ahmed writes, "Of course, we are not just talking about emotions when we talk about emotions. The objects of emotions slide and stick and they join the intimate histories of bodies, with the public domain of justice and injustice. Justice is not simply a feeling. And feelings are not always just. But justice involves feelings, which move us across the surfaces of the world, creating ripples in the intimate contours of our lives. Where we go, with these feelings, remains an open question."[27] As such, women's emotional descriptions of their hair signify the traces of justice and the moving of discourse. Resistance to the strict social norms of beauty and grooming for women must also recognize the emotional qualities of people's relationship with their hair, the way that bodies absorb emotions and how emotions take up questions about the body. Ideally, by tapping into the highly charged emotional nature of hair, women can also funnel their own discontentment

with the status quo—alongside their anger at the ongoing double standards of beauty based on gender and race—into a new vision for bodily
autonomy and freedom. If "justice involves feelings," then body hair rebels have begun to draw clear lines in the sand to separate the world they
have from the world they *want* to have.

"The Only Opinion That Matters Is My Own"

The Social Regulation of Women's Body Hair

> The body, or rather, bodies, cannot be adequately understood as
> ahistorical, precultural, or natural objects in any simple way; they
> are not only inscribed, marked, engraved, by social pressures
> external to them but are the products, the direct effects, of the very
> social constitution of nature itself.

—ELIZABETH GROSZ, *Volatile Bodies*

THE RICH AND VARIED LIFE OF THE SOCIAL WORLD AND ITS
impact on bodies, identities, and social practices underlies so much of
what people understand about themselves and others. Stories are created
and shared, molded and modified, in the social world, just as individual
narratives of self-invention and bodily autonomy all funnel through the
social. In this sense, analysis of the way women make decisions about
body hair, or any bodily decision whatsoever, must account for the enormously powerful impact of social life *onto* the body. Social life depends on
the body for its expression, just as the body yearns for definition and
expression through social life. In this sense, we must understand the
body as a social entity, indebted to the words, shapes, and definitions
given by others.

Grappling with who has control over women's bodies, and how that
control is exercised, is at the core of women's body hair politics. In the conversations I had with women who intentionally grew out their body hair,
they repeatedly struggled with, and reflected on, the painful dynamics of

how they negotiated their body hair in different social and relational spaces. From decisions about whether to wear long pants or skirts at work to conversations where they worried about dating new partners and wondered about their body hair preferences, women constantly navigated complicated and tricky terrain around the social regulation of women's body hair. Moreover, most of the women I spoke with had a genuine desire to be self-determined and to value their own opinion over others' opinions about their bodily choices in general. This tension—between the social and the personal, the contextual and the individual—forms the basis of this chapter.

I begin this chapter by examining women's feelings about body hair in different contexts, particularly work, home, while alone, and with their partners. Women described the different stakes of having body hair in these different contexts, and they reflected on how their relationships influenced their body hair choices as they moved across contexts. I then talked with them about who regulated, commented upon, or reacted to their body hair, and how this affected them. Here, women revealed the overt mechanisms of social regulation and the intricacies of power in their daily lives. I also discussed with women *who* they talked to about their body hair, and who or what inspired them to grow out their body hair. Women reflected on how they imagined permission—self-driven or other-driven—for growing out their body hair, and the various social role models they had for growing their body hair. I end the chapter by discussing women's responses to my questions about whose opinions matter to them about their body hair and how they make choices about body hair in relation to those opinions. Ultimately, this chapter highlights the contradictions and complexities of working to undermine patriarchal control of women's bodies while struggling with the weighty and contradictory parameters of the social contexts in which women live.

THE SOCIAL CONTROL FUNCTION OF SOCIAL NORMS

While many different academic fields and subfields have explored the interplay between the social world and individuals' experiences of their bodies—including sociology, psychology, women and gender studies, ethnic studies, American studies, queer studies, and many others—the specific ways that social norms impose themselves onto bodies have profound implications for women who grow out their body hair. Feminist psychologist Leonore Tiefer has suggested that social norms also serve as a mechanism of social control and that "the problem is that the very existence of standards of normality breeds negative psychological consequences for those who deviate—that is known as the 'social control' function of norms."[1] That is, social norms do not function merely as passive suggestions for how people should groom, behave, and interact but rather as standards that (sometimes violently) separate those who conform and those "deviants" who do not. The norms themselves push people into conformity by denigrating those who deviate.

For women's body hair, evidence of this "social control" function of norms permeates women's stories about their body hair. Many scholars who study women's body hair have noted the vicious and systemic ways that deviance from the hairlessness norm creates negative responses in others.[2] Sociologist Merran Toerien and psychologist Sue Wilkinson describe women growing out their hair as something subject to "interactional sanctions," writing that pressuring women to shave is "an instance of the 'policing' of women's bodies within a narrow ideal of acceptability."[3] Further, Marika Tiggemann and Sarah J. Kenyon found, when asking high school and college women about their body hair practices, that "removing body hair is a practice so normative as to go mostly unremarked, but one which contributes substantially to the notion that women's bodies are unacceptable as they are."[4] Thus, not only is deviance from the hairlessness norm met with negative reactions but also the norm has been so successfully implemented across groups of women that many women do not even recognize or reflect on it at all.

Studying the process by which social norms become mechanisms of social control, communication scholars Marina Krcmar, Steve Giles, and Donald Helme found that social norms of idealized beauty impacted young women's self-esteem in that young women who perceived that their parents and peers valued thinness, particularly if parents made comments about their body appearance, had lower body esteem. More specifically, exposure to fashion, celebrity, and fitness magazines had a negative impact on women's appearance esteem, especially if they engaged in social comparison with other women.[5] Another study found that women described their appearance more negatively than men did, and were more prone to make divisive social comparisons compared to men.[6] Further, heterosexual women seem to bear a heavier burden with regard to internalizing norms of hairlessness, with one study finding that heterosexual women reported more negative feelings about body hair and more frequent body hair removal compared to lesbian and bisexual women.[7]

Thus, to reiterate the social control function of norms, women who were made aware of their body's so-called deficiencies, and those who directly compared themselves to others (and likely felt unsatisfied) ended up feeling worse about themselves. Further, women were typically encouraged to engage in more social comparison and to feel more ashamed of their natural bodies than were men. The social control function of norms also creates a context of ambivalence, rejection, and dissonance for women who violate social norms, raising questions about how women who grow out their body hair might react to their social contexts.

HAIR IN DIFFERENT SOCIAL CONTEXTS

In my conversations with nineteen cis women, one trans woman, and two nonbinary people who grew out their body hair intentionally, I asked them about the difference in social contexts for their body hair growth, listening carefully to their stories about how different social worlds created different norms for their bodies.[8] I specifically invited participants to reflect on their body hair in four different contexts: while at work, while at home, while alone, and with a partner. They mentioned a variety of different ways that social feedback operated and how they negotiated different levels of feeling self-conscious or aware of social judgments when in different contexts of their lives.

All participants dealt with social feedback about their body hair, ranging from stares and comments to more subtle forms of social regulation. Women described a wide variety of responses to their partners' judgments about their body hair, ranging from almost no worry at all about their partners' feelings to persistent fears of being rejected by new partners. Martina (fifty/Mexican American/bisexual) linked her acceptance of her body hair directly to whether her partner liked it or not: "Since my partner likes it and would choose it, I'm fine with it. I don't think about it anymore." Ula (twenty-two/Chinese American/bisexual) also felt comfortable with her body hair because her partner expressed comfort with it: "At home, I just wear whatever. It doesn't really matter. With my partner, I guess I'm so comfortable around him. Sometimes I'm like, 'Look, I'm hairier than you!' I'm just so comfortable." Similarly, Indigo (thirty-five/white/bisexual) said that her long-term partner has fully accepted her body hair: "I've been with my partner long enough where it's like, he's just accepted it as a part of me and it's okay. It's not a weird idea. It's what a relationship is supposed to be."

A few women felt a bit self-conscious with partners, particularly if they changed partners frequently and dated new people. Bijou (twenty-two/African American/heterosexual) worried about her partners judging her body hair and said that she felt self-conscious about it: "I'm not self-conscious with a partner unless they're a new partner. If they're new, then I would feel a bit self-conscious, but if we've been together for a while and are familiar with each other, then absolutely no self-consciousness." Jasmine (twenty-eight/Taiwanese American/heterosexual) expected new partners not to interfere with her body hair decisions: "With my partners, I won't comment on other people's body hair, and I don't expect the other person to comment on my body hair. If he does, as long as it's not negative, then it's fine."

Even though I did not specifically ask about family members' judgments of women's body hair, some participants nevertheless mentioned family members as regulating and commenting upon their bodies. Dana (thirty-six/white/queer) said that their family mocked and shamed them about their body hair at a family barbecue: "Sometimes when it's the summertime and I visit, they're teasing me about it, but I don't feel self-conscious because I like who I am." Gloria (fifty-six/white/heterosexual) noted that her nieces often stared at her body hair and wondered about it:

When my nieces were young—and now they're coming of age, like eighteen to twenty-one—I know they've looked at my body hair, but they were taught not to say anything or judge. At fourteen, though, I'm sure they judged me. Recently one of my nieces asked me about that, and she said that she remembered asking me about it when she was young. She asked why I did that, and I said that it was my body. Now she's at an age where she makes her own decisions about her body, and she gets it. She thinks I'm cool for having body hair.

Quinn (twenty-one/white and Native American/lesbian) said that she recently heard negative comments from her mother, especially now that she moved back in with her during the COVID-19 quarantine: "I'm living with my parents in the 'post-corona world.' I was sitting outside in the sun with my mom the other day, and she just looked over and said, 'Oh my gosh! Your legs are so hairy,' and I was like, 'Yeah!' They're attempting to judge me, but I don't care anymore." These stories of hearing negative feedback but not caring, or working hard to define oneself in relation to one's family, show the conscious work women did to distance themselves from shaming stories and microaggressions from family members.

By far, workplaces predictably served as the most constricting context for having body hair, particularly as women negotiated the politics of respectability and feeling judged for their perceived lack of hygiene when having body hair. Vera (thirty/Chinese American/heterosexual) said that working in customer service brought up feelings of self-consciousness on a regular basis: "I work in the customer service field, so like the first impression is pretty important before I open my mouth. People just looking at my face gives them confidence or not. I think eyebrows are probably the first thing they look for. I want to be judged favorably. I can't have any hair on my upper lips." Sequoia (twenty-three/white/bisexual), who worked from home, also feared being perceived as "dirty" if she worked in an office: "If they were to actually see my body hair, like a manager or something, I wouldn't want them to think that I'm really dirty. That's just how some people think. Some people in this town are judgmental and do look at people like me as dirty people, so that would be a fear in the workplace, what people might think."

The clear sense that workplaces demand gender conformity and have tight rules about gender appeared in women's stories about having body hair at work. Kalani (twenty-one/Sri Lankan American/Heterosexual) talked about the restrictions at work and how self-conscious she felt about her body hair there: "When I'm at work, I make every effort to shave whatever is showing, to have that shaved and clean and presentable. I think that's expected in a work environment. I've worked in an office environment, and I felt that I had to be respected. It's the respectable thing to do, to show up clean and shaved and everything." Quinn (twenty-one/white and Native American/lesbian) described her past job in food service as requiring hairlessness and strict adherence to grooming norms as a job requirement, which bothered her: "When I was working in food service, shaving was something you were actively encouraged to do, to maintain within a certain set of rules. It might be written into the job requirements to have short nails and no septum jewelry and no dyed hair. One of my coworkers at the restaurant had really long body hair, and she stood out and may have gotten bullied by management."

Some women felt unfazed by having body hair at work, saying that they could manage the potential for negative social judgment at their workplaces. Ainsley (twenty-three/white/heterosexual) said having body hair at work was easily manageable and not a big deal: "At work it doesn't affect me. I'm usually covered. If I'm wearing a dress, I have to be professional, so I'd wear stockings with it too. You can't see through the stockings unless you're super-duper close, and why would someone be super-duper close at work?" Eve (thirty-eight/white/lesbian), who worked as a yoga teacher, described body acceptance as part of her job: "At work I feel fine with it. I mean, it did take me a little bit of time to get used to it, but I teach yoga, so I have a following of people who like my classes, and if my hair bothers them, then find another teacher. I just feel like people look at me as unique and probably just comfortable with myself, so it makes me feel fine."

Only three women expressed very little concern about their body hair in any context, saying that they felt comfortable with it at work and at home, with a partner and while alone. Tori (twenty-six/Asian American/bisexual) described a general sense of confidence about her body hair: "I feel really confident all the time, basically. I don't really think about it, honestly, when I'm alone or with my partner, or really even at work. I guess the only time I really think about it is if I'm showering and my underarms have gotten to the point of getting those little rashes that are forming, but apart from that, I don't think about it at all. It's so normal to me now that I'm just happy with the way it is." She added that, even as a restaurant server, she often felt confident in part because she covered her body hair up: "I wear leggings which are pretty long, and I feel like most people don't look at their waiter's bottom shin, you know what I mean? And my underarm hair, I grow it out and normally wear a T-shirt or something, so they're not going to see it one way or another." Zara (twenty-two/white and Moroccan/queer) also felt comfortable across contexts, though she occasionally critiqued her facial hair: "I'm pretty much fine with any body hair that I have except my chin hairs. I wouldn't say I'm positive, but more neutral toward my body hair, like I look down and say, 'Oh OK, that's growing.' When I'm alone, I still feel uncomfortable with my mustache hair though." Olive (sixty-three/white/heterosexual) felt confident about her body hair after growing it for nearly fifty years, though she occasionally worried it would distract others: "I don't think there's any difference in context, although if I were going to wear a dress and be in front of people, I might put on tights or something just so it doesn't come up and become a distraction for anybody. But for me personally, I don't think I have much of an opinion about it. It's just normal."

WHO REGULATES WOMEN'S BODY HAIR

The question of who regulated women's body hair, and how people expressed social regulation of body hair, also appeared in women's stories about growing out their body hair. I asked them in an open-ended way about the various reactions they have received for having body hair. While some of these stories had predictable elements—mostly in the form of male strangers feeling entitled to regulate women's bodies—the fuller story of who regulated women's body hair came into view with a variety of scenarios where people commented upon their body hair. From athletic coaches to teenage girls at the beach, many people felt entitled to weigh in on women's body hair choices.

The most common category of people who engaged in social regulation of body hair was male strangers that women encountered in various public spaces. Martina (fifty/Mexican American/bisexual) described an encounter at the bar where she felt shamed about her body hair by men: "I've had guys say stuff at a bar or something, but I'm not interested in them. They're going to make connotations. I've had people, if I raise my arms and they see my underarm hair, do a double take, but I don't care." Eve (thirty-eight/white/lesbian) described a similar experience having boys in school comment on her body hair: "The reactions were usually from men, and like a couple times it happened when I was in school. I've never experienced it unless I was undressed, like in the pool in a bathing suit." Heather (forty/white/bisexual) remembered that men sometimes commented on her underarm hair when she went out to restaurants: "Once in a while someone will be surprised if I'm out in a tank top at a restaurant or something and they notice the underarm hair. I've seen some looks or just some staring for a minute from them. I guess it's a little uncomfortable."

Other women also discussed the ways men socially regulated body hair. One participant recounted how her athletic coach openly commented on her body hair and labeled it as disgusting. Ainsley (twenty-three/white/heterosexual) described her encounter with her coach and his willingness to label her body hair as "gross": "My coach was like, 'Ew, what are you doing?' He just thought it was gross. I did 'No Shave November,' which really wasn't much of a challenge for me. I went and showed my armpits to my coach, who is a male, and he was like, 'Oh, that's disgusting! Don't show that to me!' and I'm like, 'Oh my goodness.'" Her surprise at his reaction suggests that she expected him to be unaffected by it or not to care much about it and was taken aback by his reaction of disgust.

At times, the conflict between being with men who affirmed women's body hair *verbally* but then *behaved* differently felt upsetting to women. Ula (twenty-two/Chinese American/bisexual) remembered that boyfriends would tell her that they were fine with pubic hair and then degrade her for it: "As for my pubic hair, there were a couple partners I was with that thought I was really hairy, even though they said it was fine before." Zara (twenty-two/white and Moroccan/queer) remembered that some men she had been in relationships with had used body hair to prove their feminist politics but ended up being hypocritical about it: "One thing I've noticed from being intimate with people is that a lot of guys say they're OK with body hair and see it as a very easy way to show that they're progressive, but I've found that with men, if I've even spoken about it, they say, 'Oh, I'm OK with body hair.' I've noticed that they tend to do things later on that are quite bad." She went on to add, "They try to show they understand feminist issues, but then they're coercive, so on the easy feminist issue to support, they would rally behind it, maybe to gain my trust, but I've found that the men who don't talk about it until I've said something about it tend to be more genuine. If they don't say anything about it, then they *really* don't care. It's more of a nonissue if you don't say anything at all than if you say, 'It's OK, blah blah blah blah.' I know it's OK!"

Women strangers also served as a mechanism for the social regulation of women's body hair. Jasmine (twenty-eight/Taiwanese American/heterosexual) recalled a time before she transitioned when she was shamed for shaving her leg hair: "I'm not sure if anyone has commented on my leg hair before, except when I was in high school—that was before transitioning—I did shave my legs once, and I was a guy back then, and someone commented on it, and I think from her expression she was implying that it was very strange or something." Olive (sixty-three/white/heterosexual), too, remembered that teenage girls and female college classmates found her body hair problematic: "Probably the strongest reaction I've had was the teenage girls on the beach. They were just obviously shocked by it, but I think there might have been a hallmate or two in college who didn't appear to like it either."

Women family members also regulated women's body hair decisions as well. Dana (thirty-six/white/queer) recounted that their mother expressed disgust about their body hair even while generally accepting them as a person: "People like my mom have been disgusted almost, which is weird. She's come around now, but sometimes she still teases me about it. It's not like my mom doesn't love me and accept me. I think some people don't understand that body hair doesn't equal dirtiness or whatever. It's just natural." Sequoia (twenty-three/white/bisexual) remembered that women in her family joked about her body hair in pointed ways: "My family jokes about me and says stuff, but it never hurt my feelings. They joke that I'm a wildebeest or whatever, or they show me their hair, and I'm like, 'Oh well, look at mine!' and they're like, 'Whoa!'" Whether this joking and humor signaled some kind of acceptance was unclear.

Friends also served as a source of regulation of women's body hair, even while generally showing more acceptance than others toward women's body hair. Quinn (twenty-one/white and Native American/

lesbian) noticed that friends she had not yet come out to worried about her dating prospects because of her body hair: "I notice some friends will tell me, if I haven't come out to them yet, 'Oh my God! Dudes are gonna find that so gross!' or, like, my sister's boyfriend told me that it's gnarly, or my mom has told me that it's gross or unladylike." Kalani (twenty-one/Sri Lankan American/heterosexual) remembered her sorority sisters noticing her body hair: "I just recently graduated, but I was in a sorority, so they saw me with shorts on, not shaved and whatever. No one really commented because I think they were in the same situation, but they noticed."

At times, women's body hair also brought up issues about race and identity for them, signaling another way that social regulation impacted them. Vera (thirty/Chinese American/heterosexual), who came to the United States just before middle school, related that her body hair made her feel that she was confirming negative stereotypes of "fresh off the boat" status: "When I was in middle school, someone asked me, 'Do you shave?' And I was like, 'What do you mean? What is that?' I felt again like an FOB, 'fresh off the boat,' because I was already new to the country and not super comfortable in a new environment. I didn't want to be judged differently even though I am different from my accent and my English level. I was trying to fit in, but I was thirteen, and that's such a hard age." Ruby (fifty-eight/white/heterosexual), a Southern woman who voted for Trump, felt baffled by people's association with dirtiness and likened this to her various associations with people of color: "People just assume I'm unkempt or don't wash. I think that's a lot of people's first assumption, that they don't wash. I don't look Indian, and I'm not colored, so it's not a race thing, you know? I don't really get it." The linking of immigrants and people of color to abject bodies, and the fear of being seen as "dirty" in a racialized way, is notable here.

Traveling also brought up a variety of reactions and responses to body hair that participants did not experience when living in the United States. Casey (twenty-six/white/lesbian) said their time abroad in China made them understand their body hair differently: "When I was abroad, I was in China, and some Chinese people—obviously they didn't know if I was male or female because of my androgyny—were staring at me the whole time. Back then I had very long underarms, and they're just looking at me and my legs, and I felt, 'Oh they probably don't get that a lot.' I got comments like,

'Why do you do that? Why don't you just shave?' and I'm like, 'Because it doesn't work for me.'" Indigo (thirty-five/white/bisexual) also experienced reactions to her body hair while traveling in Thailand: "It depends on the environment. When I was traveling in Thailand, even the men have a lot less body hair typically, so I would get men coming up to me, pinching my unibrow, pinching my leg hairs, just in amazement and almost like curiosity because they didn't have it. . . . When I travel and do the backpacker thing, all body hair just goes wild. I'm just letting it grow out as it wants." This awareness of shifting social norms and social relations in different cultures also reveals the permeability and fluidity of how women's body hair is regulated and controlled.

ROLE MODELS FOR WOMEN'S BODY HAIR

In line with imagining the social regulation of women's body hair, I also asked women about who inspired them to grow out their body hair, and if they had any role models of women with body hair that they looked to when making decisions to grow out their body hair. Questions about supportive friends, family members, and acquaintances are crucial to this analysis because women's feelings of empowerment are often connected to exposure to feminist models.[9] My interviewees generated a surprisingly diverse set of role models from whom they first imagined body hair as an option for women.

Friends and partners helped women to consider body hair as attractive and natural and often served as a first role model for body hair on women. Quinn (twenty-one/white and Native American/lesbian) talked about her partner giving her a first glimpse of what having body hair might be like: "The gal I was seeing in high school, she didn't shave her legs in a while, and I thought that was pretty cool. I think I kind of wanted to impress her in some way and be like her." Martina (fifty/Mexican American/bisexual) remembered that her artist friends paved the way for her to start growing her body hair alongside them: "My friends who are artists are more radical, like, 'I don't care. I don't let anybody tell me what to do.' There's kind of a stigma with it too, like a hippie or sprout-eater or whatever. I don't care if that's what people want to say." Kalani (twenty-one/Sri Lankan American/heterosexual) said that her fearless best friend helped her make the decision to grow out her body hair: "My best friend will go like a year without shaving or waxing just because, even if she's intimate with people, she just doesn't care. When we were in high school, she just stopped, and I just thought, 'Yeah, why not?' It's not like anyone is seeing anything, not like it's summer."

Some participants talked about family members inspiring them to grow out their body hair as well, again situating older family members as models for how to bravely embrace body hair. Eve (thirty-eight/white/lesbian) drew upon the role models of her mother and grandmother for growing her body hair: "My mom and my grandma, they've always been like that, where they just don't focus on it. I just did not think anything bad about it growing up. I always thought it's natural and that's fine. I always thought of it as your own kind of decision. You shouldn't be focusing on what everybody else is doing." Conversely, Casey (twenty-six/white/lesbian) felt that their male family members—older and same aged—most inspired them to grow out their body hair: "Definitely my brothers, my dad, my uncles, and some of my cousins. It was definitely, 'Well if my brother can do it, why can't I do it?' So maybe that was in some way how it went. Why do I have to do it if that guy doesn't have to do it?"

Teachers and older women also occasionally set the stage for women to imagine body hair as a possibility for them. Gloria (fifty-six/white/heterosexual) remembered that she admired her teachers in high school and her professors in college for growing body hair: "There were a couple of teachers I worked for that I really admired. I thought they had good politics and they were good humans. I knew they didn't shave, 'cause you could tell. I thought, 'Hey, I can kind of get along with them. We have similar ideas, you know, I'll hang out more with them.'" Dana (thirty-six/white/queer) felt inspired by older women in the queer community with body hair: "I went to some gay pride back in high school and I remember seeing older women with body hair, and I was like, 'Oh, that's attractive, actually.' It's more accepted in the queer community. I think maybe that was the first time I saw that and thought, 'Oh, I don't have to shave because I'm also queer.'"

The broader cultural and geographical contexts women lived in also inspired them to grow out their body hair, as living in bohemian havens like Santa Cruz, California, or Asheville, North Carolina, meant that women had more acceptance around having body hair. Indigo (thirty-five/white/bisexual) felt inspired by classmates at the University of California, Santa Cruz, a notoriously progressive college campus: "There were just several hippie women, and this one woman was the same age as me at the time, but she had really hairy armpits, and she looked like the most gorgeous pixie fairy. It's just kind of something you see around more often, and so it was definitely easier, and I would notice like when I would go back to Southern California and visit, then I would choose not to shave and watch people recoil in fear." Sequoia (twenty-three/white/bisexual), who lived in Asheville, North Carolina, also felt that living in a town more open to body hair helped her to feel comfortable with her own body hair: "In Asheville, we have topless rallies and stuff like that, and the 'free the nipple' movement, so showing your armpit hair feels more normal to me. It's definitely rubbed off on me to just accept it more." This opening up of options and possibilities occurred through direct social modeling, much like any other social process for the body; when women are deprived of such models, they may not imagine visible body hair as possible.

While some women talked about people they personally knew as body hair role models, the vast majority of participants mentioned feeling inspired by celebrities or fictional characters in the media, particularly television and social media. Heather (forty/white/bisexual) first learned about women's body hair on a television show: "I kind of picked it up from a TV show. That was my inspiration. It's called *Vida* on Starz, kind of an LGBTQ drama series, where I first noticed it, and I was like, 'Oh.' It kind of enlightened me. I wanted to try it myself." Tori (twenty-six/Asian American/bisexual), too, felt inspired by a television show that made body hair more visible: "I remember watching somebody on *The Bachelor* a couple of years ago, and in one of her posts, she mentions she grows out her underarm hair, which is quite daring. I was inspired. I thought that was kind of cool."

Social media, from Instagram posts to blogs to Facebook posts, also provided a number of role models for growing body hair. Natasha (twenty-eight/white/bisexual) drew inspiration from a blogger who went braless as a political statement: "This blogger, Alexandria Droshenya, is a body positive female, and she fights for females' rights. She doesn't wear a bra because it feels uncomfortable, and she makes posts and pictures when she just has a shirt with no bra. She doesn't wear makeup, and she looks very nice. That inspires me." Zara (twenty-two/white and Moroccan/queer) talked about celebrities with armpit hair in the media as setting the stage for publicly showing armpit hair, even if it made her self-conscious: "When I saw people in the media growing out their underarm hair, like on the red carpet, like Madonna, I realized, 'That's like half of what I have.'" Ainsley (twenty-three/white/heterosexual) appreciated the visibility of people on social media posting about their body hair: "I am seeing a trend on social media too, and that wasn't the case when I first started [growing my body hair], so it was a little hard, but when I first started, I was feeling a bit nervous about it, but after the fact, I do see a lot of people on Instagram and whatnot."

Women identified the people who posed with armpit hair on Instagram as particularly brave and inspiring to them, as they made space for hairy women on social media. Jasmine (twenty-eight/Taiwanese American/heterosexual) said user-generated pictures on Instagram and Tumblr helped her to feel less judged about her body hair: "I've seen pictures on Instagram and Tumblr before, of people who didn't remove their body hair, and I thought that was really brave, just 'cause women are judged really harshly for body hair. I thought it was interesting how they would be willing to post it online." Bijou (twenty-two/African American/heterosexual) also felt that social networking sites made space for her to imagine being hairy: "The girls I follow on Instagram, they're the type that don't shave their body hair. They're the free-spirited types. I'm inspired by them because they seem to just not care what anyone thinks." She added, "I know that having body hair is kind of taboo and not wanted by most people, and they don't care about that. They're just being themselves and being free, so that's inspiring." Thus, both interpersonal role models and celebrity and (social) media role models impacted and altered women's understandings of body hair as appealing, "no big deal," or a symbol of power and autonomy.

WHOSE OPINIONS MATTER ABOUT BODY HAIR?

Though women talked openly about the various inspirations that they drew upon for growing out their body hair, they also reflected on whose opinion mattered most to them about their body hair. I asked them, "Whose opinion do you care about with regard to your body hair practices?" As a group of body hair rebels, each of them had decided to go against the cultural norm of women's hairlessness and to flagrantly disobey invisible and unwritten social rules about women's body hair. In doing so, they had to select whose opinions about body hair mattered to them and whose opinions to disregard.

Most significantly, women stated that their partners' opinions mattered most to them when deciding to grow out their body hair. Ula (twenty-two/Chinese American/bisexual) said that her partner's opinion mattered most to her because he physically saw her the most: "First and foremost, I care about my partner's opinion because he's the person closest to me that would see those areas, every single area of my body. After that, I don't really care about strangers seeing my body hair." Dana (thirty-six/white/queer) also echoed that their partner's opinion mattered to them: "My partner, their opinion matters too but also, they're happy with me being who I am, and that's nice." Martina (fifty/Mexican American/bisexual) shared that her partner's feelings mattered because of the time spent together: "I mean, my partner's opinion matters to me, the one that I spend the most time with. I can remember even in high school when I saw girls, some girls looked really good with bushy eyebrows, so the norm doesn't always have to prevail, even if you're looking for an attractiveness factor." Finally, Eve (thirty-eight/white/lesbian) cared about only her partner's (no gender mentioned) opinion, even if she disagreed with it: "I really just care about my partner. It doesn't mean I will take that opinion and do anything about it, but I do care about the opinion because it's not something that should break or change a relationship. I'd listen to why, because maybe it's not comfortable for them or whatever. It would just have to have a reason behind it, not just like, 'It looks gross on you, so I want it off.' That's wrong to say."

Several women cared about both their partners' and their friends' opinions about their body hair, widening the social circle even further. Vera (thirty/Chinese American/heterosexual) said that she did not care about strangers' opinions but definitely cared about her partner and her friends' opinions: "My partner, my friends, yeah, they matter. I have never had the experience where strangers or acquaintances say anything.

I don't really care about those people as much." Casey (twenty-six/white/lesbian) cared about their partner's and their friend's opinions at the same time: "My partner's opinion matters to me, and there's this guy, my brother's friend, he's in law school, and he had very long hair. He shaved his whole head and donated it, and he's going to start again. So I care about his opinion, like wow, you're not doing it for you, but for someone else. That's very unselfish, very beautiful." Quinn (twenty-one/white and Native American/lesbian), too, cared about her partner and friends simultaneously, noting that many of her close friends also had body hair: "I probably would care what my partners think, like if I was in a relationship and someone told me it was gross, I would be sad. I might shave and then resent them later for it. I also care about close friends and what they think. I'm lucky enough that most of my close friends either grow their body hair out or really don't care what other people do with theirs. I think if I had grown up in a more judgmental society or with a different set of friends, then maybe I wouldn't have grown out my body hair at all."

For some women, the circle of whose opinion they cared about widened even further, to people in positions of power over them or to family members. Gloria (fifty-six/white/heterosexual) said that her boss's opinion mattered the most to her, mostly for reputational reasons: "My boss's opinion matters. I once saw him looking at my legs, and he looked kind of revolted. I only care because I need money. Anybody else can piss off." While Gloria had a rather narrow sense of whose opinion mattered to her, Ainsley (twenty-three/white/heterosexual) identified her partner, friends, and family members as having opinions that mattered to her: "They've been so close to me. I know they're all pretty positive about it. It doesn't really affect me in that aspect. They're always there to make decisions with me, to look out for me. They'll tell me, 'Hey, you have spinach in your teeth' or something, whereas other people won't."

Several women said that *everyone's* opinion about body hair mattered to them, in large part because they lived in a culture that denigrated women's body hair. Bijou (twenty-two/African American/heterosexual) talked about the difficulty of caring so much about society's opinion of her body: "I care about my opinion, I care about my partner's opinion, and I also care about the opinion of society, because I live in society, and I don't want to deal with just being looked at differently because of it. I do feel like that sometimes." Heather (forty/white/bisexual) expressed self-consciousness about strangers seeing her pubic hair alongside worries about her daughter's opinion of her body hair: "I guess I care about strangers' opinions too, if I'm talking about not showing the bikini area hair. I don't want to get attention or be judged. I care about my daughter's opinion too. She wouldn't be judgmental or give me the look, but at the same time, I worry." Zara (twenty-two/white and Moroccan/queer) talked about how she *only* cared about the opinion of strangers but not anyone close to her: "For some reason, I care about how strangers feel. I already know that my friends don't care, because I wouldn't be friends with somebody who did care about my body hair, and the same goes for a partner. I already know what my mom thinks, and she's still gonna love me even if I'm the hairiest person. I guess that leaves only strangers, which is weird, because why do I care? I don't know." This inconsistency in whose opinions mattered, and how both strangers and friends had opinions that mattered, also showed the power of social norms and the wide net they cast in people's social lives.

That said, many women vehemently said that they cared *only* about their own opinion of their body hair and that no one else's opinion mattered. Lin (thirty-four/Vietnamese American/heterosexual) said that her own opinion was the sole criterion for growing body hair: "I really don't care about anybody's opinion when it comes to body hair practices. I'm a grown woman, and I support myself and pay my own bills, so I don't really owe anything to anybody." Ruby (fifty-eight/white/heterosexual) echoed that sentiment, saying that her choices were between her and God: "No one's opinion matters to me. I mean, you're gonna have your own judgment anyway, so who are you to judge me? God knows who I am." Sequoia (twenty-three/white/bisexual) also felt that she wanted to be beholden only to herself: "Pretty much mine is the only opinion that matters. If I feel the day comes and I want to shave my legs, someone shouldn't judge me. I don't want to hear, 'Why are you shaving it today and not yesterday?' I just feel different, and some days I might want to. So, pretty much, mine is the only one that truly matters for me."

Self-determination was a key part of how women saw their body hair choices, which meant that their own opinion mattered more than anyone else's opinion. Tori (twenty-six/Asian American/bisexual) resisted the notion of seeking approval from others about her body hair: "I don't really care about anyone's opinion, to be perfectly honest. I'm really happy with the way that I've grown out my body hair and everything. I feel like I don't need to tell anyone. I don't need anyone's approval, like I feel good about myself. It's nice when someone says, 'Oh good for you,' but at the same time, I don't need to hear it, because I'm happy with the way it is, so I don't need somebody else to approve or reject what I'm doing with my body, if that makes sense." Olive (sixty-three/white/heterosexual) also felt that her own opinion mattered most: "My own judgment and nobody else's is what matters. The only opinion that matters is my own." Indigo (thirty-five/white/bisexual) offered a slightly more complicated response, saying that she cared deeply about others' opinions and also that she did not care at all about others' opinions: "I guess I want to say that no one's opinion matters, but now I'm questioning myself about why I so obsessively pluck my face all the time, so I guess it's like I don't care about anybody's opinion when I've actually chosen to grow it out. That's a tricky one, but I care about everyone's opinion, so it's like everybody and nobody, everyone and no one's opinion matters."

MAKING THE SOCIAL WORLD

The social regulation of women's body hair—and the various ways that women took cues from their social environments—permeated women's narratives about how they made decisions about their body hair. Notably, though this group of women pushed back against the norms of women's hairlessness, they, too, struggled with feelings of ambivalence and unease, particularly when they confronted their partners' negative assessments. Even for those who rebelled against body standards and norms, they struggled with the sources of social control that intruded into the public and private spheres of their lives. Tensions between boldly declaring one's own choices regardless of others' opinions and social feedback and carefully weighing the voices and judgments of others saturated the narratives about the social world of body hair.

Further, the narratives in this chapter point toward the relatively vast array of social relationships that attempt to govern, dictate, and control women's bodies. In this chapter, women described a number of surprising influences on their body hair choices: men in bars, coworkers, strangers while traveling abroad, celebrities and Instagram influencers, a sibling's friend, acquaintances they knew superficially and briefly, bosses, ex-girlfriends, and many others. In this way, women outlined the ways that their bodies felt subjected to judgment and evaluation not just by their partners and families, which was heavily emphasized in chapters 1–2, but by an array of other people in nearly every corner of their lives. Whether sitting in a bar, walking down the street, interacting with colleagues at work, or scrolling through websites, women felt the pressures on them to conform to the hairless standard for women. Even while on vacation or while traveling in other cultures, women felt subjected to social judgment and regulatory control. Thus, body hair reflected not only the values of those in our intimate lives—particularly partners and family members—but also the values of the culture at large, particularly those communicated by religion, schools, and workplaces.

These narratives also serve as a reminder that having models for growing body hair matter, as women drew from a number of different kinds of inspiration for feeling brave enough to grow out body hair. They looked toward older women and online celebrities, friends and teachers, and, at times, even just the context of the progressive and body-friendly towns they lived in. When evaluating whose opinions resonated with them about their body hair, women outlined the conflicts they face both internally and externally. For some women, many people's opinions mattered, including those of strangers, while for others, that circle shrank down to their friends, family members, and (most often) their partners. Still more, a sizable number of women said, poignantly, that the only opinion that mattered to them about their body hair was their own opinion. In this way, even in a world where so many people wanted to weigh in on their choices, they found a way to value self-determination and autonomy over the clamor of voices telling them to remove their body hair. Perhaps this is the epitome of what we can hope for when imagining the interface between the self and the social world: even when many people want to dictate what we do with our bodies, we must radically work toward crafting a self that we want to be, valuing our own opinion above all others. To be ourselves in a world hell-bent on conformity and narrow-minded conceptions of gender is indeed a hard-won battle, enacted in the daily, mundane tasks of our lives.

8 |

"In the Revolution, We Will All Be Hairy"

Redrawing the Politics of Body Hair

You cannot buy the Revolution. You cannot make the Revolution.
You can only be the Revolution. It is in your spirit, or it is nowhere.

—URSULA K. LE GUIN, *The Dispossessed*

THE STORY OF WOMEN'S BODY HAIR IS A VOLATILE ONE. HERE, a portrait of bodies being produced by their cultural and social worlds, shaped and molded (or, more precisely, shaved and waxed), reveals bodies as performances and products. Embedded within the scaffolding of patriarchal, racist, misogynist, classist, and homophobic scripts, women's bodies show the cultural stakes of jockeying between stories of individual autonomy and social sculpting. Do women control their own bodies, or are they controlled by others? Do they make decisions as individuals, or do they merely select among predetermined options that all funnel toward patriarchal fantasies of women's bodies? Can women rebel against these frameworks, or does such rebellion also reveal the limitations of bodily freedom women have? Of course, individuals do not make choices about their bodies without an array of cultural roadmaps about which choices seem "good" or "moral" and which choices are available or choosable. In this sense, the material in this book pushes back against the neoliberal model of understanding women's bodies and instead argues for a more nuanced understanding of bodies as contested, playful, rebellious, and revolting. Put more succinctly, the intentions women have about their bodily choices matter.

In this final chapter of the book, I examine, through twenty-two interviews with body hair rebels, the question of how body hair connects to gender, power, and politics, particularly as body hair moves into an explicitly rebellious framework.[1] Unlike the previous two chapters on the emotions surrounding body hair and the social and relational frameworks of body hair, the material in this chapter is explicitly political and ideological, as women constructed their body hair choices within a staunchly conservative political landscape, at the peak intensity of the Trump presidency, and in the middle of COVID-19 and the Black Lives Matter protests of 2020. In order to better understand the contexts that women reacted to, this chapter begins with women's descriptions of how they saw women's body hair in the public sphere, followed by them imagining themselves as hairless. This exercise evoked descriptions of feeling unnatural, uncomfortable, and unsettled. Next, I include women's narratives about what they would say to younger and older women, along with men and those who shame women, about women's body hair, which revealed women's anger both about restrictions placed upon women and the denigration of bodily diversity in American culture. I also look at the ways that trans and nonbinary people rewrite the gendered stories of body hair.

In the second half of this chapter, I include narratives about how women perceive the difference between the body hair choices of white women and women of color, and how those of heterosexual women and queer women might differ. These descriptions illuminate the fault lines of social inequalities that play out on the body itself. I conclude the chapter by including passages of our conversations about the other types of body norms they resisted and by asking them to explain how they had been able to defy social pressures to become hairless. These meditations on how women imagined body hair as a political tool situate women's body hair as a form of resistance written onto the body. In this light, I offer a line from a poem by Denice Frohman: "i heard a woman becomes herself / the first time she speaks without permission / then, every word out of her mouth / a riot."[2] Defining the body on one's own terms, pushing back against the forces of bodily conformity, is a revolutionary impulse.

THE STORY OF WOMEN'S BODY HAIR
IN THE PUBLIC SPHERE

Women often turn to private forms of overt or hidden resistance when the rules of heteropatriarchy become overwhelmingly punitive toward nonconformists. Hair has long been one way that women enact resistance, with feminist-minded women showing more underarm hair than nonfeminists in order to engage in embodied resistance.[3] To situate women's body hair less as an individual experience and more as a cultural phenomenon, I asked women, "What is the story of women's body hair that you see in the public sphere?" Their responses helped to give cultural and political context to how they saw women's body hair being discussed or framed in popular culture and in the broader social culture. The notion of women's bodies as inherently not good enough, or deficient unless they conformed to very specific ideas about beauty, appeared immediately in women's responses. For example, Lin (thirty-four/Vietnamese American/heterosexual) lamented that women received messages from the public sphere about the narrow beauty ideals they must conform to: "I think women are bombarded with facts that they're not good enough, there are always some other products that could make them better. It's the idea that they are not beautiful enough and they should look ten years younger or lose ten pounds, the way women are objects to be seen a certain way and to be airbrushed into impossible images of conformity. The ideal woman is a Barbie!" Martina (fifty/Mexican American/bisexual) also felt this way, referencing Barbie specifically: "The same story is told about having a Barbie doll figure, a full bust and no butt. You've got to be clean shaven, like a baby's butt everywhere, and then if you're not, they'll Photoshop it out." Olive (sixty-three/white/heterosexual), too, noted that smooth skin was a requirement for beauty norms: "I guess the primary message is that they see this ideal of smooth legs, that you should do that." Dana (thirty-six/white/queer) also felt like body hair fit into a Barbie doll mold: "You can have long hair on your head but no arm hair, no leg hair, like a Barbie doll basically."

Women acutely felt the pressures put on them by companies that sponsored commercials and advertisements for shaving products and razors.

Ainsley (twenty-three/white/heterosexual) felt pressure for smooth skin from advertisements and Instagram: "Women have to be feminine, to be clean, smooth, and have natural baby skin, but that's not really all natural! Like, silky smooth skin in every single razor commercial, and like 99 percent of those models on Instagram all have everything shaven. It's annoying." Kalani (twenty-one/Sri Lankan American/heterosexual) felt irritated about how companies branded women's razors differently than they branded men's, and how women's razors worked less well: "Why are women's razors more expensive and shittier quality? There are pink and blue Schick razors, and I went online to buy the blue one, and the brand sent me a pink one. It's just very stereotypical. I feel pushed when I buy razors and stuff to buy the pink one." She also added, "Another issue I have with the story that I see is a lot of times these ads show women shaving who are actually waxed. You don't see anything! That's how much they don't want to show body hair. They don't even want to show their product being used accurately." Sequoia (twenty-three/white/bisexual) expressed concern with how companies framed body hair removal as compulsory: "I feel like it's a corporate thing, like, 'Go buy this,' and body hair removal is one of those things pushed on us, like, 'You're supposed to do this,' and I just don't like that as a woman. It's not *supposed* to be like anything because we're all so different."

Participants felt especially irritated at the hypocrisy of advertisements manipulating women into shaving even if they did not want to. Quinn (twenty-one/white and Native American/lesbian) described the irony of seeing advertisements encouraging women with body hair to start shaving: "It's a personal pet peeve. I keep getting commercials for this type of razor that's supposed to be 'body hair friendly' and it's the most kind of cognitive dissonant thing, where they're like, 'Body hair! It's OK if you want to remove it! Here's a commercial for how you can do so!'" Similarly, Indigo (thirty-five/white/bisexual) expressed concern about how mainstream media enforced shaving norms: "Shaving has been pawned off on women. I've seen ads that are kind of like trying to trick or embrace those women who don't want to shave. They're like, 'Keep a razor around just in case you might want to,' and they're just trying to get it at any angle they can." Casey (twenty-six/white/lesbian) was alarmed by the lengths that commercials were willing to go to seduce people into shaving: "I also see those commercials and they're very, 'Oh my god, here's this woman shaving.' It's so mundane. They even have this commercial where it's the father teaching the daughter how to shave, and he's like, 'You cut yourself, here you go,' and I'm like, 'How weird and intrusive is that?' If you're a father teaching your daughter how to shave, that's a no-zone. You're not a woman understanding the pressure on a woman to do this, and you're enforcing that."

Women also felt irritated and alarmed by the negative attributes they received for having body hair, as the public sphere portrayed hairy women as lazy or dirty. Natasha (twenty-eight/white/bisexual) noticed that hairy women were portrayed in highly negative ways: "Not all people understand that females can have their choice, and they say bad words, for example, if that person has hair, like, 'She's lazy, this person is stupid, this person is mad.' Maybe if you are a server in some nightclub, they will require you to wear skirts." Ruby (fifty-eight/white/heterosexual) also perceived being accused of dirtiness when she had body hair: "Women hear that they need to shave, that they have to shave because it shows that you're clean. Of course they would think I was the dirtiest person in the world." Bijou (twenty-two/African American/heterosexual) worried about others being judged for having body hair and saw body hair as a form of resistance: "If I see a woman on social media with visible body hair and I look through the comments, it's just not pleasant, because they're making fun of her and talking about her body hair, and it seems like a woman choosing to grow out her body hair is like an act of rebellion." Vera (thirty/Chinese American/heterosexual) noticed her generation's resistance to changing their minds about women's body hair: "Maybe in the younger generation they will be more rebellious and willing to change the status quo, but I think for how I grew up, my culture and the TV and social media, it will be hard for me to change my thoughts on it. It's just something I'm judged about."

A few women felt encouraged that times were changing and that future generations may not feel as negatively about women's body hair as their own generation. Gloria (fifty-six/white/heterosexual) reflected on her generation compared to her nieces' generation: "They won't even talk about it. They just go do their thing. It's not what I hear teens talk about like I did when I was younger." Zara (twenty-two/white and Moroccan/

queer) felt encouraged that people wanted to think more about women's body hair now: "There are a lot of different stories. There's one story that it's gross and that men don't like it. Then there's another story that people tell where they're asking why, and getting people to think more about hair, and people going into the history of how and why it became popular to remove women's hair."

IMAGINING HAIRLESSNESS

To access women's feelings about their imagined selves—and to upend the narrative of hairlessness as ideal—I asked women to imagine their bodies without any body hair and how that would feel to them. This exploration of a "possible self" has been used in some research because it explores how much people cling to their current identity as well as how much they may fear, embrace, or despise alternative identities.[4] Responses spanned between relief and a feeling of conformity to society's ideals to feeling weird, foreign, or strange in their own bodies. The overwhelming sense of "not being me" pervaded women's stories about not having body hair anymore.

Affirming the notion that stigma from body hair felt exhausting, some women responded that a hairless body would bring them relief from worrying about their body hair. Ula (twenty-two/Chinese American/bisexual) said that not having body hair would free her from worry: "It could be nice actually. I don't have to worry about shaving, and I don't have to worry about society seeing me a certain way, so it's a win-win." Heather (forty/white/bisexual) celebrated the reduction of labor put into the body if she could be hairless without effort: "If I could have no body hair and then not have to do any upkeep and not ever have to have it grow back, I think I would be open to that, but also at the same time it feels on the feminine side as well." Vera (thirty/Chinese American/heterosexual) also imagined that not standing out would free her from worry: "I wouldn't need to worry. I don't need to spend time to do anything or think about it. Wouldn't it be nice if we all just had the same style and we don't need to talk about this?"

A few women also affirmed that body hair was "no big deal" and that *not* having it would also be OK with them. Bijou (twenty-two/African

American/heterosexual) expressed that she would still be herself: "I think I would feel the same but smoother. It's a neutral reaction." Jasmine (twenty-eight/Taiwanese American/heterosexual) laughed and talked about her potential athletic performance and return to a childlike state: "I suppose I would be more aerodynamic because I like to exercise a lot. It's hard now because all the gyms are closed, but I suppose if I go biking or swimming or whatever else, it would be a little bit easier. I would be like a kid again, and honestly, I wish I could be a kid again just so I don't have responsibilities as an adult. Whether or not I'm hairless doesn't really affect either. We all grow body hair eventually so whatever."

Feeling like a child again was also mentioned by two other women, as they associated hairlessness with youthfulness. Eve (thirty-eight/white/lesbian) imagined herself as a little girl if she had no hair: "It just kind of feels like a girl, kind of like too bare. When you're a little girl, you don't have any hair, so it makes me feel like a child. I'm already short and young-looking anyway so it makes me feel kind of childish. When I have hair, it makes me feel more adultlike, like I'm making my own decisions." Lin (thirty-four/Vietnamese American/heterosexual) also described feeling uncomfortably childlike and infantile without body hair: "I would feel like a baby or a child, like children and babies tend to not have that much body hair."

For other women, imagining themselves without body hair allowed them to conform to more traditional femininity, which sometimes felt sexy or more intensely gendered as feminine than their current bodily presentation. Indigo (thirty-five/white/bisexual) thought a hairless body would be fetishized and sexy in an uneasy way: "I would feel naked, but in a weird way it would be a fetishized kind of sexy if I'm being honest. I would feel more socially accepted as sexy, so I would probably feel more sexy." Sequoia (twenty-three/white/bisexual) felt like having no body hair would automatically make her more feminine: "I guess I would feel girlier in a sense. I feel like I would probably dress up if I don't have the body hair, wear my sandals and maybe a sundress and all that. I go through times where I'll dress like a boy, I'll dress like a fisherman, I'll dress in so many different styles based on the day and how I feel, but it would make me go toward being more girly." Gloria (fifty-six/white/heterosexual) said that not having body hair would change her perception of herself and make her feel cleaner: "Fresh and clean but high maintenance. I'm a fat old woman, but if someone does a wax, then it's like, 'Oh this feels really good,' but then after, when it's prickly, I hate it, so I just want to let it grow." The status of being a body hair rebel was not without ambivalence and internal conflict, as the appeal of conventional beauty standards still appeared in women's stories about body hair.

That said, the vast majority of women imagined not having body hair as weird, artificial, and foreign to them, likening it to being in a body that did not feel like their own. Tori (twenty-six/Asian American/bisexual) talked about the strange physical sensation of not having body hair: "It seems a little weird, to be honest. I'd be really smooth, like I'd fall out of bed or something. I've done it before, and I just didn't like it. It felt really fake to me, if that makes sense, just not natural. I just felt slick but not in a good way." Kalani (twenty-one/Sri Lankan American/heterosexual) likened not having body hair to changing her skin color and feeling disoriented by it: "This might be a weird analogy, but if I were to change my skin color and wake up tomorrow and be white, I don't care to be that at all. It would be extremely weird and uncomfortable. I don't know that I'd like that." Similarly, Quinn (twenty-one/white and Native American/lesbian) felt that if she had no hair, she would be performing a kind of femininity that felt depressing and uncomfortable to her: "Whenever I get into a dress, I feel really uncomfortable. I feel like I might look nice to other people and they might like it, but I would feel deeply not myself, you know? Like I'm just putting on a veneer or something that I'll be very happy to yank off later. But I think for body hair, because it's not something you can just yank off, it's something you kind of have to remove. I think I'd be really sad to shave it off."

The notion of missing one's own body hair also appeared in participants' narratives about hairlessness. Zara (twenty-two/white and Moroccan/queer) related to Kim Kardashian's public discussion of missing her body hair after lasering it off: "Kim Kardashian was a hairy person before she got all her hair removed, and she has said that she regrets lasering away her baby hairs because she thought it was such a youthful appearance, and she missed having those. I think the idea of missing my body hair if I was able to get it removed deterred me from doing that." Dana (thirty-six/white/queer) also talked about their body hair helping them to feel more genuinely human: "I would feel like an alien. Are we not human? Do we not have hair? Yeah, I wouldn't feel as human. Are you going through chemo or something? We have hair naturally on everywhere, so if you didn't have it, I think it would feel weird too. When I feel hair, it makes me feel human." Olive (sixty-three/white/heterosexual) said she would strongly dislike a return to hairlessness: "I can remember that shaving was an artificially smooth feeling. I can remember that physical sensation, but I don't think it was anything positive, really, because I was always aware that it was starting to grow out and get prickly almost immediately."

Feeling sickly or unwell also appeared in women's descriptions of hairlessness. Ainsley (twenty-three/white/heterosexual) likened hairlessness to having cancer or dying: "That would be horrible. I know a girl that has no body hair, and everyone thinks she has cancer. People are more talking about you if you don't have anything than if you have body hair, like they're like, 'Oh my god, you have cancer, this girl is dying.' I'd rather have hair than not have hair." Natasha (twenty-eight/white/bisexual) also felt that not having hair felt unsettling: "It would be like I don't have some part of me, like a person with a disease like alopecia who doesn't have hair. It wouldn't feel natural."

Poignantly, imagining hairlessness also elicited feelings of fundamentally betraying oneself or attacking one's own core self. Casey (twenty-six/white/lesbian) imagined not having body hair as a declaration of war on themselves: "Very weird, very strange, that's not me at all. I would feel—I'm getting flashbacks here—it's like going to war with my body all the time. Am I going to cut myself? Is this rusty? Is this old? Is this a new one? How do I do it? Am I going to sit? Where am I going to sit? How am I going to do it? Is it going to go down the drain? I feel like it is such a process to wake up every day and do that, that I wouldn't be able to. It feels very strange to me." Martina (fifty/Mexican American/bisexual) stated that the core of herself felt like a hairy person: "I don't think in my dreams that I'm hairless. I have body hair. I'm *me* in my dreams. Unless it started falling out—that's the only way that being without body hair is going to happen."

In order to access women's sense of generational and gender differences about body hair, I asked participants a series of questions about what they would tell different groups of people about women's body hair. I specifically asked them, "What would you tell younger women about body hair based on your own experiences and beliefs?" I also asked them about what they would tell older women, men, and those who shame women about their body hair. Responses revealed a wide variety of ways that women expressed defiance, outrage, and protectiveness about women with body hair, alongside confrontations about the damaging consequences of body shaming.

Women urgently wanted others to know that body hair was not unfeminine or incompatible with being a woman. Bijou (twenty-two/African American/heterosexual) noted that men should better understand that body hair and femininity go hand in hand: "I think I'd like them to know that having body hair isn't unfeminine. They should probably try to disassociate the two in their minds, and they should be more accepting of women who choose to grow out their own body hair and not be mean to them. Having body hair doesn't make you unfeminine, and it doesn't mean that you don't take care of yourself." Jasmine (twenty-eight/Taiwanese American/heterosexual) wanted younger women to know that body hair did not make them less feminine: "If guys think you should remove your hair 'cause it looks more feminine, then you should tell them it really isn't any of their business and they need to be more educated on how women's bodies actually are instead of what they think they are." Lin (twenty-three/Vietnamese American/heterosexual) wanted younger women to understand that pubic hair had a purpose and that removing it did not make women more feminine: "Your pubic hair is there for a reason. I wouldn't go crazy about removing the pubic hair down there as much. Men don't care either. They just care about what's for dinner or what's for lunch."

A few women immediately drew attention to the idea that men (boyfriends and husbands, in particular) still love women if they grow out body hair. Ainsley (twenty-three/white/heterosexual) noted that, while women could sometimes use shaving as a tool of seduction, they should not worry about body hair in the long run while dating men: "With the whole boy thing, they'll understand. They will get through it. You can do what I do. You can shave the first one or two times, and then they fall for you, and they're the ones that are going to be stuck with you. You have a lot more leverage over them." She went on to say to older women, "Who are you trying to impress? You shouldn't have to worry every day that if I don't trim myself my husband's going to leave me. You've got a lot of problems if that's your issue!" Ruby (fifty-eight/white/heterosexual) framed growing body hair as no big deal to men: "Do you love me, or do you love my body hair? You love all of me. You're not judging me on my body hair. What if I'm a fabulous cook or a fabulous lover? Would that bother you if I had a big pouf down there between my legs? You know, it's all about perception."

Nearly all of the participants felt adamantly against people shaming women about their body hair, talking about the importance of pushing back against those who degrade women about their bodily choices. Quinn (twenty-one/white and Native American/lesbian) advised younger women to fight back against shame and not overprioritize others' feelings: "It's nothing to be ashamed of. It's literally just hair growing out of your body, much like your eyebrows. People are going to try to make you feel bad about a lot of things in your life, and if you try to make everybody else happy, service everybody else's needs above yours, then at the end of the day, you're going to end up feeling miserable and unheard." Ula (twenty-two/Chinese American/bisexual) said to people who shamed women about their body hair: "I would tell them, 'Just because some other women don't need this, you can't categorize someone. She doesn't have to shave just because she's a woman.'"

Along these lines, several women frankly stated that no one else should be concerned about their body hair and that it was none of their business. Zara (twenty-two/white and Moroccan/queer) felt unhappy at the idea that others would care or judge her body hair and compared this to broader issues with reproductive justice: "It's not anybody's business. It's kind of the same argument for things like being pro-choice, like it's my body, my choice. The same goes for body hair. At the end of the day, why does some random person who doesn't even know me take offense to me having body hair? Why is that something that they need to spend energy being mad about or uncomfortable with?" Kalani (twenty-one/Sri Lankan American/ heterosexual) wanted men to know that women removed hair from more parts of their bodies than they knew about, together with the fact that body hair was none of their business:

> We shave a lot more places than they think, like our faces, for sure! Some of them don't know. They have no idea. But mostly it doesn't affect them at all. If I want to keep my yard overgrown, like maybe you should have a say in that because that's also your neighborhood, but this being my body or any other female's body, you don't have a say in how someone decorates their front yard even if it's your neighborhood. I know some people who would say, "I don't want to have to look at that, I don't want to see that." Well, then don't look that way. Go outside if you don't want to see it.

Vera (thirty/Chinese American/heterosexual) also believed that body hair was no one else's business: "It's none of your business. If you want to shave your hair, you can shave your *own* hair, but other people's hair is not your problem."

Most commonly, women gave advice to others that emphasized personal choice and personal happiness, especially individual control over bodies. Eve (thirty-eight/white/lesbian) wanted women to make choices based on personal happiness and feeling natural: "Do what makes you happy, what makes you feel more like yourself. If it would make you happier having it off, or make you more confident, whatever is going to make you feel better about yourself and more confident is the right thing to do." Dana (thirty-six/white/queer) also emphasized happiness in their advice to younger women: "Do whatever makes you comfortable, but also know that everybody has hair and it's fine. You're still beautiful. Whatever makes you more comfortable and happy, it has to be your choice." Sequoia (twenty-three/white/bisexual) wanted younger women to make decisions based on themselves rather than catering to others' needs or whims: "I have a little sister who just turned fifteen. I try to tell her it is fully fine, don't waste your time getting ready for boys and all that. Do everything you do for yourself, even your body hair and your appearance." Finally,

Gloria (fifty-six/white/heterosexual) wanted younger women to know that they could change their minds about their body hair and that their own happiness mattered most: "Do what you want, when you want, and you don't have to commit to stick fully with that. Things can change over time."

Women also emphasized that growing body hair was fun, enjoyable, and part of making their own decisions about their bodies. Olive (sixty-three/white/heterosexual) advised younger women to play by their own rules with regard to their bodies and body hair: "I would tell them that it's theirs to do what they want to, and it's fun to experiment with it. Don't listen to others. You can make your own decisions. You don't have to follow anybody else's rules, especially if it's someone who's going to make money off of it. That's the crazy thing—the promoters of shaving legs are the people who make the tools to remove the hair." Tori (twenty-six/Asian American/bisexual) agreed that women should not feel pressure to change their bodies: "They shouldn't conform. They should do whatever they want to do, whatever makes them happy, and not worry about what other people think. As long as you're staying healthy and being hygienic, that's all that matters." Indigo (thirty-five/white/bisexual) said that hair should be playful and fun: "Always do what you want. Let it go a little bit. Let it go, and let it grow!" Finally, Casey (twenty-six/white/lesbian) argued that self-love, fun, and aligning the body with personal beliefs matters most: "If a kid came up to me—a female kid—and said, 'Oh you have beautiful hair, why don't you shave?' I would say, 'I just love myself. I love who I am.' I care for the environment. That's really a big part of it too. Those are all my personal beliefs. I would say, 'Do what you want, period.'"

DETACHING BODY HAIR FROM GENDER: TRANS AND NONBINARY NARRATIVES

Three participants talked at length about the way that body hair interacted with their gender identity as nonbinary and trans, as two people I interviewed identified as nonbinary and one identified as a trans woman. In particular, these participants highlighted the importance of better understanding the ways that body hair becomes encoded as masculine or feminine, and how trans and nonbinary individuals can upend that dichotomy and challenge the gendering of body hair altogether. I asked each of them how there might be different things at stake for trans and nonbinary people for body hair when compared with cis women. I also asked them to talk about their own stories about body hair and how it connected to their gender identity over time.

When I asked Casey (twenty-six/white/lesbian) how body hair fit into gender for them or for others, they outlined the ways in which they identified strongly with women but also felt freer than most women by identifying as nonbinary and growing out their body hair: "I always think of women as this strong force. I consider myself, if this makes sense, a *woman* politically. Anything to do with women, I'm on board with that, because obviously, why wouldn't I? Sometimes when I see women and they're like, 'Oh, I'm so jealous of your hair,' and I've heard that before, like, 'Oh, you don't shave,' and I'm like, 'Well, you don't have to, either, if you don't want to. No one's forcing you to. No one's saying you have to.'" Casey added that their nonbinary identity helped them limit social constraints to feel more expressive with their body: "I just feel, as nonbinary, I can fit, I can squeeze into this otherness, and I don't have to say, 'Oh yeah, I'm a woman but am accepting this norm. I'm doing this so I can be more womanly.' As a nonbinary person, I can express myself in this certain light because I fit in better, I guess, than other women." When I asked Casey if they perceived a higher risk to grow body hair as a nonbinary person compared to a cis woman, they said, "Yeah, I'm definitely not accepting this weight on me. That's how I feel. I'm not accepting this weight of 'Oh, I'm a woman, so I have to be like this or look like this.' When I'm nonbinary I can just skip that, or I can be free to be who I am without accepting the consequences of being a woman. It opens up more freedom for my body and my aesthetic choices. I'm not as harassed." When I spoke with Casey about their clothing and hair choices, they described the freedom they felt in their aesthetic choices: "I don't really wear a dress, but if I wanted to, or if I wear capris or something more femme, because it fluctuates, or because it's more comfortable, like a tank top, I might get a few more stares, but I like how I dress and how people perceive me. I'm able to fit in more."

Dana (thirty-six/white/queer), who identified as nonbinary, spoke about how body hair connected to their nonbinary identity: "I'm just in the middle. I don't think body hair is necessarily male or female, so I don't feel like I need to get rid of it. I'm human. We all have hair. I guess I have female body parts, at least in the lower half, so I do feel like I am female still. I don't take hormones or anything like that." When I asked them how body hair might differ for someone who's nonbinary compared to cis women, they critiqued the dichotomous treatment of body hair: "I've heard a lot of people say that body hair sort of balances their gender because I guess it is more seen as a male thing, and to be born as female means to not have body hair. To have body hair as a female would make you be portrayed as more male. I don't necessarily agree with that, but I know that people do feel that way." Dana added that they felt less pressure to shave as a nonbinary person compared to a cis woman: "I feel like we're kind of an in-between, with more flexibility and choice in that way. I almost feel bad for [cis women]. They're tricked into feeling that they need to shave to make themselves look and feel beautiful, which is not true."

Jasmine (twenty-eight/Taiwanese American/heterosexual), who identified as a trans woman, reflected on being born male and transitioning into being a woman. She reflected on how body hair played into her gender transition: "I got a lot of hair growth on my arms before I transitioned, so I got electrolysis on my underarm hair. My leg hair I stopped actively shaving quite a few years ago. I do it intermittently, mostly to go biking or swimming or something." After deciding to let her body hair grow out, Jasmine realized that to be a woman did not mean that she had to be hairless: "In the beginning of my transition, I actually wanted all of my hair to be gone. Later on, that wasn't the case." She added that at first, she felt like being a woman meant that she must be totally hairless, but she then changed her perspective. Jasmine also believed that there were different things at stake between trans women and cis women and that having body hair as a trans woman possibly played into negative stereotypes of trans people: "There's that stereotype about trans women just being 'men in dresses,' or bearded men in dresses or something like that, which is obviously not true. If someone sees a trans woman without her hair removed, maybe other people will think she falls into that stereotype, unfortunately."

Jasmine talked about how, in order to cope with these caricatures, she developed the ability to choose her battles carefully and became more insulated to criticism: "People should just be more polite. I could engage in conversation, but most people don't care for actual conversation. It's just a lot of insults or something like that. I just fight my battles in a sense, choose my battles." Jasmine had advice for other trans women who wanted to grow their body hair: "If you think women don't have body hair, then I can understand, because I grew up like that before, but you shouldn't feel pressured to remove your body hair if you don't want to. Even for other hairy parts of your body, if you want to get rid of your facial hair too, that's fine, and if you don't, that's also fine, 'cause some people have peach fuzz or something and it's not a big deal." She went on to add, "Women come in all shapes and sizes, and if the fear of not being the right kind of woman is stopping you from transitioning and being yourself, I don't think you should be scared to do that. It's really hard 'cause society pressures women to look at certain way, and it can be harder on trans women. I just went for it despite not knowing what I would look like in the end. I just had to stop caring as much about what other people think." This defiant and gender-expansive approach to body hair gives nuance to the interplay between self, society, and gender roles.

RACE, CLASS, AND SEXUALITY IMPLICATIONS

In the same way that gender identity factored into participants' descriptions of their body hair choices, intersections of race, class, and sexuality informed the kinds of choices people made about their body hair. I asked women two questions about social identities and body hair: "How do choices about body hair differ between white women and women of color and between wealthier women and poorer women?" and "Are there different things at stake for queer women who grow body hair compared to heterosexual women?" Women explained their feelings and beliefs about social identities, bodily autonomy, and the stratification of women along race, class, and sexuality lines.

By far, the most common response to these questions about hair being experienced differently by different groups of women highlighted the notion that body hair on women of color often unfairly threatened their sense of respectability, particularly given that women of color often felt degraded about their bodies in general. Gloria (fifty-six/white/heterosexual) commented on her perception of the different pressures on white women versus women of color:

> I'm a white working-class woman; that's who I am, and that's what I got. I feel like I often am allowed to make more choices about what I do. I think in communities of color, particularly African American communities as well as Middle Eastern cultures, you have to turn out looking prim and trimmed up, cleaned up, perfectly groomed, patted down, and I feel like that is a sort of pressure to show who you are and what you can do, and that you are ably human. As a white woman, I have been afforded a privilege to be able to choose whether I do that or not.

Quinn (twenty-one/white and Native American/lesbian) echoed this, saying that women of color experienced worse backlash against their body hair than did white women: "For any behavior that could be penalized for women of color and white women, women of color are gonna get more whiplash and hit back against it worse. I have different coarser, darker, curlier body hair than my sister who is blond. I had a roommate who was from India, and I know that she was always really encouraged to remove her body hair because, like mine, it's dark and coarse." Women of color also faced threats to perceptions of their femininity based on having body hair. Bijou (twenty-two/African American/heterosexual) reflected on her experiences as a Black woman and how she felt pressured to overcompensate for being seen as less feminine: "I know that women of color—I'm a woman of color—we have coarser hair, and I know that women of color, especially Black women, sometimes we are seen as not as feminine as other types of women. I think sometimes we try to overcompensate for that, and maybe that might lead to Black women partaking in hair removal activities more often."

Participants also noted that women of color typically had more visible body hair than white women did and that darker hair could become more stigmatized. Vera (thirty/Chinese American/heterosexual) talked about women of color having visible body hair and being judged more harshly: "White women's body hair is in a lighter color, and unless you dye it, it's not visible, versus people of color, where it is very visible. People of color are judged harsher. It's not just about body hair." Jasmine (twenty-eight/ Taiwanese American/heterosexual) linked race and class with an analysis of women of color and poorer women being perceived as dirtier when they had body hair: "For poor women, they won't have as many resources, and they might be judged more harshly because if they don't remove their hair, people will end up thinking that the hairy body is dirty, and they will be judged because of it. For white women [versus] women of color, it might be the same thing, because most of the people in the minority group are also poorer, so they won't have as many resources, and they'll be seen as dirty." Eve (thirty-eight/white/lesbian) felt that women of color received harsher judgments than light-haired white women because of the visibility of the hair: "I would think they would get made fun of more because they have darker hair, so they'd stand out more." Zara (twenty-two/white and Moroccan/queer) also felt that the visibility of women of color's body hair, combined with the lack of role models for women of color growing out body hair, led to more stigma: "Women of color tend to have more body hair sometimes, or it could just be darker because if they have darker hair instead of blond hair, that definitely plays into it. A lot of celebrities I saw growing out their body hair were white. I think that comes into play a lot."

While women gave a wider variety of responses about race, their responses about class tended to focus more on the consumeristic framework of the specific amount of money women had to pay for shaving products and treatments. They largely left out a more systemic analysis of how class shaped options, social perceptions, and consciousness about the body more broadly. Lin (thirty-four/Vietnamese American/heterosexual) immediately referenced the high price of salon visits: "I think for wealthier women, they can afford salon visits. They could have more things done to them, like threading a certain part, while some of the poor women might use an old razor blade over and over again." Tori (twenty-six/Asian American/bisexual) struggled to imagine race and class differences but eventually noted the ability to pay for body hair removal for wealthier women: "I feel like it's younger women that go to these waxing places and are really intense about having body hair removed. Wealthier women go there." Martina (fifty/Mexican American/bisexual), who had no opinion about race at all, offered an immediate analysis of how class impacts ability to pay for hair removal services: "I'm sure that wealthier women have more expendable income to get treatments." Sequoia (twenty-three/white/bisexual) added that wealthier women had more money than (what she called) "normal" women: "Probably it's quite expensive to go to the salon and get a European wax and things like that. Normal women would probably stay at home and use a razor."

A few women noted that wealthier women faced more social pressures for total hairlessness and also paid a steeper social price for not removing their body hair when compared to poorer women. Natasha (twenty-eight/white/bisexual) imagined that wealthier women had to invest more in their image and were therefore burdened by their social status: "I think poor women are in a better situation, because wealthier women are connected to social media, and they have to be in different conferences at work, but if they can do it in pants, it's OK. But if she has some disease on her legs or doesn't want to show her legs, it's more difficult for a wealthier woman. People can say, 'She has so much money, and she doesn't even want to go to the salon!'" Ainsley (twenty-three/white/heterosexual) compared the grooming expectations for wealthier and poorer women by noting the burdens on wealthier women: "I feel like the wealthier you are, the more expected you are to groom and to have different resources like laser hair or wax or super nice razors or people doing it for you, with your pedicure or whatever. For lower-class people, not that they don't care about their appearance, but sometimes they're super busy. The working class has a whole bunch of stuff going on and sometimes can't do that, can't afford those expensive treatments, so the working class is more relaxed about it." Again, the lack of structural analysis and class consciousness about why different bodies feel burdened with different aesthetic expectations seemed notable here, as being "busy" as a working-class person did not link up with an analysis of social class as a system of privileges and disadvantages.

In contrast, structural inequalities appeared more as women recognized the different conditions of women's jobs and labor playing into perceived class differences. Quinn (twenty-one/white and Native American/lesbian) noted that there were different expectations on her working a manual labor job than for professional jobs: "I've had a lot of blue collar, physical jobs. I think shaving is less of a priority when you're doing a lot of manual labor jobs. You're usually wearing more clothing, and you're not selling yourself as a product, but more as your time and your labor, so you don't have to polish yourself up as much. But if you're working at a higher-salaried job, like at an office, and you're of a higher class, then there's almost like an insidious need to maintain appearances in some way, so you might even catch harder flak if you don't shave."

In their responses about the different stakes for queer and heterosexual women, women tended to imagine that queer women would be in a community more accepting of body hair than heterosexual women. Quinn (twenty-one/white and Native American/lesbian) reflected on her friendships with heterosexual and queer women and how the queer women cared so much less about their body hair: "I think for straight women, they're also dealing with that layer of a lot of dudes don't know that women can grow body hair, and so that's probably another battle that has to be waged within relationships. Men do really care! I've found it really almost kind of liberating when I'm hanging out with a bunch of other queer people and we tend to really not care about body hair at all." Similarly, queer women were also seen as simultaneously more chastised for their body hair and freer to have body hair, leaving an unresolved tension. Heather (forty/white/bisexual) highlighted this tension: "I think queer women are probably judged more. I think they're judged more based on that, but they're also more liberated to do what they want to do and not follow the social norms. As far as body hair, I feel like they're more liberated to do what they want and not care about what people think or what the social norms are or being judged on them."

The belief that having body hair signaled to others a queer or lesbian identity also appeared in women's narratives. Gloria (fifty-six/white/heterosexual) described growing up with lots of queer people and having her body hair associated with lesbian identity: "Half the time I show up and I've got hairy legs, and I might even have Birkenstocks on, somebody's going to think I'm a lesbian, you know? I didn't care about that, but I have thought about that. I think society sometimes links those two together." Dana (thirty-six/white/queer) wondered whether only queer women grew leg hair out and felt that the queer community was more open to women's body hair: "I would think that maybe only women that were queer would not shave, just because straight people want to please the guy in some way. I think in the queer community, it's definitely more acceptable to present however you want to present with hair. With straight women, it's almost a culture of shaving their legs or having smooth armpits." Indigo (thirty-five/white/bisexual) agreed that queer women had more freedom to express themselves with body hair: "For some of the butch women I knew, it was like all of a sudden they were just so free to present themselves with their leg hair all of a sudden." The tangled associations women had with social identities and body hair revealed a muddled picture of freedoms and constraints patterned chaotically along race, class, and sexuality lines. Tensions between structural and individual readings of inequalities, and ability to recognize pressures on different groups of women about their body hair, highlight some of the political undercurrents of body politics.

USING THE BODY AS A FORM OF RESISTANCE

Resisting body hair norms also went hand in hand with using the body for other forms of social and political resistance. For example, in previous research, those who identified as feminist reported less of a drive toward thinness, fewer eating disorders, a more public sense of using their bodies as a tool of resistance, and a better impression of their bodies than women who did not call themselves feminists.[5] Thus, in tandem with growing body hair, women also engaged in a wide variety of other forms of revolt with their bodies. To better understand this, I asked women, "What other norms related to the body do you resist?" Responses ranged from small aesthetic choices that they consciously made to delineating their entire identity—as a fat woman or a trans/nonbinary person, for example—as a form of rebellion. Women imagined their bodies as rebellious by valuing their natural bodies, fighting back against patriarchy with their bodies, or by choosing to make modifications to their bodies that emphasized their autonomy, personality, and individuality.

Most commonly, women identified their clothing choices as a form of personal rebellion, particularly when they rebelled against typical kinds of "feminine" clothing. Olive (sixty-three/white/heterosexual) described her aesthetic choices as rebelling against restrictive and stereotypically fashionable clothing: "Fashion, hairstyling, dyeing, and jewelry—I don't do jewelry. Heels? Never! I'm just very practical, and I wear gardening clothing a lot. We have a farm, and I dress like a farm girl. It feels great, and I'm really proud of it." Natasha (twenty-eight/white/bisexual) also signaled that she felt pride in embracing practical and down-to-earth clothing and aesthetic choices, particularly as she reimagined self-love: "I just wear unisex and oversized clothing because it's more comfortable. I don't do too much. I don't sit in the bathroom and do makeup and masks and waxing. I just clean myself very fast. To look better for someone else doesn't mean you love yourself. You love yourself if you are eating healthy foods, if you are doing exercises, wearing comfortable clothes."

In particular, women described not wearing a bra as particularly freeing and rebellious. Quinn (twenty-one/white and Native American/lesbian) talked about enjoying not wearing a bra even though it caused tension between her and her mother: "This one might even be more of a stickler between me and my mom, but I don't wear a bra. I've been living at home, so I'll wear a tank top like a second skin now. She'll be like, 'Dude, I can see your nipple,' and I'm like, 'I mean, I have them. I'd be more concerned if you didn't see them.'" Quinn went on to describe her bond with friends over not wearing a bra: "It's kind of a well-known thing for my friends. My friends and I don't wear one. I think I have a lot of room to get away with it because I don't have boobs that are big or that physically hurt me." Bijou (twenty-two/African American/heterosexual) also embraced the concept of not wearing a bra as a personal form of bodily resistance: "I don't wear a bra most of the time. I don't even think I own any bras right now. It's definitely a 'I feel more comfortable' thing. Bras are very uncomfortable, and if it's not in a professional setting, I don't feel the need to wear one. I don't think I have to, and I don't." Ainsley (twenty-three/white/heterosexual) also refused to wear a bra in most settings: "I don't usually wear bras. I'm lucky, like I'm littler, like I get away with it, whereas some people it would be a little bit harder to." Eve (thirty-eight/white/lesbian) linked her refusal of bras to her general rebellious hippie aesthetic: "I dress how I want to dress, like a hippie. I like kind of not wearing a bra."

Several women also explicitly mentioned not wearing makeup as another form of resistance. (I noticed, as the interviewer, that almost none of the participants wore any makeup for our interview together.) Ula (twenty-two/Chinese American/bisexual) experimented with not wearing makeup and eventually decided to keep doing it as a form of resistance: "I don't wear makeup. I was wearing a lot of makeup when I started working at my current company, but then I noticed a lot of women didn't, and it was OK for me not to. I didn't look absolutely hideous without it." Zara (twenty-two/white and Moroccan/queer) also has started to wear makeup much less often, with a few exceptions: "I don't really wear makeup. I only fill in my eyebrows because I have a habit of touching them a lot, so that kind of weakened my roots at the end." Tori (twenty-six/Asian American/bisexual) resisted the high-maintenance versions of femininity around her and linked this to her refusal to wear makeup: "I remember even in college, I felt like a lot of my girlfriends would take so long to get ready and that kind of stuff, primping and pampering themselves like that. I just could never do that."

Women also described getting tattoos as a form of bodily rebellion and linked this to their individuality and willingness to push back against norms of "respectability." Sequoia (twenty-three/white/bisexual) talked about her long history of loving tattoos and ear gauges as an expression of her individuality: "I think getting tattoos, piercings, anything like that is all just on your own behalf. I have ear gauges. My sister said, 'You're starting to get weird,' but I was just changing, doing what I like as a person." She went on to say, "Me and my sister were pretty wild when we were thirteen or fourteen. We both got matching tattoos, stuff that wasn't even accepted at our school. They weren't even going to allow us to dye our hair, or wear a bunch of piercings, and we were like, 'We're not going to listen to that. It's our bodies!" Casey (twenty-six/white/lesbian) described getting tattoos as an important aesthetic choice: "I have tattoos. It was my choice. No one forced me to do anything that I didn't want to do because I have a choice. I'm practicing my voice that we all have, that we all should say something."

As another twist on bodily rebellion, Indigo (thirty-five/white/bisexual) described her history of performative dancing as a form of bodily rebellion. She described dance as a way of asserting her freedom of movement and her bodily agency: "As a dancer, I kind of like do a lot of public prancing, like Prancercise stuff, dancing in public. I've had a few emotional reactions to that at times. I was presenting more masculine and dancing in public, and I experienced some homophobia on the street, so I definitely think that freedom of movement is just such a huge interest of mine." She added, "It's something I want to explore for my own body autonomy, and doing that publicly is a way of showing people that I'm not just limited to those rigid movements of, like, left, right. Dancing is just this freedom of movement or exploring your potentials of how free you can be with your movement."

In a related way, two participants identified their being trans or non-binary as itself a form of daily bodily rebellion. Jasmine (twenty-eight/Taiwanese American/heterosexual) noted that her resistance to having an hourglass figure and refusal to present as stereotypically feminine constituted her bodily rebellion as a trans woman: "I think the pressure to have a female body shaped in a certain way, like an hourglass figure, or a skeletal structure, is something I can't get even if I am thin. It depends on my state of mind, 'cause sometimes I really feel bad about not being able to have that body, but sometimes I don't care, 'cause other people do think I'm attractive in spite of that, and it doesn't really matter to me anymore. As a trans woman, I still went for it and transitioned, and you don't have to look any certain way." Dana (thirty-six/white/queer) talked about their top surgery as a form of bodily rebellion against gender norms: "I got top surgery, so I don't have breasts. It was great. I got it because I identify as nonbinary and I don't think I'm male or female, but these were very female-presenting, so I feel like I can wear the clothes I want to wear, and I feel a lot more comfortable. I know some people will be like, 'Why would you do that?' like my family was. I think they still feel weird about it, but I'm still the same person. It actually makes sense to me. This is who I am."

Finally, two participants imagined their fat bodies as a form of bodily rebellion as well, seeing fat acceptance as part of their rebelliousness as women. Kalani (twenty-one/Sri Lankan American/heterosexual) talked about embracing her weight and stretch marks as a form of activism:

> I would say mostly the weight thing. I definitely felt way more comfortable in my body in the past couple of years, and I think totally as a result of socially what I see, whether it's a song saying

that they want to see a real ass with stretch marks, or whatever it is, so I feel like I've looked at my body and thought my thighs are fat, but these are the thighs that carry me everywhere. I feel like that is some sort of activism just by being comfortable and proud of my body for doing its job.

Finally, Gloria (fifty-six/white/heterosexual) talked about embracing her fat body and her age as ways of rebelling against a culture that denigrates fatter and older women: "I've never been a totally slim woman. I've only been fat in the last probably ten years. I am somewhat doing this as a way to protest that you don't have to be a perfectly slim person as well as an excuse that I don't want to go run ten miles like I used to. It's a way to say, 'I'm still a good human. I'm still wonderful and beautiful.'" She added, "You don't have to be size zero, like I watch my sister struggle with that her whole life, the size of her clothes that she links to her feelings of self-worth, and it really, really upsets me."

BECOMING BODY HAIR REBELS

Though participants did not always imagine that growing their body hair constituted a direct act of gendered rebellion, many of them did see the links between having body hair and resisting gender norms. At the end of the interviews with them, I asked two questions about their feelings about resistance and body hair: "If body hair is so often considered gross or dirty in the broader culture, how have you been able to resist these constructions of body hair as gross or dirty?" and "How did you become a body hair rebel?" Women's responses touched on the political implications of their bodies, their feelings of wanting to define beauty and normality on their own terms, the potential for the body to serve as a form of resistance, and imagining a future where all people can make choices about their bodies without shame.

As one of the immediate responses to these questions, some women argued against the notion that body hair is dirty, claiming instead that they felt clean and perfectly hygienic with body hair. Bijou (twenty-two/African American/heterosexual) talked about her beliefs that ideas about body hair need to move away from associating hair with dirtiness: "I take care of myself, by showering and making sure I'm clean. It releases that idea of body hair being dirty. I try to shoot down the idea of body hair as dirty. It's not logical. It's just untrue. If you take care of yourself, it's not gross or dirty, so yeah, that helps me to resist." Eve (thirty-eight/white/lesbian) framed herself as not dirty and said that she did not care what others thought of her: "I just stay clean, and to me, it's not gross or dirty. I don't really care what other people really say about it, but I guess I can see why they would think it's gross. But if you're a clean person, then it's not dirty. It's important to be confident in yourself and do what is important to you and not really think about what anybody else thinks about it." Natasha (twenty-eight/white/bisexual) felt committed to resisting the double standard between men and women: "It's just weird. Why is men's hair not dirty, and why is female hair dirty? It's a double standard. It's discrimination."

Women also claimed that being a body hair rebel freed up time and felt convenient. Tori (twenty-six/Asian American/bisexual) celebrated both the ease of not shaving and the implications of rebelling against men: "Honestly, it started off as a convenience thing, and then as I heard stories of people who were shaving their body hair because of things that men or society told them to do, I realized that's ridiculous." Martina (fifty/Mexican American/bisexual) said that she operated more from laziness than from rebellion: "It just kind of happened organically. I'm kind of a puny lightweight. I'm lazy, and that's how it worked for me." Olive (sixty-three/white/heterosexual) embraced the joy of how easy not shaving has been for her: "It's not hard at all to not shave! It's very easy. The act of not doing it is wonderful, and it's only difficult if you still buy into the need to do it. I never thought it was needed or expected or that I was any better if I shaved. It's practical and easy, and I never looked back, and I'm really grateful that I was able to get that perspective when I was eighteen years old."

Challenging society's ideals for women and not caring about one's appearance also appeared in these narratives. Jasmine (twenty-eight/Taiwanese American/heterosexual) said that she has greatly benefited from caring less about what others think of her: "It's not specific to body hair. I just stopped caring about my appearance unless I'm going to an interview or something. Before, I used to wear makeup every single day for my transition period when I looked more androgynous and before I looked more feminine, but afterwards, I stopped using makeup as often, and I stopped caring about that. I expanded that to body hair as well. I just stopped caring. I'll take care of myself, shower, wash my hair, but I'm not looking to impress anyone." Sequoia (twenty-three/white/bisexual) also used body hair as a way to not care about others' judgment of her: "I'm just open with it and not caring, like I'll explain to people why if you take too many showers, you're rubbing off your own pH. Body hair is just part of my own skin."

Appreciating body hair as a reflection of the natural body also appeared in women's responses to the body hair rebel questions. Ula (twenty-two/ Chinese American/bisexual), who was adopted by a white father in the Midwest, said that she saw body hair as a part of accepting herself as a whole: "It's just a part of accepting who I am in a broader sense, accepting that I'm not ever gonna be blond hair, blue eyes. I remember when I was young, I really wanted to be white, and I also thought I was straight, and I'm not, so I guess body hair is a part of accepting who I am in general." Kalani (twenty-one/Sri Lankan American/heterosexual) saw body hair as completely natural and biologically normal: "It's very, very natural. Sweating is natural, and you have hair in those areas for that reason. Biologically, you grow it out for that, so it's very natural and very normal." Ainsley (twenty-three/white/heterosexual) embraced the natural qualities of her body hair as well: "It's natural. We have hair on our head, which isn't considered dirty. Why is body hair dirty for a female and not for men? It's natural! It's not going to do me any harm. It's not going to kill me. Why not do it?" Dana (thirty-six/white/queer) also saw body hair as a way to embrace their natural body and to celebrate their queer identity: "I shower, and that's how you get clean. You don't need to shave all your hair off. Your hair isn't dirty until you shave your head, you know? But how did I become a rebel? I guess it was in college. I just felt more comfortable and free to be queer and who I am. I just stopped believing what other people were saying."

Poignantly, women also saw growing body hair as a conscious rebellion against restrictive and oppressive gender norms. Zara (twenty-two/ white and Moroccan/queer) said that she grew her body hair out of anger about gendered double standards and the need to take action about her anger: "Definitely spite, I think, because I hear these things, and I disagree with them, and I would like to actively disagree with them and not just disagree with them in my head but then continue to wax and shave and stuff. The idea that body hair is wrong in some way just makes me angry, and I don't want to participate in it, and I hope I don't remove any body hair." Casey (twenty-six/white/lesbian) saw growing body hair as a conscious move toward not being passive about gender: "I see my brother my dad and my cousins and my uncles and other guys running, walking, being without a shirt, and they're hairy, and wearing shorts, and they look good and comfortable. Why can't I do that? Besides my boobs, why can't I do that? Why can't I grow out my hair? Why can't I show off who I am? I don't want to be passive." Indigo (thirty-five/white/bisexual) saw herself as a lifelong warrior working to accept her body: "It's like a whole different way of just accepting yourself as you are and just kind of seeing the hair as a living part of my organism. It just gave me compassion for my own body, and it gave myself compassion for the little girl I was, who had so much pressure on her for no reason. While that manifested as lots of anger in my youth, it almost just feels like I've been a warrior on a long road, and at this point I've come to a place of acceptance with it."

As a final expression of body hair rebellion, some women also saw their body hair as an explicit and pointed part of their fight against misogyny and patriarchy. Quinn (twenty-one/white and Native American/lesbian) claimed space for her body to be wild and free: "I think camping and being physically gross and dirty and accepting of that reality really helped. When you go backpacking, you're out in the wilderness for four days and accepting it's OK to be gross and dirty and it's kind of a reality of being a human being." She added that she disliked feeling that she should prove her cleanliness to others as a woman: "It's a weird implicit assumption that if you have body hair, you don't shower. It's like, 'No, my pits don't reach out and stop me from turning the water on!' I mean, maybe it's because body hair is so untamed." Quinn also recalled the impact of having her head hair cut against her will by her father after he felt it was too out of control: "I had a tiny little Afro, and it was a pain in the ass to brush, so he took me to his barber, and they sheared me like a sheep. It was super traumatic. I thought, 'No one's ever gonna cut my hair again.' I cut my own hair now. I make my own choices about my body." Gloria (fifty-six/white/

heterosexual) reflected on the bravery and willpower that not shaving has sometimes taken: "You just gotta be strong. You just gotta be ready for battle."

THE REVOLUTIONARY POTENTIAL OF BODY HAIR

Looking back on these twenty-two interviews, I am struck with the intimacy of them, the ways that women imagined things about themselves, shared their stories, and saw their body hair as both symbolic and literal, easy and difficult, rebellious and ordinary, silly and serious. They showed us a huge range of perspectives, in their identities and geographies, in their relationship and work stories, and in their struggles for freedom of expression and beauty choices. In doing so, they worked—albeit often unintentionally—to carve out more space for everyone who feels suffocated and oppressed by the narrow standards of gender; they are, in their own way, and whether they recognize it or not, making more space for the body to exist as diverse and multiple. Some women saw their everyday grooming practices as simply an individual set of habits, while many women connected their personal choices to the power dynamics produced in a society where women are treated as objects and products. To the extent that they connected their body hair choices to their political and social environments, they also did the hard work of politicizing the body, understanding it as immensely powerful, and laying down the foundations needed for people of all genders to fight back against the painfully narrow constraints of gender.

To imagine the body as explicitly political and tied to battles for bodily autonomy, gender diversity, and resistance to patriarchy is a crucial part of understanding the links between embodiment and justice. As one of the great contributions of the feminist movement, the linking of the body to its political context, and the explicit ways that women have started to use their bodies for political resistance, has created a powerful affront to status quo patriarchal politics. The narratives in this chapter, from questioning double standards to imagining bodies as permanently in revolt against oppressors and oppressions, show the possibilities of seemingly mundane bodily choices in the broader political landscape. More importantly, even when women themselves do not ascribe political meaning to their actions, they still enter a discursive space where they unsettle and remake the rules of gender.

The narratives in this chapter powerfully illustrate how the body operates as a *social text*, one written (and written upon) within an elaborate web of powerful influences, trappings, and pitfalls, and, perhaps, unexpected doorways into what feels like freedom. Speaking to women about their body hair showed me the ways that the body can be a force of confinement or a site of rebellion. It can operate both as something that constrains and holds people back and as something that can change and evolve and grow into something new. It has, I think, revolutionary potential. There is no prescription for how to fight back against patriarchy, white supremacy, homophobia, racism, and the insidious oppression of the poor and working class. Many tactics can undermine the workings of oppression, just as many roads can lead to a different, brighter future. Bodies that revolt in these ways are but one of these approaches to a more just world. And while women growing body hair may seem like the tiniest of things—a mundane choice made daily alongside so many other mundane choices—it often gives women a taste of freedom. The nature of freedom, of course, is that once we sense it, smell it, taste it, and feel it, we almost always want more.

We are freer than we feel. This claim is a meditation, a hope, a small comfort, an act of defiance, a reckoning, a call to the future.

Epilogue |

They Are Going to Be Mad at Us

IN THE DIZZYING FLURRY OF DEATHS DURING THE HEIGHT OF COVID-19, conservative shock jock Rush Limbaugh died of lung cancer on February 17, 2021, putting an end to a career defined by taunting rants and a buffet of hateful phobias targeting the political left. A friend of mine texted me the news: "Your nemesis is dead." There is a certain truth to this "nemesis" characterization. Limbaugh symbolizes so much of what my work opposes, particularly his deep hatred of women, queer people, and people of color, and he did personally target me about my body hair assignment on his show, resulting in weeks of tormenting, absurdist emails and threats from his right-wing cadre of followers. He had a cancerous quality, certainly, a villainous persona to those of us characterized as "femi-Nazis" (a term coined by Limbaugh and widely utilized starting in 1991). And while the seriousness of his legacy is a startling thing to reflect upon, I also continue to feel amused by how much the simple act of women growing their body hair seemed to scare and anger him. It has been my experience—as documented closely throughout this book—that body hair has a surprising amount of power to unsettle and unnerve. I have written about many topics in my career, several of which are, in my view, more controversial, radical, political, and frankly risky than body hair, and yet body hair continues to be the topic that gets under the skin of misogynists with the greatest efficiency and speed.

When I was in high school, I used to drive around listening to an Ani DiFranco song called "Shameless," in which she defiantly sings,

We better have a good explanation for all the fun that we had
'Cuz they are coming for us, baby, and they are going to be mad[1]

I think about myself at age seventeen, just as I started to imagine how the workings of power played out upon my body. I realized then, in the tiniest of ways, that there was something delightful in using the body to provoke, in dreaming up small forms of bodily resistance, even in private. I loved the idea that "they are going to be mad at us," and I wanted to know all about that reality. I sensed, rightly, that it would be easy to make them mad. I wanted to imagine a space where women could exist just outside of the reach of patriarchy, on the outer limits of that known world, on the edges of those maps and grids. I wondered what kinds of troublemaking I could get away with there and how much fun it really might be.

By the time I graduated college, I had managed the dual educational experiences of earning an undergraduate degree from a progressive liberal arts college and getting into all sorts of political trouble. By the time I was twenty, I had joined forces with fellow radicals on campus to petition my college to allow Mumia Abu-Jamal, a death-row inmate and prolific writer, to record and deliver a graduate speech in lieu of a more traditional choice of graduation speaker. When the college refused, citing concerns about donors pulling their money and the "respectability" of the institutional practices of graduation ceremonies, we called press conferences, had fiery meetings with the campus president (who later became Obama's education secretary), rallied students to the cause, protested the Los Angeles Police Department convening on campus, and played Abu-Jamal's recording at our baccalaureate ceremony, much to the chagrin of the unsuspecting parents of the wealthy kids in the crowd. As a consequence of these efforts, my fellow organizer and I earned the dubious title of *Hustler Magazine*'s "Assholes of the Month." *They are going to be mad.*

At age twenty-eight and just out of graduate school, I first interviewed radical feminist Ti-Grace Atkinson for a two-day span of time in her home in Cambridge, Massachusetts. While the interview was mostly about her experiences interacting with Valerie Solanas (author of *SCUM Manifesto* and would-be assassin of Andy Warhol), she spent a substantial amount of time talking about the radical feminist civil rights lawyer Flo (Florynce) Kennedy and the lessons she learned from Flo.[2] Among these were understanding small acts of resistance as having a potentially huge impact; the value of collective acts of revolt (e.g., Flo organized the "pee-in" protests, where women poured urine from glass jars down the steps of the Harvard library to protest the lack of women's restrooms in the building where they took entrance exams);[3] the necessity of using defiance and humor in full force; and the vital importance of radicals finding ways to sustain themselves for the long haul. Ti-Grace Atkinson herself told me when reflecting on her radical feminist activist experiences of the late 1960s and early 1970s,

> I think that if you have anything really corrupt, like sexism, like the way women are treated and it's accepted, you have a poison. You have something at the core. It's going to infect everyone, and it's the foundation. You have to get all the way back into it, and you start understanding things. I understood other oppressions when I understood the oppression of women. I think that the most horrifying part is that we are at least half of the problem because if we only say "no" and just refuse, it's over! It's over! Just a few people speaking up, the whole world practically came to an end. It's amazing! It can't be all that secure.[4]

In nearly all the academic and political work I have done subsequent to that interview, I think about these lessons, particularly when I reflect about the bizarre reactivity people have to the deceptively simple act of women growing their body hair. Over and over in this book, the collision of the seemingly trivial and mundane with the political and provocative appears, from zine makers and artists making body hair visible to audiences to students refusing to ask their boyfriends for permission to grow their body hair to activists using a body hair contest to confront the colossal power of the Chinese government to office workers quietly rebelling against stories that body hair is unprofessional. In their use of the body as a political canvas, these body hair rebellions represent hyperrealized versions of "the personal is political."

The norm of body hair removal is both entrenched and slippery, hard to change and easy to resist; these contradictions pervade these pages. Pressures about body hair removal trap women in a sticky spider web of stories about bodies, identity, power, respectability, and cleanliness. In the decisions women make about their bodies, the social world is made and remade. Many facets of women's body hair removal demonstrate the bridges between the body and its sociocultural context: widespread body hair removal for women is a norm that is less than a hundred years old and consciously invented; it is premised not on health or hygiene but on changing standards of beauty; it requires the purchasing of products and objects to assist with achieving hairlessness and thus obviously connects to consumerism; it is temporary, reversible, and requires constant exertions of labor to maintain; and it insists on the belief that a feature of most adults' bodies is "gross" or "disgusting." In the face of women's extraordinary compliance with body hair removal, starting at a young age and often encouraged by family members, friends, partners, and coworkers, this norm persists almost unconsciously. Women's body hair removal is a ubiquitous element of modern grooming and beauty routines for nearly all women in the United States, much of Europe, and Australia and New Zealand, despite there being no obvious benefit to it other than social conformity and the meeting of gendered expectations of bodily presentation. Body hair removal is a social norm experienced by women as overwhelming in its force and deeply engrained within them as *required*, not chosen.

And yet, women from many corners of the world have pushed back against this norm with subtlety or force, cleverness or in-your-face defiance, within communities and while going it alone. These actions serve as a reminder that the rules of the body are not really rules after all, that mandates for how women groom or look or behave can be undone and discarded, privately and publicly. It cannot be overstated how new—and thus fragile—the norm of women's body hair removal actually is. In this book, I have detailed how body hair removal emerged in the 1910s and 1920s as a conscious effort to sell products to women by insisting that they can and should remove their body hair. Prior to that, body hair removal existed mostly as an act of more direct coercion, particularly coercion exerted onto the bodies of women and men of color in contexts of colonial abuses of power. Perhaps if readers collectively imagine that fashion magazine editors and Gillette razor makers (at the time, these were nearly all white wealthy men) sat around and made a conscious choice to tell women, or rather, *instruct women*, to remove their body hair, this might inspire a more defiant reaction. Or, if readers understand the history of hair removal as one of forcibly removing hair as an act of colonial humiliation to consolidate the power of nation-states, they might better situate bodies as landscapes upon and within which power is enacted and exerted.

The power of social norms lies not only in how readily they inform social life but also in how easily they can be undone and rewritten. Working on body hair politics all these years has taught me that one does not need to intentionally provoke in order to unsettle existing social norms. We do not *only* need activists and radicals to change the world, though they of course have an enormously important role in dismantling existing oppressive structures. Rather, the simple act of abstaining from hair removal and allowing body hair to grow can show flagrant disregard for the hairlessness norm and all that it symbolizes. Put more pointedly, once women sense their own freedom and imagine it in relation to their bodies, the whole system of objectification, self-objectification, patriarchal control of bodies, internalized body shame, careful compliance with sexist and misogynist body norms, control of bodies in relation to labor and work, and the ceding of control over reproductive freedom (and much more) begins to topple.

This whole book is an exercise in that very premise. Making space for merely imagining or sensing the freedom that comes from growing body hair presents a new set of logics and possibilities perhaps previously unseen or unknown. I want readers to move in this book from student narratives to artist images to political battlegrounds to body hair rebellions and find what they need to sustain themselves for the long haul. The struggle for bodily autonomy and women's collective right to self-define has many fault lines and battlegrounds, has been won and lost many times before, and will be won and lost many times again. Still, Ti-Grace Atkinson knew then and the pandemic has shown us now: The system isn't secure or inevitable. We don't have to experience the world in the way we've been told to. We can make something new, something better.

Maybe that sounds trite or idealistic or foolish, and if so, perhaps we can shrink our ambitions down to this: *they are going be mad at us*. And when they are—when we hit a nerve in the circuitry of patriarchal power or laugh in the face of hatefulness or find our way off the existing maps and into the wilder and less-explored terrain—we know that we are headed in the right direction.

ACKNOWLEDGMENTS |

One of the great gifts of the COVID-19 period was its ability to refocus energies toward the people I love and the work I most want to do. I wrote the majority of this book from March through November of 2020, surrounded on all sides by cultural narratives of fear and uncertainty, death and dying, despair and sorrow. And yet, in the tiny world of my home office, I felt the deep resonances of the kindness, care, and love of my friends, family, mentors, and students. Crafting this book kept me company, in a sense, but the work itself would have been impossible without the people who invested in me during this time. I am, now and always, in their debt.

A book about body hair would never exist without a vast network of feminist scholars who helped to conjure it into existence. I feel grateful to each of these women for writing and thinking so beautifully, and for understanding that feminist solidarity is the only way out of this nightmare we've all just lived through: Jane Caputi, Leonore Tiefer, Abby Stewart, Ti-Grace Atkinson, Roxanne Dunbar-Ortiz, Virginia Braun, Marlene Tromp, Jessa Crispin, Michelle Tea, Soraya Chemaly, Rebecca Plante, Deborah Tolman, Carla Golden, Diana Álvarez, Jill Wood, Chella Quint, Louisa Allen, Mary Lou Rasmussen, Leta Hong Fincher, Kimberly Dark, and Monica Casper. Thank you to the Society for Menstrual Cycle Research and all of the incredible people who study and work in critical menstrual studies, particularly Chris Bobel, Inga Winkler, Liz Kissling, Tomi-Ann Roberts, Jane Ussher, Janette Perz, Ingrid Johnston, Jessica Barnack-Tavlaris, Joan Chrisler, Maureen McHugh, David Linton, Mindy Erchull,

Peggy Stubbs, Heather Dillaway, Evelina Sterling, Sheryl Mendlinger, Rachel Fikslin, Saniya Lee Ghanoui, and Alex Hawkey.

I give a special shout-out to the Feminist Research on Gender and Sexuality Group—the FROGS—who had a dizzying number of roles in this book. Many participated in the body hair assignment, helped to design research questions, found articles, pushed my thinking about body hair, and embodied body hair rebellion in their own right. I owe a special debt to Mikhail Collins for their boundless energy and enthusiasm, deep understanding of abject bodies, relentless work ethic, and generosity to me and to the whole group. A whip-smart gang of FROGS helped me edit and transcribe material for this book: Claire Halling, Marli Mayon, Camille Edelstein, Alexis Starks, John Payton, Jakob Salazar, Kiley Romano, Farhat Ali, Felicya Ptak, Caroline Rudel, Tatiana Crespo, Mam Marie Sanyang, Loralei Cook, and Kalen Aradia. I marvel at your goodwill and am always humbled by it. Thank you also to the rest of the FROGS, for infusing my work with your vitality and passion: Decker Dunlop, Michael Karger, Stephanie Voelker, Laisa Schweigert, Madison Carlyle, Laura Martinez, Carolyn Anh Thu Dang, Atlas Pillar, Emma DiFrancesco, Crystal Zaragoza, Natali Blazevic, Jax Gonzalez, Kimberly Koerth, Chelsea Pixler Charbonneau, Corie Cisco, Nic Santos, Rachel Caldwell, and Jennifer Bertagni. And to Adrielle Munger, the oldest and wisest, who kept us laughing and who never ceases to amaze, thank you.

For helping to get this book started, I thank the Center for Critical Inquiry and Cultural Studies at Arizona State University for a small grant that came at just the right time. I am deeply grateful to the Institute for Humanities Research at Arizona State University for helping to fund and support this project in ways big and small. Thank you to my colleagues in New College who made room for me to write and work: Sarah Stage, Annika Mann, Sharon Kirsch, Miriam Mara, Ramsey Eric Ramsey, Gloria Cuádraz, Eduardo Pagán, Heather Smith-Cannoy, Majia Nadesan, Lucy Berchini, and Tracy Encizo. Thanks especially to Rose Carlson, for transformative kindness and care. I also want to offer thanks to my interview participants, a group of incredible women from all over the US who shared their stories so generously; their words became my fuel for this book and so richly captured the complexities of feminist body hair politics.

I am grateful for the journal and book editors who saw promise and value in my earlier work on women's body hair. Note that parts of an earlier version of chapter 1 appeared as "Perilous Patches and Pitstaches: Imagined versus Lived Experiences of Women's Body Hair Growth," *Psychology of Women Quarterly* 38, no. 2 (2014): 167–80. An earlier version of chapter 2 was published as "Body Hair Battlegrounds: The Consequences, Reverberations, and Promises of Women Growing Their Leg, Pubic, and Underarm Hair," in *Body Battlegrounds: Transgressions, Tensions, and Transformations*, ed. Chris Bobel and Samantha Kwan (Nashville: Vanderbilt University Press, 2019), 11–22.

I have deep gratitude for my editor, Larin McLaughlin, who has now edited three of my books and has thrown not only institutional support behind me but also her profound warmth, compassion, and insight. Truly, none of this would exist without her. Thanks also to the entire University of Washington Press team, especially Julie Fergus, Laura Fish, Kait Heacock, Neecole Bostick, Elizabeth Mathews, David Schlangen, and Joeth Zucco. I am so grateful to Mikhail Collins for helping to index the book, and to Derek George for designing the beautiful cover. Special thanks to Ben Hopper for allowing me to use one of his photographs on the book's cover, and to the variety of artists and photographers who allowed me to reprint their work here, particularly Ayqa Khan and Eleanor Antin. Thanks also to Jessie Kindig and Amy Scholder, editors extraordinaire, who have made my life fuller and richer in every way imaginable.

Truly, the love of friendship animates my life and, by extension, this book. As Zadie Smith writes, life without love is just "passing time." Thank you to my tribe: Lori Errico-Seaman, Sean Seaman, Mary Dudy, Jennifer Tamir, Sarah Stage, Sara McClelland, Claire Croft, Steve DuBois, Elizabeth Brake, Ela Przybylo, Annika Mann, Garyn Tsuru, Denise Delgado, Jan Habarth, Marcy Winokur, Connie Hardesty, Katie Goldey, Patrick Grzanka, Toby Oshiro, Pat Hart, Damon Whittaker, Karen Swank-Fitch, Lucy Phelps, Lanie Saunders, and Sadie Mohler. To my niece and nephews—Simon, Ryan, Fiona, and Matthew—and to my friends' kids—Thomas, Tess, Matthew, Frannie, Faye, Hazel, Micah, Francesca, and Jacob—may you continue the fight for a world that lets you live in your bodies without shame. To Elmer Griffin, the architect of possibilities, the dearest of friends, I write through and because of you. To Kristen (Fahs) Nusbaum,

I'm lucky to have a sister who talks freely about bodies and shares my anger about the body shaming of women. And to my mom, who takes pride in my studying abject and difficult subjects that make her friends blush, thank you for your abundant love. To Eric Swank, who even made lockdown during a pandemic feel uniquely joyful and beautiful, and who never wavered in throwing his weight and his energy behind my work, I love and adore you. Finally, I dedicate this book to my dear friend Chris Bobel, who has fought for women to embrace their bodies—however messy, leaky, and imperfect—and who understands, better than most, that we can make and remake the world many times over.

NOTES |

1 Throughout this book, I make reference at times to concepts of the "natural" when discussing women having body hair. I do this as a reference to the body *not* as a precultural entity but as a site at times working to evade the more heavy-handed impositions of commercialism, capitalism, and patriarchal molding. Most women have the capacity to grow body hair, and to remove it is a gesture away from the natural body; this action also separates the normative from the natural and exposes both as socially and politically constructed. See Gail Weiss, "The Normal, the Natural, and the Normative: A Merleau-Pontian Legacy to Feminist Theory, Critical Race Theory, and Disability Studies," *Continental Philosophy Review* 48, no. 1 (2015): 77–93. I nevertheless maintain that the body is *always* in relation to its social context (Michel Foucault's "inscribed surface of events" or Elizabeth Grosz's notion of women's bodies as "socially inscribed") and that there is no natural outside of the cultural, no body outside of its context. The body is constructed through language and discourse. Any reference to the "natural" thus comes with the caveat that I understand that no such thing can actually exist, as the body is a cultural entity. See Pippa Brush, "Metaphors of Inscription: Discipline, Plasticity and the Rhetoric of Choice," *Feminist Review* 58, no. 1 (1998): 22–43; Judith Butler, "Foucault and the Paradox of Bodily Inscriptions," *Journal of Philosophy* 86, no. 11 (1989): 601–7. Further, performance artists and scholars studying gender and beauty have both convincingly argued that one can pursue a "natural look" but not the *actual* material experience of a natural body, claims I agree with. See Jane Goodall, "An Order of Pure Decision: Un-natural Selection in the Work of Stelarc and Orlan," *Body & Society* 5, no. 2–3 (1999): 149–70; Laura Hurt Clarke and Meridith Griffin, "The Body Natural and the Body Unnatural: Beauty Work and Aging," *Journal of Aging Studies* 21, no. 3 (2007): 187–201.

2 Marika Tiggemann and Sarah J. Kenyon, "The Hairlessness Norm: The Removal of Body Hair in Women," *Sex Roles* 39, no. 11–12 (1998): 873–85; Marika Tiggemann and Christine Lewis, "Attitudes toward Women's Body Hair: Relationship with Disgust Sensitivity," *Psychology of Women Quarterly* 28, no. 4 (2004): 381–87; Merran Toerien, Sue Wilkinson, and Precilla Y. L. Choi, "Body Hair Removal: The 'Mundane' Production of Normative Femininity," *Sex Roles* 52, no. 5–6 (2005): 399–406.

3 Tiggemann and Kenyon, "Hairlessness Norm."

4 Marika Tiggemann and Suzanna Hodgson, "The Hairlessness Norm Extended: Reasons for and Predictors of Women's Body Hair Removal at Different Body Sites," *Sex Roles* 59, no. 11–12 (2008): 889–97.

5 Toerien, Wilkinson, and Choi, "Body Hair Removal"; Tiggemann and Lewis, "Attitudes toward Women's Body Hair."

6 Lenore Riddell, Hannah Varto, and Zoë G. Hodgson, "Smooth Talking: The Phenomenon of Pubic Hair Removal in Women," *Canadian Journal of Human Sexuality* 19, no. 3 (2010): 121–30; Scott M. Butler, Nicole K. Smith, Erika Collazo, Lucia Caltabiano, and Debby Herbenick, "Pubic Hair Preferences, Reasons for Removal, and Associated Genital Symptoms: Comparisons between Men and Women," *Journal of Sexual Medicine* 12, no. 1 (2015): 48–58.

7 Tami S. Rowen, Thomas W. Gaither, Mohannad A. Awad, et al., "Pubic Hair Grooming Prevalence and Motivation among Women in the United States," *JAMA Dermatology* 152, no. 10 (2016): 1106–13.

8 Rebecca Herzig, *Plucked: A History of Hair Removal* (New York: New York University Press, 2015), 10; see also "Women Spend up to $23,000 to Remove Hair," UPI.com, June 24, 2008, www.upi.com/Health_News/2008/06/24/Women-spend-up-to-23000-to-remove-hair/64771214351618/?hsFormKey=6c23 6b2fe21f331cdf53ce23f1415097&ur3=1.

9 Yuan Ren, "Why Chinese Women Like Me Aren't Ashamed of Our Body Hair," *Telegraph*, June 24, 2015; Matthew Boyle, "Veet's Hairy Strategy for Chinese Women," SF Gate, October 21, 2012, www.sfgate.com/business/article/Veet-s-hairy-strategy-for-Chinese-women-3969580.php.

10 "What Women in These 7 Countries Shave and What They Don't," *Life*, May 30, 2017, https://life.laseraway.com/smile/what-women-in-these-7-countries-shave-and-what-they-dont.

11 Ada Borkenhagen, Ursula Mirastschijski, Bernhard Strauss, Uwe Gieler, and Elmar Braehler, "Body Hair Removal: Prevalence, Demographics, and Body Experience among Men and Women in Germany," *Journal of Cosmetic Dermatology*, 19, no. 11 (2020): 2886–92.

12 Anne E. Becker, "Television, Disordered Eating, and Young Women in Fiji: Negotiating Body Image and Identity during Rapid Social Change," *Culture, Medicine and Psychiatry* 28, no. 4 (2004): 533–59; Marwan M. Kraidy and Katherine Sender, *The Politics of Reality Television: Global Perspectives* (New York: Routledge, 2010).

13 Allison S. Glass, Herman S. Bagga, Gregory E. Tasian, Patrick B. Fisher, et al., "Pubic Hair Grooming Injuries Presenting to U.S. Emergency Departments," *Urology* 80, no. 6 (2012): 1187–91.

14 Andrea L. DeMaria, Marissa Flores, Jacqueline M. Hirth, and Abbey B. Berenson, "Complications Related to Pubic Hair Removal," *American Journal of Obstetrics and Gynecology* 210, no. 6 (2014): 528-e1.

15 Meike Schild-Suhren, Amr A. Soliman, and Eduard Malik, "Pubic Hair Shaving Is Correlated to Vulvar Dysplasia and Inflammation: A Case-Control Study," *Infectious Diseases in Obstetrics and Gynecology* (2017), 1–5.

16 The Joanna Briggs Institute, "Preoperative Hair Removal and Surgical Site Infection: Long-Accepted Practices Aren't Always Best," *American Journal of Nursing* 5 (2006): 6411–64NN; Giovanni Battista Orsi, Federica Ferraro, and Cristiana Franchi, "Preoperative Hair Removal Review," *Annali Di Igiene: Medicina Preventiva e Di Comunita* 17, no. 5 (2005): 401–12.

17 Butler, Smith, Collazo, Caltabiano, and Herbenick, "Pubic Hair Preferences."

18 Kris G. McGrath, "An Earlier Age of Breast Cancer Diagnosis Is Related to More Frequent Use of Antiperspirants/Deodorants and Underarm Shaving," *European Journal of Cancer Prevention* 12, no. 6 (2003): 479–85.

19 Linda Smolak and Sarah K. Murnen, "Gender, Self-Objectification and Pubic Hair Removal," *Sex Roles* 65, no. 7–8 (2011): 506–17.

20 See chapter 1 of this book.

21 Ruth Igielnik, "Most Americans Say They Regularly Wore a Mask in Stores in the Past Month; Fewer See Others Doing It," Pew Research Center, June 23, 2020, www.pewresearch.org/fact-tank/2020/06/23/most-americans-say-they -regularly-wore-a-mask-in-stores-in-the-past-month-fewer-see-others-doing-it; see also Kendall Karson, "More than Half of Americans Wear Masks as Coronavirus' New Normal Takes Hold: Poll," ABC News, April 10, 2020, https://abcnews.go.com/Politics/half-americans-masked-coronavirus-normal -takes-hold-poll/story?id=70073942; Jake Gammon, "United States of Bad Habits and Hygiene," YouGov, July 14, 2014, https://today.yougov.com/topics /lifestyle/articles-reports/2014/07/14/united-states-bad-hygiene; Maggie Fox, "You're Still Not Eating Enough Vegetables," NBC News, July 9, 2015, www .nbcnews.com/health/diet-fitness/youre-still-not-eating-enough-vegetables -n389466; Jamie Ducharme, "Only 23% of Americans Get Enough Exercise, A New Report Says," *Time*, June 28, 2018; Christopher Ingraham, "Here's How Good (or Awful) Your Hometown Drivers Are at Wearing a Seat Belt," *Washington Post*, April 4, 2017; Centers for Disease Control and Prevention, "Current Cigarette Smoking among Adults in the United States: 2018," www .cdc.gov/tobacco/data_statistics/fact_sheets/adult_data/cig_smoking/index .htm.

22 North American Precis Syndicate, "Women and High Heels: A Love/Hate Relationship," accessed June 1, 2021, www.mynewstouse.com/stories/women -and-high-heels,16493; see also American Podiatric Medical Association, "New

Study Shows High Heels Are Biggest Culprit of Female Foot Pain," *Ciston*,
May 19, 2014, www.prnewswire.com/news-releases/new-study-shows-high
-heels-are-biggest-culprit-of-female-foot-pain-259775731.html.

23 Alexander Kunst, "Frequency of Makeup Use among U.S. Consumers 2017, by
Age," Statista, December 20, 2019, www.statista.com/statistics/713178/makeup
-use-frequency-by-age; Renfrew Center Foundation, "New Survey Results
Indicate There's More to Makeup Use than Meets the Eye," February 22, 2012,
www.prnewswire.com/news-releases/new-survey-results-indicate-theres-more
-to-makeup-use-than-meets-the-eye-140012233.html.

24 Kirsten Dellinger and Christine L. Williams, "Makeup at Work: Negotiating
Appearance Rules in the Workplace," *Gender & Society* 11, no. 2 (1997): 151–77;
Rebecca Nash, George Fieldman, Trevor Hussey, Jean-Luc Lévêque, and Patricia
Pineau, "Cosmetics: They Influence More than Caucasian Female Facial
Attractiveness," *Journal of Applied Social Psychology* 36, no. 2 (2006): 493–504.

25 Adrienne Rich, "Compulsory Heterosexuality and the Lesbian Existence," *Signs*
5, no. 4 (1980): 631–60; Breanne Fahs, *Performing Sex: The Making and Unmaking of
Women's Erotic Lives* (Albany: State University of New York Press, 2011); Ela
Przybylo, *Asexual Erotics: Intimate Readings of Compulsory Sexuality* (Columbus:
Ohio State University Press, 2019).

26 Elizabeth Grosz, *Volatile Bodies: Toward a Corporeal Feminism* (Bloomington:
Indiana University Press, 1994), 23.

27 Christine Hope, "Caucasian Female Body Hair and American Culture," *Journal
of American Culture* 5, no. 1 (1982): 93–99.

28 Herzig, *Plucked*, 12.

29 Herzig, *Plucked*, 121.

30 Herzig, *Plucked*, 122.

31 Herzig, *Plucked*, 122–23.

32 G. Bruce Retallack, "Razors, Shaving and Gender Construction: An Inquiry into
the Material Culture of Shaving," *Material Culture Review* 49, no. 1 (1999): 6.

33 Hope, "Caucasian Female Body Hair," 94.

34 Hope, "Caucasian Female Body Hair," 94.

35 Herzig, *Plucked*, 125–26.

36 Hope, "Caucasian Female Body Hair," 95.

37 Hope, "Caucasian Female Body Hair," 95.

38 Helena Rubinstein, *The Art of Feminine Beauty* (London: Victor Collancz, 1930),
116–17, as cited in Hope, "Caucasian Female Body Hair," 96.

39 Hope, "Caucasian Female Body Hair," 98.

40 Herzig, *Plucked*, 126.

41 Herzig, *Plucked*, 126–27.

42 "Advice for Women Who Shave," *Today's Health*, July 1964, 37, as cited in Herzig,
Plucked, 127; Rose Weitz, *Rapunzel's Daughters: What Women's Hair Tells Us about
Women's Lives* (New York: Macmillan, 2004).

43 Breanne Fahs, *Firebrand Feminism: The Radical Lives of Ti-Grace Atkinson, Kathie Sarachild, Roxanne Dunbar-Ortiz, and Dana Densmore* (Seattle: University of Washington Press, 2018).

44 Fahs, *Firebrand Feminism*.

45 Herzig, *Plucked*, 131.

46 Herzig, *Plucked*, 132.

47 Susan A. Basow, "Women and Their Body Hair," *Psychology of Women Quarterly* 15, no. 1 (1991): 83–96.

48 Chris Bobel, "'Our Revolution Has Style': Contemporary Menstrual Product Activists 'Doing Feminism' in the Third Wave," *Sex Roles* 54, no. 5 (2006): 331–45; Chris Bobel and Breanne Fahs, "From Bloodless Respectability to Radical Menstrual Embodiment: Shifting Menstrual Politics from Private to Public," *Signs* 45, no. 4 (2020): 955–83.

49 Vanessa Cecil, Louise F. Pendry, Jessica Salvatore, Hazel Mycroft, and Tim Kurz, "Gendered Ageism and Gray Hair: Must Older Women Choose between Feeling Authentic and Looking Competent?" *Journal of Women & Aging* (2021), online first; Ulpukka Isopahkala-Bouret, "'It's a Great Benefit to Have Gray Hair!': The Intersection of Gender, Aging, and Visibility in Midlife Professional Women's Narratives," *Journal of Women & Aging* 29, no. 3 (2017): 267–77; Mary Ane Mohandraj, "My Feminist Revolution at 40: Why I Let My Gray Show, and Why It's a Political Act," *Salon*, June 2, 2014, www.salon.com/2014/06/02/my _feminist_revolution_at_40_why_i_let_my_gray_show_and_why_its_a _political_act.

50 Roger Melick and H. Pincus Taft, "Observations on Body Hair in Old People," *Journal of Clinical Endocrinology & Metabolism* 19, no. 12 (1959): 1597–607.

51 Harry Barbee and Douglas Schrock, "Un/gendering Social Selves: How Nonbinary People Navigate and Experience a Binarily Gendered World," *Sociological Forum* 34, no. 3 (2019): 572–93; M. Paz Galupo, Lex Pulice-Farrow, and Emerson Pehl, "'There Is Nothing to Do About It': Nonbinary Individuals' Experience of Gender Dysphoria," *Transgender Health* 6, no. 2 (2021): 101–110.

52 Herzig, *Plucked*, 133.

53 Herzig, *Plucked*, 3. Herzig references a 2007 Red Cross report on the treatment of US-held detainees at Guantánamo Bay.

54 Herzig, *Plucked*, 4.

55 Herzig, *Plucked*, 4.

56 Herzig, *Plucked*, 5.

57 Anne McClintock, *Imperial Leather: Race, Gender, and Sexuality in the Colonial Contest* (New York: Routledge, 2013), 50.

58 Madina Tlostanova, "A Ricochet of Desiring Gazes: Inter-racial Eroticism and the Modern Colonial Gender System," *Interlitteraria* 12, no. 12 (2007): 73–90. See also McClintock, *Imperial Leather*.

59 Herzig, *Plucked*, 10–11.

60 Julie C. Nack Ngue, "Colonial Discourses of Disability and Normalization in Contemporary Francophone Immigrant Narratives: Bessora's 53cm and Fatou Diome's *Le Ventre de l'Atlantique*," in *Wagadu*, ed. Pushpa Parekh, vol. 4, *Intersecting Gender and Disability Perspectives* (Bloomington, IN: Xlibris, 2008), 51–65, 56–59.

61 Herzig, *Plucked*, 5.

62 Michele Bacci, *The Many Faces of Christ: Portraying the Holy in the East and West, 300 to 1300* (London: Reaktion Books, 2014).

63 Emma Tarlo, *Entanglement: The Secret Lives of Hair* (London: One World, 2016), 52, 70–71.

64 Tarlo, *Entanglement*; Natalie Venclová, "The Venerable Bede, Druidic Tonsure and Archaeology," *Antiquity* 76, no. 292 (2002): 458–71.

65 Weitz, *Rapunzel's Daughters*, xv.

66 Lynn Davidman, *Becoming Un-Orthodox: Stories of Ex-Hasidic Jews* (New York: Oxford University Press, 2015).

67 Rose Weitz, "Women and Their Hair: Seeking Power through Resistance and Accommodation," *Gender & Society* 15, no. 5 (2001): 667–86; Claire Anderson, *Discourses of Ageing and Gender* (London: Palgrave, 2019).

68 Weitz, *Rapunzel's Daughters*, 4.

69 Weitz, *Rapunzel's Daughters*, 4.

70 Weitz, *Rapunzel's Daughters*, 4.

71 Ingrid Pfluger-Schindlbeck, "On the Symbolism of Hair in Islamic Societies: An Analysis of Approaches," *Anthropology of the Middle East* 1, no. 2 (2006): 72–88.

72 For a description of her reactions to some of these right-wing attacks, see Brenda Jones and Krishan Trotman, *Alexandria Ocasio-Cortez* (New York: Penguin, 2020); Amanda R. Matos, "Alexandria Ocasio-Cortez and Cardi B Jump through Hoops: Disrupting Respectability Politics When You Are from the Bronx and Wear Hoops," *Harvard Journal of Hispanic Policy* 31 (2019): 89–93.

73 Tarlo, *Entanglement*, 51.

74 Tarlo, *Entanglement*, 53.

75 Weitz, *Rapunzel's Daughters*, 8; See also Clifford E. Trafzer, Jean A. Keller, and Lorene Sisquoc, *Boarding School Blues: Revisiting American Indian Educational Experiences* (Lincoln: University of Nebraska Press, 2006).

76 Tarlo, *Entanglement*, 43.

77 Tarlo, *Entanglement*, 47, 53.

78 Weitz, *Rapunzel's Daughters*, xiii.

79 Weitz, *Rapunzel's Daughters*, xv.

80 Karin Lesnik-Oberstein, "The Last Taboo: Women, Body Hair and Feminism," in *The Last Taboo: Women and Body Hair*, ed. Karin Lesnik-Oberstein (Manchester: Manchester University Press, 2006), 1–17. Note that this has not always been the case, which is illustrated by the pubic merkin used in the seventeenth and eighteenth centuries by gentry to cover baldness or blemishes that resulted from venereal disease treatments and the removal of lice. See Louise Tondeur,

"A History of Pubic Hair, or Reviewers' Responses to Terry Eagleton's *After Theory*," in *The Last Taboo: Women and Body Hair*, ed. Karin Lesnik-Oberstein (Manchester: Manchester University Press, 2006), 61.

81 Daniella Caselli, "'The Wives of Geniuses I Have Sat With': Body Hair, Genius, and Modernity," in *The Last Taboo: Women and Body Hair*, ed. Karin Lesnik-Oberstein (Manchester: Manchester University Press, 2006), 19.

82 Tiggemann and Hodgson, "Hairlessness Norm Extended"; Megdala Peixoto Labre, "The Brazilian Wax: New Hairlessness Norm for Women?" *Journal of Communication Inquiry* 26, no. 2 (2002): 113–32; Hope, "Caucasian Female Body Hair."

83 Barbara L. Fredrickson and Tomi-Ann Roberts, "Objectification Theory: Toward Understanding Women's Lived Experiences and Mental Health Risks," *Psychology of Women Quarterly* 21, no. 2 (1997): 173–206; Bonnie Moradi and Yu-Ping Huang, "Objectification Theory and Psychology of Women: A Decade of Advances and Future Directions," *Psychology of Women Quarterly* 32, no. 4 (2008): 377–98; Amy Shields Dobson, "'Sexy' and 'Laddish' Girls: Unpacking Complicity between Two Cultural Imag(inations)es of Young Femininity," *Feminist Media Studies* 14, no. 2 (2014): 253–69.

84 Casey Ryan Kelly and Kristen E. Hoerl, "Shaved or Saved? Disciplining Women's Bodies," *Women's Studies in Communication* 38, no. 2 (2015): 141–45.

85 Sara Ramsey, Clare Sweeney, Michael Fraser, and Gren Oades, "Pubic Hair and Sexuality: A Review," *Journal of Sexual Medicine* 6, no. 8 (2009): 2102–10; Riddell, Varto, and Hodgson, "Smooth Talking."

86 Virginia Braun, Gemma Tricklebank, and Victoria Clarke, "'It Shouldn't Stick Out from Your Bikini at the Beach': Meaning, Gender, and the Hairy/Hairless Body," *Psychology of Women Quarterly* 37, no. 4 (2013): 478–93; Patricia Obst, Katherine White, and Ebony Matthews, "A Full Brazilian or All Natural: Understanding the Influences on Young Women's Decision to Remove Their Pubic Hair," *BMC Women's Health* 19, no. 1 (2019): 164–74.

87 Stephanie L. Grossman and Rachel A. Annunziato, "Risky Business: Is Pubic Hair Removal by Women Associated with Body Image and Sexual Health?" *Sexual Health* 15, no. 3 (2018): 269–75.

88 Dawn M. Szymanski, Lauren B. Moffitt, and Erika R. Carr, "Sexual Objectification of Women: Advances to Theory and Research," *Counseling Psychologist* 39, no. 1 (2011): 6–38; Melanie S. Hill and Ann R. Fischer, "Examining Objectification Theory: Lesbian and Heterosexual Women's Experiences with Sexual- and Self-Objectification," *Counseling Psychologist* 36, no. 5 (2008): 745–76.

89 Mary Douglas, *Purity and Danger: An Analysis of the Concepts of Pollution and Taboo* (London: Ark-Routledge and Kegan Paul, 1966), 15.

90 For a longer analysis of this, see Alice Macdonald, "Hairs on the Lens: Female Body Hair on the Screen," in *The Last Taboo: Women and Body Hair*, ed. Karin Lesnik-Oberstein (Manchester: Manchester University Press, 2006), 69.

91 Macdonald, "Hairs on the Lens," 69.

92 Julia Kristeva, *The Powers of Horror: An Essay on Abjection* (New York: Columbia University Press, 1982), 4.

93 Kristeva, *Powers of Horror*, 4.

94 Macdonald, "Hairs on the Lens," 70.

95 Emily Martin, *The Woman in the Body: A Cultural Analysis of Reproduction* (Boston: Beacon, 2001).

96 Martin, *Woman in the Body*, 13.

97 For a compelling analysis of how much attention is paid to women's body weight and the industries around dieting, how little is paid to women's body hair, and how women's body hair is far more invisible and thus carries the weight of patriarchy more silently than fatness, see Lesnik-Oberstein, "Last Taboo."

98 Catherine Hakim, "Erotic Capital," *European Sociological Review* 26, no. 5 (2010): 499–518.

99 Herzig, *Plucked*, 187.

100 Herzig, *Plucked*, 188.

101 Tondeur, "History of Pubic Hair," 56.

102 Tondeur, "History of Pubic Hair."

103 Herzig, *Plucked*, 190.

104 Weitz, *Rapunzel's Daughters*, xii.

105 Lesnik-Oberstein, *Last Taboo*, 1.

106 Pierce Alexander Dignam and Deana A. Rohlinger, "Misogynistic Men Online: How the Red Pill Helped Elect Trump," *Signs: Journal of Women in Culture and Society* 44, no. 3 (2019): 589–612. For a thorough discussion of the financial backing behind right-wing attacks of professors, see Isaac Kamola, "Dear Administrators: To Protect Your Faculty from Right-Wing Attacks, Follow the Money," *AAUP Journal of Academic Freedom* 10 (2019).

107 Herzig, *Plucked*, 78.

108 Dorothy Allison, *Two or Three Things I Know for Sure* (New York: Penguin, 1995), 71.

1. HAIRY SUBJECTS

1 Michel Foucault, *The History of Sexuality*, vol. 1 (New York: Vintage Books, 1990), 86.

2 Alicia Wallace, "Walmart CEO Says We're in the 'Hair Color' Phase of Panic Buying," CNN Business, April 11, 2020, www.cnn.com/2020/04/11/business /panic-buying-walmart-hair-color-coronavirus/index.html; Krisann Chasark, "Coronavirus Impact: Hair Dye Becoming Next High-Demand Item amid COVID-19 Pandemic," ABC, April 11, 2020, https://abc13.com/coronavirus -shopping-out-of-stock-hair-color-dye-items-selling/6095606.

3 Sara Ahmed, *The Cultural Politics of Emotion* (Edinburgh: Edinburgh University Press, 2014), 9.

4 Sara Rodrigues and Ela Przybylo, "Introduction: On the Politics of Ugliness," in *On the Politics of Ugliness*, ed. Sara Rodrigues and Ela Przybylo (London: Palgrave, 2018), 5.

5 Marika Tiggemann and Christine Lewis, "Attitudes toward Women's Body Hair: Relationship with Disgust Sensitivity," *Psychology of Women Quarterly* 28, no. 4 (2004): 381–87.

6 Marika Tiggemann and Suzanna Hodgson, "The Hairlessness Norm Extended: Reasons for and Predictors of Women's Body Hair Removal at Different Body Sites," *Sex Roles* 59, no. 11–12 (2008): 889–97; Breanne Fahs, "Imagining Ugliness: Failed Femininities, Shame, and Disgust Written onto the 'Other' Body," in *On the Politics of Ugliness*, ed. Sara Rodrigues and Ela Przybylo (London: Palgrave, 2018), 237–58.

7 Breanne Fahs and Denise A. Delgado, "The Specter of Excess: Race, Class, and Gender in Women's Body Hair Narratives," in *Embodied Resistance: Breaking the Rules, Challenging the Norms*, ed. Chris Bobel and Samantha Kwan (Nashville, TN: Vanderbilt University Press, 2011), 13–25.

8 Roxanne Dunbar-Ortiz, *Outlaw Woman: A Memoir of the War Years, 1960–1975* (Norman: University of Oklahoma Press, 2014), 210.

9 Diane Ponterotto, "Trivializing the Female Body: A Cross-Cultural Analysis of the Representation of Women in Sports Journalism," *Journal of International Women's Studies* 15, no. 2 (2014): 94–111; Gregory A. Cranmer, Maria Brann, and Nicholas D. Bowman, "Male Athletes, Female Aesthetics: The Continued Ambivalence toward Female Athletes in ESPN's *The Body Issue*," *International Journal of Sport Communication* 7, no. 2 (2014): 145–65.

10 Martha Rosler, *Semiotics of the Kitchen*, 1975, Collection of the Modern Museum of Art, New York, NY, www.moma.org/collection/works/88937; Judy Chicago, *Womanhouse*, 1972, for commentary, see Balasz Takac, "Inside *Womanhouse*, a Beacon of Feminist Art," *Widewalls*, June 2, 2019, www.widewalls.ch/judy-chicago -womanhouse; Mierle Laderman Ukeles, *Hartford Wash: Washing, Tracks, Maintenance—Outside and Inside*, July 22, 1973, Wadsworth Atheneum Museum, Hartford, CT, for commentary, see Rachel Wetzler, "Meet the Artist Who Called Out a Museum by Scrubbing the Floor for Hours," Timeline, December 15, 2016, https://timeline.com/mierle-ukeles-cleaning-museum-64d274a0a19c.

11 Deborah Morrison Thomson, "Big Food and the Body Politics of Personal Responsibility," *Southern Communication Journal* 74, no. 1 (2009): 2–17.

12 David Harvey, *A Brief History of Neoliberalism* (New York: Oxford University Press, 2007); Rosalind Gill and Christina Scharff, "Introduction," in *New Femininities: Postfeminism, Neoliberalism and Subjectivity*, ed. Rosalind Gill and Christina Scharff (New York: Palgrave, 2011), 2; Aihwa Ong, *Neoliberalism as Exception: Mutations in Citizenship and Sovereignty* (Durham, NC: Duke University Press, 2006).

13 A recent article found that only 8.6 percent of women had never groomed their pubic hair, a marked decrease from the past four decades. See Andrea L.

DeMaria and Abbey B. Berenson, "Prevalence and Correlates of Pubic Hair Grooming among Low-Income Hispanic, Black, and White Women," *Body Image* 10, no. 2 (2013): 226–31.

14 Amelia Thomson-Deveaux, "40 Percent of Men Have Asked Their Partner to Change Their Pubic Hair," *Cosmopolitan*, April 26, 2017, www.cosmopolitan.com /sex-love/a9535211/pubic-hair-removal-trends-stats.

15 Andrea L. DeMaria, Marissa Flores, Jacqueline M. Hirth, and Abbey B. Berenson, "Complications Related to Pubic Hair Removal," *American Journal of Obstetrics and Gynecology* 210, no. 6 (2014): 528-e1–e5.; Abigail C. Mancuso and Ginny L. Ryan, "Normal Vulvovaginal Health in Adolescents," *Journal of Pediatric and Adolescent Gynecology* 28, no. 3 (2015): 132–35.

16 Allison S. Glass, Herman S. Bagga, Gregory E. Tasian, Patrick B. Fisher, et al., "Pubic Hair Grooming Injuries Presenting to U.S. Emergency Departments," *Urology* 80, no. 6 (2012): 1187–91.

17 Kris G. McGrath, "An Earlier Age of Breast Cancer Diagnosis Is Related to More Frequent Use of Antiperspirants/Deodorants and Underarm Shaving," *European Journal of Cancer Prevention* 12, no. 6 (2003): 479–85.

18 Imelda Whelehan, *Overloaded: Feminism and Popular Culture* (London: Women's Press, 2000), 11.

19 Gill and Scharff, "Introduction," 3.

20 Gill and Scharff, "Introduction," 4; Angela McRobbie, "Post-feminism and Popular Culture," *Feminist Media Studies* 4, no. 3 (2004): 255–64.

21 Kristen A. Gonzalez, Johanna L. Ramirez, and M. Paz Galupo, "Increase in GLBTQ Minority Stress Following the 2016 Presidential Election," *Journal of GLBT Family Studies* 14, no. 1–2 (2018): 130–51; Ashley-Marie Daftary, Paul Devereux, and Marta Elliott, "Discrimination, Depression, and Anxiety among College Women in the Trump Era," *Journal of Gender Studies* 29, no. 7 (2020): 765–78.

22 Joanna Walters and Erin Durkin, "'I Feel Outraged, Exhausted and Betrayed': Kavanaugh Nomination—The Feminist Response," *Guardian*, October 6, 2018; Patt Morrison, "Column: A Year after the Election, There's Still Ferocious Power in the Phrase 'Nasty Woman,'" *Los Angeles Times*, November 8, 2017; Elise Andaya and Joanna Mishtal, "The Erosion of Rights to Abortion Care in the United States: A Call for a Renewed Anthropological Engagement with the Politics of Abortion," *Medical Anthropology Quarterly* 31, no. 1 (2017): 40–59.

23 Dana R. Fischer, *American Resistance: From the Women's March to the Blue Wave* (New York: Columbia University Press, 2019); Kaitlynn Mendes, Jessica Ringrose, and Jessalynn Keller, "#MeToo and the Promise and Pitfalls of Challenging Rape Culture through Digital Feminist Activism," *European Journal of Women's Studies* 25, no. 2 (2018): 236–46.

24 Breanne Fahs, *Firebrand Feminism: The Radical Lives of Ti-Grace Atkinson, Kathie Sarachild, Roxanne Dunbar-Ortiz, and Dana Densmore* (Seattle: University of Washington Press, 2018).

25 Bianca Fileborn and Rachel Loney-Howes, # *MeToo and the Politics of Social Change* (New York: Springer Nature, 2019); Nancy S. Love, "Ani DiFranco: Making Feminist Waves," in *Political Rock*, ed. Mark H. Pedelty and Kristine Weglarz (New York: Routledge, 2016), 185–202; Russell Rickford, "Black Lives Matter: Toward a Modern Practice of Mass Struggle," *New Labor Forum* 25, no. 1 (2016): 34–42; Anna Leigh, *Alexandria Ocasio-Cortez: Political Headliner* (Minneapolis: Lerner Books, 2020).

26 WITCH PDX, Twitter, https://twitter.com/witchpdx?lang=en. For a more thorough feminist analysis of witch symbolism in general, see Jessie Kindig, "All the Witches They Could Not Burn," *Boston Review*, December 2, 2018, http://bostonreview.net/gender-sexuality/jessie-kindig-all-witches-they-could-not-burn.

27 Andrea Long Chu, *Females* (New York: Verso, 2019); Andrea Long Chu, "On Liking Women," *n+1 Magazine* 30 (2018), https://nplusonemag.com/issue-30/essays/on-liking-women; KJ Cerankowski, "Praying for Pieces: A Practice in Building the Trans Body," *CrossCurrents* 68, no. 4 (2018): 515–24; Thea Cacchioni, *Big Pharma, Women, and the Labour of Love* (Toronto: University of Toronto Press, 2015); Chandan Reddy, "Neoliberalism Then and Now: Race, Sexuality, and the Black Radical Tradition," *GLQ* 25, no. 1 (2019): 150–55.

28 Helen Malson and Maree Burns, *Critical Feminist Approaches to Eating Dis/orders* (New York: Routledge, 2009); Sara Rodrigues and Ela Przybylo, *On the Politics of Ugliness* (London: Palgrave, 2018); Michelle Tea, *Against Memoir: Complaints, Confessions & Criticisms* (New York: Feminist Press, 2018); Anna Freixas, Bárbara Luque, and Amalia Reina, "Critical Feminist Gerontology: In the Back Room of Research," *Journal of Women & Aging* 24, no. 1 (2012): 44–58; Caroline Faria and Sharlene Mollett, "Critical Feminist Reflexivity and the Politics of Whiteness in the 'Field,'" *Gender, Place & Culture* 23, no. 1 (2016): 79–93; Jane Ussher, "A Critical Feminist Analysis of Madness: Pathologising Femininity through Psychiatric Discourse," in *Routledge International Handbook of Critical Mental Health*, ed. Jane Ussher (New York: Routledge, 2017), 96–102.

29 Amy L. Best, *Representing Youth: Methodological Issues in Critical Youth Studies* (New York: New York University Press, 2007); Joschka Philipps, "A Global Generation? Youth Studies in a Postcolonial World," *Societies* 8, no. 1 (2018): 1–18.

30 Audre Lorde, *Sister Outsider: Essays and Speeches* (Toronto: Crossing Press, 2012); Kimberlé Williams Crenshaw, "Twenty Years of Critical Race Theory: Looking Back to Move Forward," *Connecticut Law Review* 43, no. 5 (2010): 1253–1352; Sara Ahmed, *On Being Included: Racism and Diversity in Institutional Life* (Durham, NC: Duke University Press, 2012); bell hooks, *Teaching to Transgress* (New York: Routledge, 2014); Mireille Miller-Young, *A Taste for Brown Sugar: Black Women in Pornography* (Durham, NC: Duke University Press, 2014); James Baldwin, *Collected Essays*, vol. 2 (Washington, DC: Library of America, 1998).

31 Carolee Schneemann, *Interior Scroll*, August 1975, Women Here and Now, East Hampton, New York; Patty Chang, *Shaved (At a Loss)*, 1998, SD Video, www .pattychang.com/shaved-at-a-loss.

32 VALIE EXPORT, *Genital Panics: Action Pants*, 1969, Munich, Germany, for commentary, see Ruth Askey, "VALIE EXPORT Interviewed by Ruth Askey in Vienna 9/18/79," *High Performance* 4, no. 1 (1981): 14–19.

33 Kathy Davis, *Reshaping the Female Body: The Dilemma of Cosmetic Surgery* (New York: Routledge, 2013); Shelley Eriksen and Sara Goering, "A Test of the Agency Hypothesis in Women's Cosmetic Surgery Usage," *Sex Roles* 64, no. 11–12 (2011): 888–901; Anna Kirkland and Rosemarie Tong, "Working within Contradiction: The Possibility of Feminist Cosmetic Surgery," *Journal of Clinical Ethics* 7 (1996): 151–59; Samantha Crompvoets, "Comfort, Control, or Conformity: Women Who Choose Breast Reconstruction Following Mastectomy," *Health Care for Women International* 27, no. 1 (2006): 75–93; Patricia Gagné and Deanna McGaughey, "Designing Women: Cultural Hegemony and the Exercise of Power among Women Who Have Undergone Elective Mammoplasty," *Gender & Society* 16, no. 6 (2002): 814–38; Virginia Braun, "'The Women Are Doing It for Themselves': The Rhetoric of Choice and Agency around Female Genital 'Cosmetic Surgery,'" *Australian Feminist Studies* 24, no. 60 (2009): 233–49; Vanessa R. Schick, Sarah K. Calabrese, Brandi N. Rima, and Alyssa N. Zucker, "Genital Appearance Dissatisfaction: Implications for Women's Genital Image Self-Consciousness, Sexual Esteem, Sexual Satisfaction, and Sexual Risk," *Psychology of Women Quarterly* 34, no. 3 (2010): 394–404; Linda Duits and Liesbet Van Zoonen, "Headscarves and Porno-Chic: Disciplining Girls' Bodies in the European Multicultural Society," *European Journal of Women's Studies* 13, no. 2 (2006): 103–17; Adrienne Evans, Sarah Riley, and Avi Shankar, "Technologies of Sexiness: Theorizing Women's Engagement in the Sexualization of Culture," *Feminism & Psychology* 20, no. 1 (2010): 114–31; Catherine Hakim, "Erotic Capital," *European Sociological Review* 26, no. 5 (2010): 499–518; Beverly Yuen Thompson, "Myself, Covered," in *Embodied Resistance: Breaking the Rules, Challenging the Norms*, ed. Chris Bobel and Samantha Kwan (Nashville, TN: Vanderbilt University Press, 2011), 177–78.

34 Joan Chrisler, "Leaks, Lumps, and Lines: Stigma and Women's Bodies," *Psychology of Women Quarterly* 35, no. 2 (2011): 202–14.

35 Abbey Hyde, Jean Nee, Etaoine Howlett, Michelle Butler, and Jonathan Drennan, "The Ending of Menstruation: Perspectives and Experiences of Lesbian and Heterosexual Women," *Journal of Women & Aging* 23, no. 2 (2011): 160–76; Roseann M. Mandziuk, "'Ending Women's Greatest Hygienic Mistake': Modernity and the Mortification of Menstruation in Kotex Advertising, 1921–1926," *Women's Studies Quarterly* 38, no. 3/4 (2010): 42–62; Bernice Hausman, "The Feminist Politics of Breastfeeding," *Australian Feminist Studies* 19, no. 45 (2004): 273–85; Margrit Shildrick, *Leaky Bodies and Boundaries: Feminism, Postmodernism and (Bio)Ethics* (New York: Routledge, 2015); Samantha Warren

and Joanna Brewis, "Matter over Mind? Examining the Experience of Pregnancy," *Sociology* 38, no. 2 (2004): 219–36; Shannon K. Carter, "Beyond Control: Body and Self in Women's Childbearing Narratives," *Sociology of Health & Illness* 32, no. 7 (2010): 993–1009; Jan Draper, "Blurring, Moving and Broken Boundaries: Men's Encounters with the Pregnant Body," *Sociology of Health & Illness* 25, no. 7 (2003): 743–67; Shari L. Dworkin and Faye Linda Wachs, "'Getting Your Body Back': Postindustrial Fit Motherhood in *Shape Fit Pregnancy* Magazine," *Gender & Society* 18, no. 5 (2004): 610–24; Susan A. Basow and Amie C. Braman, "Women and Body Hair: Social Perceptions and Attitudes," *Psychology of Women Quarterly* 22, no. 4 (1998): 637–45; Breanne Fahs, "Dreaded 'Otherness': Heteronormative Patrolling in Women's Body Hair Rebellions," *Gender & Society* 25, no. 4 (2011): 451–72; Tiggemann and Kenyon, "Hairlessness Norm"; Merran Toerien and Sue Wilkinson, "Gender and Body Hair: Constructing the Feminine Woman," *Women's Studies International Forum* 26, no. 4 (2003): 333–44.

36 Janet K. Swim and Laurie L. Cohen, "Overt, Covert, and Subtle Sexism: A Comparison between the Attitudes toward Women and Modern Sexism Scales," *Psychology of Women Quarterly* 21, no. 1 (1997): 103–18.

37 Tiggemann and Kenyon, "Hairlessness Norm"; Tiggemann and Lewis, "Women's Body Hair"; Merran Toerien, Sue Wilkinson, and Precilla Y. L. Choi, "Body Hair Removal: The 'Mundane' Production of Normative Femininity," *Sex Roles* 52, no. 5–6 (2005): 399–406.

38 Wendy Cooper, *Hair: Sex, Society, Symbolism* (London: Aldus, 1971); Tiggemann and Kenyon, "Hairlessness Norm"; Toerien, Wilkinson, and Choi, "Body Hair Removal."

39 Sara Ramsey, Clare Sweeney, Michael Fraser, and Gren Oades, "Pubic Hair and Sexuality: A Review," *Journal of Sexual Medicine* 6, no. 8 (2009): 2102–10; Debra Herbenick, Vanessa Schick, Michael Reece, Stephanie Sanders, and J. Dennis Fortenberry, "Pubic Hair Removal among Women in the United States: Prevalence, Methods, and Characteristics," *Journal of Sexual Medicine* 7, no. 10 (2010): 3322–30; Vanessa R. Schick, Brandi N. Rima, and Sarah K. Calabrese, "*Evulvalution*: The Portrayal of Women's External Genitalia and Physique across Time and the Current Barbie Doll Ideals," *Journal of Sex Research* 48, no. 1 (2011): 74–81.

40 Linda Smolak and Sarah K. Murnen, "Gender, Self-Objectification and Pubic Hair Removal," *Sex Roles* 65, no. 7–8 (2011): 506–17.

41 Virginia Braun, Gemma Tricklebank, and Victoria Clarke, "'It Shouldn't Stick Out from Your Bikini at the Beach': Meaning, Gender, and the Hairy/Hairless Body," *Psychology of Women Quarterly* 37, no. 4 (2013): 478–93.

42 Susan A. Basow and Joanna Willis, "Perceptions of Body Hair on White Women: Effects of Labeling," *Psychological Reports* 89, no. 3 (2001): 571–76; Toerien, Wilkinson, and Choi, "Body Hair Removal."

43 Tiggemann and Hodgson, "Hairlessness Norm Extended"; Whelehan, *Overloaded.*

44 Christine Hope, "Caucasian Female Body Hair and American Culture," *Journal of American Culture* 5, no. 1 (1982): 93–99; Rebecca Herzig, *Plucked: A History of Hair Removal* (New York: New York University Press, 2015).

45 Meredith Dault, "The Last Triangle: Sex, Money, and the Politics of Pubic Hair" (master's thesis, Queen's University, 2011); Megan Duesterhaus, Liz Grauerholz, Rebecca Weichsel, and Nicholas A. Guittar, "The Cost of Doing Femininity: Gendered Disparities in Pricing of Personal Care Products and Services," *Gender Issues* 28, no. 4 (2011): 175–91.

46 Candace West and Don H. Zimmerman, "Doing Gender," *Gender & Society* 1, no. 2 (1987): 125–51; Kristen Schilt and Laurel Westbrook, "Doing Gender, Doing Heteronormativity: 'Gender Normals,' Transgender People, and the Social Maintenance of Heterosexuality," *Gender & Society* 23, no. 4 (2009): 440–64.

47 Sandra C. Anderson and Mindy Holliday, "Normative Passing in the Lesbian Community: An Exploratory Study," *Journal of Gay & Lesbian Social Services* 17, no. 3 (2004): 25–38; Margaret L. Stubbs and Daryl Costos, "Negative Attitudes toward Menstruation: Implications for Disconnection within Girls and between Women," *Women & Therapy* 27, no. 3–4 (2004): 37–54; Ayana D. Byrd and Akiba Solomon, *Naked: Black Women Bare All about Their Skin, Hair, Hips, Lips, and Other Parts* (New York: Penguin, 2005); Judith Kegan Gardiner, "Can Ms. Prozac Talk Back? Feminism, Drugs, and Social Constructionism," *Feminist Studies* 21, no. 3 (1995): 501–17.

48 Toerien, Wilkinson, and Choi, "Body Hair Removal," 405.

49 Toerien and Wilkinson, "Gender and Body Hair"; Merran Toerien and Sue Wilkinson, "Exploring the Depilation Norm: A Qualitative Questionnaire Study of Women's Body Hair Removal," *Qualitative Research in Psychology* 1, no. 1 (2004): 69–92.

50 Basow and Braman, "Women and Body Hair"; Basow and Willis, "Perceptions of Body Hair."

51 Tiggemann and Hodgson, "Hairlessness Norm Extended."

52 Tiggemann and Hodgson, "Hairlessness Norm Extended"; Herbenick, Schick, Reece, Sanders, and Fortenberry, "Pubic Hair Removal"; Tiggemann and Hodgson, "Hairlessness Norm Extended."

53 Toerien and Wilkinson, "Exploring the Depilation Norm"; Wendy Chapkis, *Beauty Secrets: Women and the Politics of Appearance* (Boston: South End Press, 1986); Tiggemann and Hodgson, "Hairlessness Norm Extended."

54 Breanne Fahs, *Performing Sex: The Making and Unmaking of Women's Erotic Lives* (Albany: State University of New York Press, 2011); Adrienne Rich, "Compulsory Heterosexuality and the Lesbian Existence," *Signs* 5, no. 4 (1980): 631–60.

55 Fahs and Delgado, "Specter of Excess."

56 Rose Weitz, "Women and Their Hair: Seeking Power through Resistance and Accommodation," *Gender & Society* 15, no. 5 (2001): 667–86.

57 Maxine Craig, *Ain't I a Beauty Queen? Black Women, Beauty, and the Politics of Race* (New York: Oxford University Press, 2002).

58 Sarah A. Vannier, Anna B. Currie, and Lucia F. O'Sullivan "Schoolgirls and Soccer Moms: A Content Analysis of Free 'Teen' and 'MILF' Online Pornography," *Journal of Sex Research* 51, no. 3 (2014): 253–64; A. Dana Ménard and Peggy J. Kleinplatz, "Twenty-One Moves Guaranteed to Make His Thighs Go up in Flames: Depictions of 'Great Sex' in Popular Magazines," *Sexuality & Culture* 12, no. 1 (2008): 1–20.

59 Meg Butler, "Do You Let It Grow? Women Who Don't Shave," *Madame Noire*, 2015, http://madamenoire.com/528409/do-you-let-it-grow-celebrity-women-who-dont-shave/5.

60 Peter Holley, "Why Women Are Dyeing Their Armpit Hair," *Washington Post*, December 13, 2014; Andrea Adam Newman, "Women Who Dye Their (Armpit) Hair," *New York Times*, July 14, 2015.

61 Kimberley Fry and Cheryl Lousley, "Girls Just Want to Have Fun with Politics: Out of the Contradictions of Popular Culture, Eco-Grrrls Are Rising to Define Feminism, Environmentalism, and Political Action," *Alternatives Journal* 27, no. 2 (2001): 24–28.

62 Toerien and Wilkinson, "Gender and Body Hair."

63 Susan A. Basow, "Women and Their Body Hair," *Psychology of Women Quarterly* 15, no. 1 (1991): 83–96; Toerian and Wilkinson, "Gender and Body Hair."

64 Michael Boroughs, Guy Cafri, and J. Kevin Thompson, "Male Body Depilation: Prevalence and Associated Features of Body Hair Removal," *Sex Roles* 52, no. 9 (2005): 637–44; Alan Dixson, Rebecca East, Gayle Halliwell, and Praveen Wignarajah, "Masculine Somatotype and Hirsuteness as Determinants of Sexual Attraction to Women," *Archives of Sexual Behavior* 32, no. 1 (2003): 29–39; Breanne Fahs, "Shaving It All Off: Examining Social Norms of Body Hair among College Men in a Women's Studies Course," *Women's Studies* 42, no. 5 (2013): 559–77.

65 Basow, "Women and Their Body Hair."

66 Fahs, "Dreaded 'Otherness.'"

67 Fahs and Delgado, "Specter of Excess."

68 Fahs, "Shaving It All Off."

69 Breanne Fahs, "Breaking Body Hair Boundaries: Classroom Exercises for Challenging Social Constructions of the Body and Sexuality," *Feminism & Psychology* 22, no. 4 (2012): 482–506. I did not ask directly about students' sexual identities, but most students referred in their response papers to the gender of their current or past sexual partners (e.g., "my boyfriend") or specifically mentioned their sexual identity as part of their narratives. Roughly forty (65 percent) described having exclusively male partners or suggested a heterosexual identity, whereas roughly thirteen (21 percent) described having exclusively female partners or mentioned a lesbian identity, and nine (14 percent) described both male and female partners and/or a bisexual identity.

70 Fahs and Delgado, "Specter of Excess."

71 Foucault, *History of Sexuality*, 96.

72 Foucault, *History of Sexuality*, 101.

2. BODY HAIR BATTLEGROUNDS

1 Breanne Fahs and Denise A. Delgado, "The Specter of Excess: Race, Class, and Gender in Women's Body Hair Narratives," in *Embodied Resistance: Breaking the Rules, Challenging the Norms*, ed. Chris Bobel and Samantha Kwan (Nashville, TN: Vanderbilt University Press, 2011), 13–25; Breanne Fahs, "Dreaded 'Otherness': Heteronormative Patrolling in Women's Body Hair Rebellions," *Gender & Society* 25, no. 4 (2011): 451–72; Breanne Fahs, "Breaking Body Hair Boundaries: Classroom Exercises for Challenging Social Constructions of the Body and Sexuality," *Feminism & Psychology* 22, no. 4 (2012): 482–506; Breanne Fahs, "Shaving It All Off: Examining Social Norms of Body Hair among College Men in a Women's Studies Course," *Women's Studies* 42, no. 5 (2013): 559–77.

2 Nancy A. Naples and Karen Bojar, *Teaching Feminist Activism: Strategies from the Field* (New York: Routledge, 2013); Suki Ali, "Black Feminist Praxis: Some Reflections on Pedagogies and Politics in Higher Education," *Race Ethnicity and Education* 12, no. 1 (2009): 79–86.

3 Gareth Terry and Virginia Braun, "To Let Hair Be, or to Not Let Hair Be? Gender and Body Hair Removal Practices in Aotearoa/New Zealand," *Body Image* 10, no. 4 (2013): 599–606; Victoria Clarke and Virginia Braun, "How Can a Heterosexual Man Remove His Body Hair and Retain His Masculinity? Mapping Stories of Male Body Hair Depilation," *Qualitative Research in Psychology* 16, no. 1 (2019): 96–114.

4 Karen McCarthy, Meghan Ballog, Maria Mayela Carranza, and Katie Lee, "Doing Nonbinary Gender: The Occupational Experience of Nonbinary Persons in the Environment," *Journal of Occupational Science* (2020): 1–16, published online in advance of print publication; Harry Barbee and Douglas Schrock, "Un/gendering Social Selves: How Nonbinary People Navigate and Experience a Binarily Gendered World," *Sociological Forum* 34, no. 3 (2019): 572–93.

5 Suzanne Staggenborg and Verta Taylor, "Whatever Happened to the Women's Movement?" *Mobilization: An International Quarterly* 10, no. 1 (2005): 37–52.

3. HAIRY, NOT SO SCARY

1 Dana Mastro and Andrea Figueroa-Caballero, "Measuring Extremes: A Quantitative Content Analysis of Prime Time TV Depictions of Body Type," *Journal of Broadcasting & Electronic Media* 62, no. 2 (2018): 320–36.

2 Red Chidgey, "The Resisting Subject: Per-Zines as Life Story Data," *University of Sussex Journal of Contemporary History* 10 (Spring 2006), www.sussex.ac.uk /webteam/gateway/file.php? name=10-a-chidgey-perzines-final&site=15.

3 Chris Bobel, *New Blood: Third-Wave Feminism and the Politics of Menstruation* (New Brunswick, NJ: Rutgers University Press, 2010), 113; Stephen Duncombe, *Notes from the Underground: Zines and the Politics of Alternative Culture* (Portland: Microcosm, 2014), 6–7.

4 Duncombe, *Notes from Underground*, 9–13. For a look at some of the feminist zines that have been digitally archived, see the Queer Zine Archive Project, 2014, https: //archive.qzap.org/index.php/Search/Index/search/ca_objects .keywords% 3Afeminism#.

5 Jennifer Bleyer, "Cut-and-Paste Revolution: Notes from the Girl Zine Explosion," in *The Fire This Time: Young Activists and the New Feminism*, ed. Vivien Labaton and Dawn Lundy Martin (New York: Anchor Books, 2004), 49.

6 Bobel, *New Blood*, 114; Susan Lurie, Ann Cvetkovich, Jane Gallop, Tania Modleski, and Hortense Spillers, "Roundtable: Restoring Feminist Politics to Poststructuralist Critique," *Feminist Studies* 27, no. 3 (2001): 702.

7 Bobel, *New Blood*, 114; Dawn Bates and Maureen McHugh, "Zines: Voices of Third Wave Feminists," in *Different Wavelengths: Studies of the Contemporary Women's Movement*, ed. Jo Reger (New York: Routledge, 2014), 209–24.

8 Bobel, *New Blood*, 114; Julie Chu, "Navigating the Media Environment: How Youth Claim a Place through Zines," *Social Justice* 24, no. 3 (1997): 71–85.

9 Bobel, *New Blood*, 114.

10 Michelle Kempson, "'My Version of Feminism': Subjectivity, DIY and the Feminist Zine," *Social Movement Studies* 14, no. 4 (2015): 459–72.

11 Elke Zobl, "Cultural Production, Transnational Networking, and Critical Reflection in Feminist Zines," *Signs: Journal of Women in Culture and Society* 35, no. 1 (2009): 1–12.

12 Red Chidgey, "Reassess Your Weapons: The Making of Feminist Memory in Young Women's Zines," *Women's History Review* 22, no. 4 (2013): 658–72.

13 Kimberly Creasap, "Zine Making as Feminist Pedagogy," *Feminist Teacher* 24, no. 3 (2014): 155–68.

14 Adela C. Licona, "(B)orderlands' Rhetorics and Representations: The Transformative Potential of Feminist Third-Space Scholarship and Zines," *NWSA Journal* 17, no. 2 (2005): 104–29.

15 The poem that follows the title of this section is attributed to @alokvmenon, as cited by Dena Lake, *Hairy: A Zine Braiding Personal + Political Strands of Hair* (2020), 19.

16 For a more detailed description of the history of qualitative content analysis and its strengths and weaknesses as a method, see Philipp Mayring, "Qualitative Content Analysis," in *A Companion to Qualitative Research*, ed. Uwe Flick, Ernst von Kardoff, and Ines Steinke (London: Sage, 2004), 156–76.

17 Eddie Jude, "From a Young Age You Learn It's Never a Good Idea to Stray from the Pack," *Static Zine* 7 (Body Issue, May 2015), 7.

18 Janice Quiles-Reyes, *Frida at My Table*, vol. 2 (2019), 1.

19 Crash Reynolds and Edd Castillo, *Why Does Society Care So Much about My Body Hair* (June 2019), 1.

20 Olga Alexandru, *Body Hair: A Love/Hate Story* (n.d.), 1.

21 Lubadalu, *Affirmations* (2020), 6, 10.

22 Reynolds and Castillo, *Why Does Society Care.*

23 Lake, *Hairy*, 5.

24 Janice Quiles-Reyes, *Frida at My Table*, vol. 1 (2016), 1–2.

25 Quiles-Reyes, *Frida at My Table*, vol. 2, 4.

26 Janice Quiles-Reyes, *Hairy, Not So Scary* (2018), 10.

27 Alexandru, *Body Hair*, 14.

28 Bitter Tooth, *a lil zine about shaving and me not doing it*, 1–2.

29 Alexandru, *Body Hair*, 4.

30 Jen Venegas, *Hairy Femme Mother*, vol. 3 (n.d.), 32–33.

31 Bitter Tooth, *lil zine about shaving*, 3–4.

32 Lake, *Hairy*, 12.

33 Reynolds and Castillo, *Why Does Society Care*, 3.

34 Quiles-Reyes, *Hairy, Not So Scary*, 16.

35 Maryam Adib, *A Journey into Body Hair* (n.d.), 2.

36 Jen Venegas, *Hairy Femme Mother*, vol. 1 (n.d.), 34–35.

37 Alexandru, *Body Hair*, 5.

38 Venegas, *Hairy Femme Mother*, vol. 1, 21–22.

39 Bitter Tooth, *lil zine about shaving*, 6.

40 Bitter Tooth, *lil zine about shaving*, 9–12.

41 Venegas, *Hairy Femme Mother*, vol. 3, 32–33.

42 Venegas, *Hairy Femme Mother*, vol. 1, 29–30.

43 Olivia M., "Hairy Disabled Latina Femme," in *Hairy Femme Mother*, vol. 2, ed. Jen Venegas (n.d.), 13–17.

44 Venegas, *Hairy Femme Mother*, vol. 1 (n.d.), 3–5.

45 Dayanita Ramesh, *Hairy Hair* (July 2015), 1.

46 Ramesh, *Hairy Hair*, 1.

47 Jaliessa Sipress, "Hairy while Black," in *Hairy Femme Mother*, vol. 2, ed. Jen Venegas (n.d.), 52–53.

48 Venegas, *Hairy Femme Mother*, vol. 1, 22.

49 Alexandru, *Body Hair*, 3.

50 Nancy Aragon, "Open Letter to: White Supremacist, Capitalist, Hetero Patriarchal Hairless America," in *Hairy Femme Mother*, vol. 2, ed. Jen Venegas (n.d.), 42. The Spanish text translates to "Because we are seeds and we will continue to grow."

51 Jamie Squire, *Hairy & Happy* (n.d.), 11.

52 Quiles-Reyes, *Frida at My Table*, vol. 2, 4.

53 Adib, *Journey into Body Hair*, 4.

54 Quiles-Reyes, *Frida at My Table*, vol. 1, 3–4.

55 Quiles-Reyes, *Hairy, Not So Scary*, 19.

56 Lake, *Hairy*, 13.

57 Adib, *Journey into Body Hair*, 6.

58 Venegas, *Hairy Femme Mother*, vol. 1, 36.

59 Squire, *Hairy & Happy*, 6–7.

60 Noor Bhangu, "Self-Preservation," *Nat. Brut.*, 2016, www.natbrut.com/ayqa -khan.

61 Bhangu, "Self-Preservation."

62 WYSK, "After Receiving Hate Comments, Artist Ayqa Khan Took to Tumblr 'to Talk about Body Hair,'" Women You Should Know, January 20, 2016, https: //womenyoushouldknow.net/after-receiving-hate-comments-artist-ayqa-khan -took-to-tumblr-to-talk-about-body-hair.

63 Katherine Brooks, "A Young Artist Wants to Give South Asian Women the Spotlight They Deserve," Huffington Post, October 28, 2016, www.huffpost .com/entry/ayqa-khan-south-asian-artist_n_569d6c21e4b00f3e9862ab98 ?guccounter=1.

64 Brooks, "Young Artist."

65 WYSK, "After Receiving Hate Comments."

66 Brooks, "Young Artist."

67 Brooks, "Young Artist"; Imaan Sheikh, "Meet the Pakistani-American Artist Taking a Stand to Normalise Body Hair," BuzzFeed, January 19, 2016, www .buzzfeed.com/imaansheikh/ayqa-khan#.cdqpbBZEX; Alison Roberts, "A Space of Her Own: Ayqa Khan Raises a Voice," *Vice*, July 6, 2016, www.vice.com/en_us /article/nz4g4m/ayqa-khan-raises-a-voice-for-south-asian-women; Fariha Roisin, "Youth Artists Ayqa Khan and Goth Shakira Discuss the Pressures of Being in the Public Eye," *Teen Vogue*, April 13, 2017, www.teenvogue.com/story /youth-artists-ayqa-khan-and-goth-shakira-discuss-the-pressures-of-being-in -the-public-eye.

68 Roberts, "Space of Her Own."

69 Michel Foucault, *The History of Sexuality*, vol. 1 (New York: Vintage Books, 1990), 96.

4. EXPANDING THE BODY HAIR IMAGINARY

1 Rebecca Herzig, *Plucked: A History of Hair Removal* (New York: New York University Press, 2015), 78.

2 "Abject Art," Tate Modern, accessed July 20, 2020, www.tate.org.uk/art/art -terms/a/abject-art.

3 Julia Kristeva, *The Powers of Horror: An Essay on Abjection* (New York: Columbia University Press, 1982).

4 Georges Bataille, *The Story of the Eye (Histoire de l'Oeil)* (New York: Urizen Books, 1977), originally published in 1928 under the pseudonym Lord Auch; Georges Bataille, *Blue of Noon (Le Bleu du Ciel)* (Paris: J. Pauvert, 1957), originally written in 1935 but not published until 1957.

5 "Abject Art."

6 Betsy Sussler and Cindy Sherman, "An Interview with Cindy Sherman," *Bomb* 12 (1985): 30–33; Jennifer Dalton, Nikki S. Lee, Anthony Goicolea, and David Henry Brown, "Look at Me: Self-Portrait Photography after Cindy Sherman," *PAJ: A Journal of Performance and Art* 22, no. 3 (2000): 47–56; "Cindy Sherman," Museum of Modern Art, accessed July 20, 2020, www.moma.org/artists/5392.

7 Andrea Juno, "Interview with Carolee Schneemann," in *Angry Women*, ed. V. Vale (San Francisco: Re/Search, 1991), 66–77; Carolee Schneemann, *Imagining Her Erotics: Essays, Interviews, Projects* (Boston: MIT Press, 2003).

8 Mignon Nixon, *Fantastic Reality: Louis Bourgeois and a Story of Modern Art* (Boston: MIT Press, 2005); Helen Chadwick and Mark Holburn, *Enfleshings: Helen Chadwick* (New York: Aperture, 1989); Amna Malik, *Sarah Lucas: Au Naturel* (London: Afterall Books, 2009); Wendy Weitman, Kiki Smith, and John Coletti, *Kiki Smith: Prints, Books & Things* (New York: Museum of Modern Art, 2003).

9 Arthur Lubow, *Diane Arbus* (New York: Random House, 2016); Diane Arbus, *In the Beginning*, Metropolitan Museum of Art, New York, NY, July 12–November 27, 2016, www.metmuseum.org/exhibitions/listings/2016/diane-arbus.

10 Herzig, *Plucked*, 76.

11 Herzig, *Plucked*, 76–82.

12 Herzig, *Plucked*, 77.

13 Herzig, *Plucked*, 77. For a broader discussion of whiteness, race, immigration, and xenophobia, see David R. Roediger, *Working toward Whiteness: How America's Immigrants Became White* (New York: Basic Books, 2006).

14 Herzig, *Plucked*, 79.

15 Peter Stearns, *Battleground of Desire: The Struggle for Self-Control in Modern America* (New York: New York University Press, 1999), 99–100.

16 Herzig, *Plucked*, 90.

17 Zara Kenyon, "Hairy Armpits Are 'Natural Beauty' in Ben Hopper's Exhibition," *Cosmopolitan*, April 17, 2014, www.cosmopolitan.com/uk/beauty-hair/news/a26312/ben-hopper-natural-beauty-exhibition.

18 Isaac Saul, "Striking Photos Aim to Redefine 'Natural' Female Beauty," Huffington Post, April 7, 2014, www.huffpost.com/entry/ben-hopper-photos-natural-beauty_n_5104969.

19 Kenyon, "Hairy Armpits Are 'Natural Beauty.'"

20 Margot Peppers, "Body Hair Is Natural, NOT Gross: Striking Images of Women with Unshaven Underarms Protest Conventional Standards of Beauty," *Daily Mail*, April 8, 2014.

21 Katy Young, "Natural Beauty: The Exhibition Making a Statement about Armpit Hair," *Telegraph*, April 15, 2014.

22 Katherine Toland Frith, Hong Cheng, and Ping Shaw, "Race and Beauty: A Comparison of Asian and Western Models in Women's Magazine Advertisements," *Sex Roles* 50, no. 1–2 (2004): 53–61; Michelle Lazar, "Consuming Personal Relationships: The Achievement of Feminine Self-Identity through

Other-Centeredness," in *Gender Identity and Discourse Analysis*, ed. Jane Sunderland and Lia Litosseliti (Amsterdam: John Benjamins Press, 2002), 111–28.

23 Christopher Koulouris, "Ben Hopper Natural Beauty: Do Hairy Armpits Make Skinny Girls Hot?" Scallywag and Vagabond, April 8, 2014, https://scallywagandvagabond.com/2014/04/ben-hopper-natural-beauty-hairy-armpits-make-skinny-girls-hot.

24 Peppers, "Body Hair Is Natural."

25 Ben Hopper, *Natural Beauty*, Ben Hopper, accessed September 1, 2020, www.therealbenhopper.com/Projects/Natural-Beauty/1/thumbs.

26 Young, "Natural Beauty."

27 Brenda Pitt, "Models Protest Beauty Standards by Growing Fabulous Armpit Hair," *Bust*, 2014, https://bust.com/arts/11990-models-protest-beauty-standards-by-growing-fabulous-armpit-hair.html#.U1hOjuZdW5Z.

28 Michelle, "Hairy Armpits and Natural Beauty," *Thou Shall Not Covet* (blog), https://thoushaltnotcovet.net/2014/04/21/hairy-armpits-natural-beauty.

29 Bre Payton, "Dear Ladies: Growing Out Your Armpit Hair Is a Terrible Idea," Federalist, June 15, 2015, https://thefederalist.com/2015/06/15/armpit-hair-bad-idea.

30 Payton, "Dear Ladies."

31 "Meet Zuly Garcia," *Voyage LA*, October 24, 2018, http://voyagela.com/interview/meet-zuly-garcia/?doing_wp_cron=1569225659.4327249526977539062500.

32 "Meet Zuly Garcia."

33 Araceli Cruz, "Latina Artist Is Tearing apart European Beauty Standards One Picture at a Time," HipLatina, July 31, 2017, https://hiplatina.com/beauty-standards-art/.

34 "Meet Zuly Garcia." Notably, the Slumber Party Barbie, released in 1965, came with a plastic pink scale, a book on how to lose weight, and miniature diet pills. See Martha De Lacey, "'Don't Eat!': Controversial 1965 Slumber Party Barbie Came with Scales Permanently Set to Just 100lbs and a Diet Book Telling Her Not to Eat," *Daily Mail*, November 29, 2012, www.dailymail.co.uk/femail/article-2239931/1965-Slumber-Party-Barbie-came-scales-set-110lbs-diet-book-telling-eat.html.

35 Zuly Garcia, "Flores Politicos," @dolescent, June 29, 2018, www.adolescent.net/a/flores-politicos; for information about the Politics of Womanhood show, see Cruz, "Latina Artist."

36 "This Oaxaqueña Is Using Her Photography to Challenge Body Hair Beauty Norms," HipLatina, June 10, 2018, https://hiplatina.com/zuly-garcia-photography-body-hair.

37 "Zuly de la Rose," 22 *West Magazine*, November 11, 2017, https://medium.com/22westmag/zuly-de-la-rose-f49824a75715; see also Alejandra Martinez, "'Flores Politicos' Photos Highlight Oaxacan Culture and Break Down Beauty Norms," NPR Latino USA, July 27, 2017, www.latinousa.org/2017/07/27/flores-politicos-photos-highlight-oaxacan-culture-break-beauty-norms.

38 "Meet Zuly Garcia."

39 "This Oaxaqueña."

40 "This Oaxaqueña."

41 "This Oaxaqueña."

42 Kimberly Drew, "Pussy Power," *Playboy*, September 17, 2019, www.playboy.com /read/pussy-power-marilyn-minter.

43 Drew, "Pussy Power."

44 Drew, "Pussy Power."

45 Drew, "Pussy Power."

46 Drew, "Pussy Power."

47 Drew, "Pussy Power."

48 Joseph Keckler, "Artist Marilyn Minter on Her First Retrospective, Anti-censorship, and Pubes," *Vice*, August 11, 2015, www.vice.com/en_us/article /qbxw5m/enough-success-to-keep-going-0000713-v22n8.

49 Eliza Jordan, "Marilyn Minter: Art, Activism, Glamour, and Sex," *Whitewall*, May 25, 2017, www.whitewall.art/art/marilyn-minter-art-activism-glamour-sex.

50 Alanna Martinez, "Marilyn Minter's First Artist's Book Examines the Beauty of Female Pubic Hair," *Observer*, December 2, 2014, https://observer.com/2014 /12/marilyn-minters-first-artists-book-examines-the-beauty-of-female-pubic -hair.

51 Drew, "Pussy Power."

52 Priscilla Frank, "Glorious NSFW Art Book Examines the Beauty of Female Pubic Hair," Huffington Post, December 6, 2017, www.huffpost.com/entry/plush -marilyn-minter_n_6290050.

53 Marilyn Minter, *Plush* (New York: Fulton Ryder, 2014).

54 Martinez, "Marilyn Minter's First Artist's Book."

55 Frank, "Glorious NSFW Art Book."

56 Drew, "Pussy Power."

57 Alex Fialho, "Marilyn Minter," April 17, 2015, www.artforum.com/interviews /marilyn-minter-talks-about-her-touring-retrospective-51525.

58 Drew, "Pussy Power."

59 Sarah Trigg, "A Peek at Marilyn Minter's Bush Book," Vulture, December 1, 2014, www.vulture.com/2014/12/peek-at-marilyn-minters-bush-book-nsfw .html.

60 "Marilyn Minter's 'Plush' Book Celebrates Female Hair Down There," Cause and Yvette, December 26, 2014, https://causeandyvette.com/marilyn-minters -plush-book-celebrates-female-hair-down-there.

61 Chelsea G. Summers, "A Brief History of Pubic Hair in Art," Vulture, Decem-ber 16, 2014, www.vulture.com/2014/12/brief-history-of-pubic-hair-in-art.html.

62 Jordan, "Marilyn Minter."

63 Owen Campbell, "Humid and Moist, a High-Definition Look at Bush in Minter's 'Plush,'" ASX, January 5, 2015, https://americansuburbx.com/2015/01 /marilyn-minter-plush.html.

64 Alice Butler, "Eleanor Antin on Art, Ageing and Grief," Frieze, May 29, 2019, https://frieze.com/article/eleanor-antin-art-ageing-and-grief.

65 Butler, "Eleanor Antin on Art."

66 Clare Johnson, "Traces of Feminist Art: Temporal Complexity in the Work of Eleanor Antin, Vanessa Beecroft, and Elizabeth Manchester," Feminist Theory 7, no. 3 (2006): 309–31; 315–16.

67 Eleanor Antin, as quoted in Butler, "Eleanor Antin on Art."

68 Jori Finkel, "Eleanor Antin Revisits Her Dieting Diary, 45 Years on, for LACMA Show," Art Newspaper, November 15, 2018, www.theartnewspaper.com/news /artist-takes-on-the-naked-truth.

69 Butler, "Eleanor Antin on Art."

70 Finkel, "Eleanor Antin Revisits."

71 Elizabeth Freeman, Time Binds: Queer Temporalities, Queer Histories (Durham, NC: Duke University Press, 2010).

72 Johnson, "Traces of Feminist Art."

73 Johnson, "Traces of Feminist Art," 316.

74 Butler, "Eleanor Antin on Art."

5. CHINA'S ARMPIT HAIR CONTEST

1 Aisha Mirza, "Why Body Hair Is on the Frontline of Feminist Action," Independent, August 16, 2012, www.independent.co.uk/voices/comment/why -body-hair-is-on-the-frontline-of-feminist-action-8457424.html; Christian Shepherd, "Four Chinese Activists Shave Heads to Protest 'Persecution' of Husbands," Reuters, December 17, 2018, www.reuters.com/article/us-china -rights/four-chinese-activists-shave-heads-to-protest-persecution-of-husbands -idUSKBN1OGoYB; Millicent Cooke, "Januhairy: Why Women Are Growing Out Their Body Hair," BBC News, January 4, 2019, www.bbc.com/news/uk -england-46747452.

2 C. Fred Blake, "Foot Binding in Neo-Confucian China and the Appropriation of Female Labor," Signs 19, no. 3. (1994): 676–712.

3 Tina Mai Chen, "Dressing for the Party: Clothing, Citizenship, and Gender-Formation in Mao's China," Fashion Theory 5, no. 2 (2001): 143–71; Wenqi Yang and Fei Yan, "The Annihilation of Femininity in Mao's China: Gender Inequality of Sent-Down Youth During the Cultural Revolution," China Information 31, no. 1 (2017): 63–83.

4 Manya Koetse, "Is There No Chinese Feminism?," What's on Weibo, May 20, 2015, www.whatsonweibo.com/is-there-no-chinese-feminism.

5 Leta Hong Fincher, Betraying Big Brother: The Feminist Awakening in China (New York: Verso Books, 2018), 4.

6 Koetse, "Is There No Chinese Feminism?"

7 Koetse, "Is There No Chinese Feminism?"

8 Yingchun Ji, "Between Tradition and Modernity: 'Leftover' Women in Shanghai," *Journal of Marriage and Family* 77, no. 5 (2015): 1057–73.

9 Koetse, "Is There No Chinese Feminism?" For the image itself, see www.whatsonweibo.com/wp-content/uploads/2015/05/69cc29ofjw1erd5ma7hbwj2oc8ogb75i.jpg.

10 Xiao-yuan Dong and Xinli An, "Gender Patterns and Value of Unpaid Care Work: Findings from China's First Large-Scale Time Use Survey," *Review of Income and Wealth* 61, no. 3 (2015): 540–60.

11 Leta Hong Fincher, *Leftover Women: The Resurgence of Gender Inequality in China* (Chicago: Zed Books, 2016).

12 Leta Hong Fincher, "China's Feminist Five," *Dissent*, Fall 2016, www.dissentmagazine.org/article/china-feminist-five.

13 Fincher, "China's Feminist Five"; see also Fincher, *Leftover Women*.

14 Anna Fifield, "Two-Husband Strategy May Be a Remedy for China's One-Child Policy, Professor Posits," *Washington Post*, June 10, 2020.

15 Xiao Ban, as quoted in Koetse, "Is There No Chinese Feminism?"

16 Xiao Meili, "China's Feminist Awakening," *New York Times*, May 13, 2015.

17 Xiao, "China's Feminist Awakening."

18 Wei Wei, "Street, Behavior, Art: Advocating Gender Rights and the Innovation of a Social Movement Repertoire," *Chinese Journal of Sociology* 1, no. 2 (2015): 279–304.

19 Fincher, "China's Feminist Five."

20 Fincher, "China's Feminist Five."

21 Lu Pin, "Two Years On: Is China's Domestic Violence Law Working?," Amnesty International, March 7, 2018, www.amnesty.org/en/latest/campaigns/2018/03/is-china-domestic-violence-law-working.

22 "Half of Men Report Using Violence and a Quarter Perpetrate Rape According to UN Survey of 10,000 Men in Asia-Pacific," UN Women, September 10, 2013, www.unwomen.org/en/news/stories/2013/9/half-of-men-report-using-violence-and-a-quarter-perpetrate-rape-according-to-un-survey.

23 Hongwei Bao, "'Anti–Domestic Violence Little Vaccine': A Wuhan-Based Feminist Activist Campaign during COVID-19," *Interface: A Journal for and about Social Movements* (2020), www.interfacejournal.net/wp-content/uploads/2020/05/Bao.pdf.

24 Fincher, *Betraying Big Brother*, 91.

25 William L. Parish, Ye Luo, Edward O. Laumann, Melissa Kew, and Zhiyuan Yu, "Unwanted Sexual Activity among Married Women in Urban China," *Journal of Sex Research* 44, no. 2 (2007): 158–71; Kai Lin, Ivan Y. Sun, Yuning Wu, and Jianhong Liu, "College Students' Attitudes toward Intimate Partner Violence: A Comparative Study of China and the US," *Journal of Family Violence* 31, no. 2 (2016): 179–89.

26 Lu, "Two Years On."

27 Lu, "Two Years On."

28　Xiao Meili, "China Must Combat On-Campus Sexual Harassment: An Open Letter," SupChina, January 8, 2018, https://supchina.com/2018/01/08/china -must-combat-on-campus-sexual-harassment-an-open-letter.

29　Xiao, "China's Feminist Awakening"; see also Leanne Italie, "Shorn or Hairy: Female Underarms Having a Mainstream Moment," AP News, June 16, 2015, https: //apnews.com/56450d2ba7a74576aee1bf906ea354f7.

30　Matt Sheehan, "If You Got It, Flaunt It: Chinese Feminists Bare Their Armpit Hair for Contest," Huffington Post, June 12, 2015, www.huffpost. com/entry/chinese-armpit-hair-contest_n_7568528; Fincher, *Betraying Big Brother*, 53.

31　Xiao, "China's Feminist Awakening."

32　Xiao, "China's Feminist Awakening"; Lu, "Two Years On."

33　Lu, "Two Years On."

34　Fincher, "China's Feminist Five."

35　Diana Fu and Greg Distelhorst, "Grassroots Participation and Repression under Hu Jintao and Xi Jinping," *China Journal* 79, no. 1 (2018): 100–122.

36　Fincher, "China's Feminist Five."

37　Fincher, *Betraying Big Brother*.

38　Fincher, *Betraying Big Brother*, 102.

39　Fu and Distelhorst, "Grassroots Participation and Repression."

40　Fincher, "China's Feminist Five."

41　Fincher, "China's Feminist Five."

42　Fincher, "China's Feminist Five."

43　Fincher, "China's Feminist Five."

44　Fincher, "China's Feminist Five."

45　Fincher, "China's Feminist Five"; Fincher, *Betraying Big Brother*, 15–18.

46　Fincher, "China's Feminist Five."

47　Fincher, "China's Feminist Five."

48　Fincher, "China's Feminist Five."

49　Jinyan Zeng, "China's Feminist Five: 'This Is the Worst Crackdown on Lawyers, Activists and Scholars in Decades,'" *Guardian*, April 17, 2015.

50　Koetse, "Is There No Chinese Feminism?"

51　Fincher, *Betraying Big Brother*, 2.

52　Xiao, "China's Feminist Awakening."

53　Zeng, "China's Feminist Five."

54　Wang Zheng, as quoted in Koetse, "Is There No Chinese Feminism?"

55　Zeng, "China's Feminist Five."

56　Fincher, *Betraying Big Brother*, 2.

57　Fincher, "China's Feminist Five."

58　Koetse, "Is There No Chinese Feminism?"

59　Xiao, "China's Feminist Awakening."

60　Fincher, "China's Feminist Five."

61 Vanessa Piao and Didi Kirsten Tatlow, "In Women's Rights Battle, a Call to Underarms," *New York Times*, June 9, 2015.

62 Jennifer Newton, "Why Are Chinese Women Taking Photographs of Their Underarm Hair? Bizarre 'Competition' Sweeps Country's Version of Twitter . . . Despite There Being No Prize on Offer," *Daily Mail*, August 1, 2014.

63 Xu Lin, "Armpit Hair to Stay, Some Women Say," *China Daily*, August 15, 2014, http: //usa.chinadaily.com.cn/life/2014–08/15/content_18314593. htm.

64 In an email exchange in September 2014, I was asked by a Chinese reporter why I "ruined China." Subsequently, in April 2015, I was asked by a *Global Times* reporter about the body hair assignment and its meaning. I told the reporter from the *Global Times* that I felt body hair had revolutionary potential: "I enjoy thinking of my body as a social text upon which I can write many stories. I encourage other women to do the same. I am a supporter of women using their bodies to resist and seeing their bodies as a part of social movements that have revolutionary spirit." See Yin Lu, "To Shave or Not to Shave," *Global Times*, June 8, 2015, www.globaltimes.cn/content/925931.shtml.

65 Lu, "To Shave or Not to Shave"; for key coverage of my body hair assignment, see Jaleesa Jones, "Viewpoint: Hairy Experiment Isn't Just about Shock Factor," *USA Today*, July 15, 2014, www.usatoday.com/story/college/2014/07/15/viewpoint-hairy-experiment-isnt-just-about-shock-factor/37392815; Erin Mayer, "Female Armpit Hair Still Grosses Everyone Out, According to Science," *Bustle*, June 27, 2014, www.bustle.com/articles/29617-female-armpit-hair-still-grosses-everyone-out-according-to-science; Hadley Freeman, "Should Women Shave Their Legs and Under-Arms?" *Guardian*, August 4, 2014; Lizzie Crocker, "Meet the Professor of Hairy Studies," Daily Beast, July 9, 2014, www.thedailybeast.com/meet-the-professor-of-hairy-studies.

66 Flora Macdonald Johnston, "Why Hair Removal Is Now out of Fashion," *Financial Times*, January 24, 2019, www.ft.com/content/5d1ac70a-1a5c-11e9-b93e-f4351a53f1c3.

67 Lin, "Armpit Hair to Stay."

68 Italie, "Shorn or Hairy."

69 Shepherd, "Four Chinese Activists."

70 Shepherd, "Four Chinese Activists."

71 Note that Sina Weibo has over four hundred million users and has attracted attention for actively censoring "controversial" content. See Andrew Bylund, "Weibo Added 15 Million Users in Q3," Motley Fool, November 28, 2018, www.fool.com/investing/2018/11/29/weibo-added-15-million-users-in-q3.aspx; Margaret Anderson, "How Feminists in China Are Using Emoji to Avoid Censorship," *Wired*, March 30, 2018, www.wired.com/story/china-feminism-emoji-censorship.

72 Yiying Fan, "Weibo Women's 'Armpit Hair Contest,'" What's on Weibo, June 12, 2015, www.whatsonweibo.com/weibo-womens-armpit-hair-contest.

73 Piao and Tatlow, "In Women's Rights Battle."

74 Alyssa Toomey, "Are You Listening, Miley Cyrus? There's Female Armpit Hair Competition in China," E News, June 11, 2015, www.eonline.com/news/665892 /are-you-listening-miley-cyrus-there-s-female-armpit-hair-competition-in -china.
75 Xiao Meili, as quoted in Piao and Tatlow, "In Women's Rights Battle."
76 Lu, "To Shave or Not to Shave."
77 Piao and Tatlow, "In Women's Rights Battle."
78 Fan, "Weibo Women's 'Armpit Hair Contest.'"
79 Lu, "To Shave or Not to Shave."
80 Fan, "Weibo Women's 'Armpit Hair Contest.'"
81 Fan, "Weibo Women's 'Armpit Hair Contest.'"
82 Fan, "Weibo Women's 'Armpit Hair Contest.'"
83 Lu, "To Shave or Not to Shave."
84 Lu, "To Shave or Not to Shave."
85 Fan, "Weibo Women's 'Armpit Hair Contest.'"
86 Piao and Tatlow, "In Women's Rights Battle."
87 Piao and Tatlow, "In Women's Rights Battle."
88 Italie, "Shorn or Hairy."
89 Fan, "Weibo Women's 'Armpit Hair Contest.'"
90 Victoria Sherrow, *Encyclopedia of Hair: A Cultural History* (Westport, CT: Greenwood, 2006).
91 Lu, "To Shave or Not to Shave."
92 Yuan Ren, "Why Chinese Women Like Me Aren't Ashamed of Our Body Hair," *Telegraph*, June 24, 2015.
93 Ren, "Why Chinese Women Like Me."
94 Ren, "Why Chinese Women Like Me."
95 Jaehee Jung, "Young Women's Perceptions of Traditional and Contemporary Female Beauty Ideals in China," *Family and Consumer Sciences Research Journal* 47, no. 1 (2018): 56–72.
96 Dorothy Ko, "The Body as Attire: The Shifting Meanings of Footbinding in Seventeenth-Century China," *Journal of Women's History* 8, no. 4 (1997): 8–27.
97 Ko, "The Body as Attire."
98 Meng Zhang, "A Chinese Beauty Story: How College Women in China Negotiate Beauty, Body Image, and Mass Media," *Chinese Journal of Communication* 5, no. 4 (2012): 437–54; Eileen Otis, "China's Beauty Proletariat: The Body Politics of Hegemony in a Walmart Cosmetics Department," *Positions: Asia Critique* 24, no. 1 (2016): 155–77.
99 Matthew Boyle, "Veet's Hairy Strategy for Chinese Women," SF Gate, October 21, 2012, www.sfgate.com/business/article/Veet-s-hairy-strategy-for -Chinese-women-3969580.php.
100 "Challenge for Veet: Sell Products That Have Never Been Sold in China Before," Marketing to China, July 5, 2019, www.marketingtochina.com/challenge-for -veet-sell-products-have-never-been-sold-in-china-before.

101 Boyle, "Veet's Hairy Strategy for Chinese Women."
102 Kerry McDermott, "Fuzz Phobia in the Far East: How One Marketing Company Convinced Chinese Women They Are Too Hairy," *Daily Mail*, October 25, 2012.
103 Lu, "To Shave or Not to Shave."
104 Lu, "To Shave or Not to Shave."
105 Piao and Tatlow, "In Women's Rights Battle."
106 Piao and Tatlow, "In Women's Rights Battle."
107 Sheehan, "If You Got It, Flaunt It."
108 Fincher, "China's Feminist Five."
109 Fincher, *Betraying Big Brother*, 103.
110 "Chinese Armpit Hair Competition Triggers Online Debate," BBC News, June 8, 2015, www.bbc.com/news/blogs-china-blog-33053826.
111 Fincher, *Betraying Big Brother*, 104.

6. GROWING A THICKER SKIN

1 I often use the term *women* throughout chapters 6–8 to refer to the twenty-two participants interviewed for this study. The two nonbinary participants said they prefer they/them pronouns and that, as AFAB (assigned-female-at-birth) people, they do not object to being included in an aggregate group called *women*. This use is done consciously and with permission of participants. When referring to them as individuals, I use they/them pronouns, but when referring to the entire group of interviewees, I use the term *women*.
2 Sara Ahmed, *The Cultural Politics of Emotion* (Edinburgh: Edinburgh University Press, 2014), 3.
3 Ahmed, *Cultural Politics of Emotion*, 4.
4 Annika Mann, *Reading Contagion: The Hazards of Reading in the Age of Print* (Charlottesville: University of Virginia Press, 2018).
5 Ahmed, *Cultural Politics of Emotion*, 12.
6 Lisa Blackman, "The Subject of Affect: Bodies, Process, Becoming," in *Immaterial Bodies: Affect, Embodiment, Mediation*, ed. Lisa Blackman (London: Sage, 2012), 3–4; Melissa Gregg and Gregory J. Seigworth (eds.), *The Affect Theory Reader* (Durham, NC: Duke University Press, 2010).
7 Gregg and Seigworth, *Affect Theory Reader*.
8 Blackman, "Subject of Affect," 4.
9 Blackman, "Subject of Affect," 4.
10 Gregory J. Seigworth and Melissa Gregg, "An Inventory of Shimmers," in *The Affect Theory Reader*, ed. Melissa Gregg and Gregory J. Seigworth (Durham, NC: Duke University Press, 2010), 1.
11 Seigworth and Gregg, "Inventory of Shimmers," 3.
12 Ingun Klepp and Mari Rysst, "Deviant Bodies and Suitable Clothes," *Fashion Theory* 21, no. 1 (2017): 79–99.

13 Lucia Ruggerone, "The Feeling of Being Dressed: Affect Studies and the Clothed Body," *Fashion Theory* 21, no. 5 (2017): 573–93. See also Lucia Ruggerone and Renate Stauss, "The Deceptive Mirror: The Dressed Body Beyond Reflection," *Fashion Theory* (2020), published online first.

14 Ruggerone and Stauss, "Deceptive Mirror," 3.

15 Ruggerone and Stauss, "Deceptive Mirror."

16 Joel Watson, "'Why Did You Put That There?': Gender, Materialism, and Tattoo Consumption," *Advances in Consumer Research* 25 (1998): 453–60.

17 Mary Kosut, "Tattoo Narratives: The Intersection of the Body, Self-Identity, and Society," *Visual Studies* 15, no. 1 (2000): 79–100; Jeremy Sierra, Ravi Jillapalli, and Vishag Badrinarayanan, "Determinants of a Lasting Purchase: The Case of the Tattoo Patron," *Journal of Retailing and Consumer Services* 20, no. 4 (2013): 389–99.

18 Michelle Lipton, Lorraine Sherr, Jonathan Elford, Malcolm Rustin, and William Clayton, "Women Living with Facial Hair: The Psychological and Behavioral Burdens," *Journal of Psychosomatic Research* 61, no. 2 (2006): 161–68.

19 Toks Oyedemi, "Beauty as Violence: 'Beautiful' Hair and the Cultural Violence of Identity Erasure," *Social Identities* 22, no. 5 (2016): 537–53; Druann Maria Heckert and Amy Best, "Ugly Duckling to Swan: Labeling Theory and the Stigmatization of Red Hair," *Symbolic Interaction* 20, no. 4 (1997): 365–84.

20 Druann Maria Heckert, "Mixed Blessings: Women and Blond Hair," *Free Inquiry in Creative Sociology* 31, no. 1 (2003): 47–72.

21 Kelly Reddy-Best, "'I Cut It Real Short Right after I Got the Job': Queer Coding During the Interview for LGBTQ+ Women," *Fashion, Style & Popular Culture* 5, no. 2 (2018): 221–34.

22 Although the consequences of doing interviews through video conferencing are not yet well known, Zoom offers greater accessibility to respondents throughout the country while minimizing the health risks of being exposed to COVID-19. See Lia M. Gray, Gina Wong-Wylie, Gwen R. Rempel, and Karen Cook, "Expanding Qualitative Research Interviewing Strategies: Zoom Video Communications," *The Qualitative Report* 25, no. 5 (2020): 1292–1301.

23 While using Craigslist to recruit subjects can lead to selection biases, this approach often allows for a more diverse sample than qualitative studies that rely upon social media sites like Facebook or megadata sites like Amazon Turk. See Christopher Antoun, Chan Zhang, Frederick G. Conrad, and Michael F. Schober, "Comparisons of Online Recruitment Strategy for Convenience Samples: Craigslist, Google AdWords, Facebook, and Amazon Mechanical Turk," *Field Methods* 28, no. 3 (2016): 231–46.

24 D. Clayton Smith, "Environmentalism, Feminism, and Gender," *Sociological Inquiry* 71, no. 3 (2001): 314–34; Corey Lee Wrenn, "Trump Veganism: A Political Survey of American Vegans in the Era of Identity Politics," *Societies* 7, no. 4 (2017): 32–45.

25 Breanne Fahs, "Dreaded 'Otherness': Heteronormative Patrolling in Women's Body Hair Rebellions," *Gender & Society* 25, no. 4 (2011): 451–72; Mark Michael Smith, *How Race Is Made: Slavery, Segregation, and the Senses* (Chapel Hill: University of North Carolina Press, 2016); Janice McCabe, "Racial and Gender Microaggressions on a Predominantly-White Campus: Experiences of Black, Latina/o and White Undergraduates," *Race, Gender & Class* 16, no. 1–2 (2009): 133–51.

26 Lipton, Sherr, Elford, Rustin, and Clayton, "Women Living with Facial Hair."

27 Ahmed, *Cultural Politics of Emotion*, 202.

7. "THE ONLY OPINION THAT MATTERS IS MY OWN"

1 Leonore Tiefer, *Sex Is Not a Natural Act and Other Essays* (Boulder, CO: Westview, 2004), 11.

2 Marika Tiggemann and Sarah J. Kenyon, "The Hairlessness Norm: The Removal of Body Hair in Women," *Sex Roles* 39, no. 11–12 (1998): 873–85; Merran Toerien and Sue Wilkinson, "Gender and Body Hair: Constructing the Feminine Woman," *Women's Studies International Forum* 26, no. 4 (2003): 333–44; Breanne Fahs, "Imagining Ugliness: Failed Femininities, Shame, and Disgust Written onto the 'Other' Body," in *On the Politics of Ugliness*, ed. Sara Rodrigues and Ela Przybylo (London: Palgrave, 2018), 237–58; Breanne Fahs and Denise A. Delgado, "The Specter of Excess: Race, Class, and Gender in Women's Body Hair Narratives," in *Embodied Resistance: Breaking the Rules, Challenging the Norms*, ed. Chris Bobel and Samantha Kwan (Nashville, TN: Vanderbilt University Press, 2011), 13–25.

3 Merran Toerien and Sue Wilkinson, "Exploring the Depilation Norm: A Qualitative Questionnaire Study of Women's Body Hair Removal," *Qualitative Research in Psychology* 1, no. 1 (2004): 69–92.

4 Tiggemann and Kenyon, "Hairlessness Norm," 873; see also Marika Tiggemann and Suzanna Hodgson, "The Hairlessness Norm Extended: Reasons for and Predictors of Women's Body Hair Removal at Different Body Sites," *Sex Roles* 59, no. 11–12 (2008): 889–97.

5 Marina Krcmar, Steve Giles, and Donald Helme, "Understanding the Process: How Mediated and Peer Norms Affect Young Women's Body Esteem," *Communication Quarterly* 56, no. 2 (2008): 111–30.

6 Erin Strahan, Anne Wilson, Kate Cressman, and Vanessa Buote, "Comparing to Perfection: How Cultural Norms for Appearance Affect Social Comparisons and Self-Image," *Body Image* 3, no. 2 (2006): 211–17.

7 Nikki Hayfield, Emma Halliwell, and Victoria Clarke, "An Exploration of Bisexual, Lesbian, and Heterosexual Women's Body Dissatisfaction, and Body Hair and Make-Up Practices," *Psychology of Sexualities Section Review* 8, no. 2 (2017): 55–67.

8 For a detailed overview of the methods for these interviews, see chapter 6 and the description of the research methods, questions, and demographics of the current sample.

9 Jaclyn A. Nelson, Miriam Liss, Mindy J. Erchull, Molly M. Hurt, Laura R. Ramsey, Dixie L. Turner, and Megan E. Haines, "Identity in Action: Predictors of Feminist Self-Identification and Collective Action," *Sex Roles* 58 (2008): 721–28.

8. "IN THE REVOLUTION, WE WILL ALL BE HAIRY"

1 For a detailed overview of the methods for these interviews, see chapter 6 and the description of the research methods, questions, and demographics of the current sample.

2 Denice Frohman, "A Woman's Place," in *Women of Resistance: Poems for a New Feminism*, ed. Danielle Barnhart and Iris Mahan (New York: O/R Books, 2018), 9–11.

3 Samantha Kwan, Scott V. Savage, and Mary Nell Trautner, "Adorning the Female Body: Feminist Identification, Embodied Resistance, and Esthetic Body Modification Practices," *Sociological Focus* 53, no. 1 (2020): 67–88.

4 Breanne Fahs and Eric Swank, "Exploring Stigma of 'Extreme' Weight Gain: The Terror of Fat Possible Selves in Women's Responses to Hypothetically Gaining One Hundred Pounds," *Women's Studies International Forum* 61 (2017): 1–8; Ellen Granberg, "'Is That All There Is?' Possible Selves, Self-Change, and Weight Loss," *Social Psychology Quarterly* 69, no. 2 (2006): 109–26.

5 Sarah K. Murnen and Linda Smolak, "Are Feminist Women Protected from Body Image Problems? A Meta-analytic Review of Relevant Research," *Sex Roles* 60, no. 3–4 (2009): 186–97.

EPILOGUE

1 Ani DiFranco, "Shameless," *Dilate* (Buffalo, NY: Righteous Babe Records, 1996).

2 Breanne Fahs, *Valerie Solanas: The Defiant Life of the Woman Who Wrote SCUM (and Shot Andy Warhol)* (New York: Feminist Press, 2014); Breanne Fahs, *Firebrand Feminism: The Radical Lives of Ti-Grace Atkinson, Kathie Sarachild, Roxanne Dunbar-Ortiz, and Dana Densmore* (Seattle: University of Washington Press, 2018).

3 Clara J. Bates, "The Harvard Pee-in of 1973, *Crimson*, November 1, 2018, www .thecrimson.com/article/2018/11/1/harvard-pee-in-1973.

4 Breanne Fahs, "Ti-Grace Atkinson and the Legacy of Radical Feminism," *Feminist Studies* 37, no. 3 (2011): 586.

INDEX |

"Open Letter to: White Supremacist, Capitalist, Hetero Patriarchal Hairless America," 114

oppression, 6, 7, 26, 28, 38, 44, 62, 69–72, 125, 145, 151, 155, 249–50, 253

Palmer, Amanda, 66

patriarchy, 7, 12, 19, 24–26, 29, 42–44, 64, 89, 100, 102, 110–11, 114, 150, 221, 223, 241, 248–50, 252; control by the, 28, 32, 38, 41, 73–77, 128, 155–56, 201, 255–56

performance art, 30, 41–42, 46, 127–28, 131, 142–47, 149, 153, 168

personal choice, 4, 7, 20–22, 25, 27–28, 41–44, 46, 52–59, 63–65, 163–64, 232–33. *See also* neoliberalism

Playboy, 122, 139

Plucked, 126

Plush, 30, 127, 139–42

Poisonwood Bible, The, 99

Politics of Womanhood, 136

Porn Grid, 139

pornography, 17, 47, 48, 49, 53, 92, 126, 139–40

postfeminism, 43–44

Powers of Horror, 128

Probyn, Elspeth, 173

Przybylo, Ela, 5, 40

Psychology of Women Quarterly, 92

pubic hair removal, 3–4, 17, 42–43, 46, 47–49, 56, 70, 85–86, 105, 108, 183, 191; complications, 4, 43

Quiles-Reyes, Janice, 103, 105, 106, 108, 109, 115

racism, 7, 14, 16, 32, 44, 45, 46, 49, 50, 64, 65, 72–73, 94, 112, 114, 129–30, 210, 221, 236–38, 250, 251, 254–55

radical feminism, 12, 23, 45, 61, 252–53

Ramesh, Dayanita, 103, 113

religious hairlessness, 15

reproduction, 12, 18, 19, 150, 155; reproductive rights, 25, 142, 231, 255

resistance, 7, 12, 28–29, 44–45, 63–65, 83, 100–101, 104, 110, 116, 124, 153, 249, 253; body hair, 13, 25–27, 94–95, 103, 114–16, 124–25, 148–49, 171, 198, 222, 225, 245–50; embodied, 26, 31–32, 37–38, 45–46, 68, 94, 147, 178, 223, 241–45, 249, 250, 252

respectability politics, 28, 38, 40, 49, 61–62, 67, 72–73, 91, 205, 236–37, 243, 252, 254

Reuters, 161

Reynolds, Crash, 103, 105, 106, 109

Rich, Adrienne, 5,

right-wing, 7, 24, 251

Roberts, Alison, 123

Roberts, Julia, 49

Rodrigues, Sara, 40

"rogue" body hair, 31, 172, 193

Rosler, Martha, 41

Ruggerone, Lucia, 175

Russo, Maria Del, 160

Scharff, Christina, 43

Schneemann, Carolee, 46, 128

SCUM Manifesto, 253

Sehgal, Aditya, 166

Seigworth, Gregory, 174

Semiotics of the Kitchen, 41

sexism, 28, 45, 46, 50, 68, 74, 80, 94, 150–52, 155, 158, 185, 186, 253, 255

"Shameless," 251–52

Shaved (At Loss), 46

shaving, men, 8–9, 28, 38, 50, 67, 79–82

Sherman, Cindy, 128

Shilling, Chris, 173

Shit Kicker, 139

Silverman, Sarah, 49

slavery, 14, 16

Smith, Kiki, 128

Smith, Zadie, 1

social intervention, 29, 30, 126–27, 139, 147, 162

CPSIA information can be obtained
at www.ICGtesting.com
Printed in the USA
BVHW070440150522
636924BV00003B/10